Praise for *A Spell in the Wild*

'These enchanting words make the world feel less broken'
Emma Mitchell, author of *The Wild Remedy*

'Part-primer, part-chronicle; a fresh and personal account of
a contemporary witch's year told with lucidity and verve'
Eley Williams, author of *The Liar's Dictionary*

'*A Spell in the Wild* is a beautiful and intimate set of
reflections on the persistence and necessity of magic, not
just in our mythologies but in our daily accommodations
with the changing natural world'
Paraic O'Donnell, author of *The Maker of Swans*

'The wise words in *A Spell in the Wild* offer solace for
our hearts and homes in a changing world. Every reader
will find themselves under her spell'
Nancy Campbell, author of *The Library of Ice*

'A joyful foray into wild landscapes, celebrating nature's
calendar and harnessing the power of lunar phases'
The Herald

A Spell in the Wild

A Year (and six centuries) of Magic

ALICE TARBUCK

First published in Great Britain in 2020 by Two Roads
An Imprint of John Murray Press
An Hachette UK company

This paperback edition published in 2021

1

Copyright © Alice Tarbuck 2020

A CIP catalogue record for this title is available from the British Library

Paperback ISBN 978 1 529 38086 6
eBook ISBN 978 1 529 38087 3

Typeset in Hoefler Text by
Palimpsest Book Production Ltd, Falkirk, Stirlingshire

Printed and bound in Great Britain by Clays Ltd, Elcograf S.p.A.

John Murray policy is to use papers that are natural, renewable and
recyclable products and made from wood grown in sustainable forests.
The logging and manufacturing processes are expected to conform
to the environmental regulations of the country of origin.

Two Roads
Carmelite House
50 Victoria Embankment
London EC4Y 0DZ

www.tworoadsbooks.com

This book is dedicated to Simone Kotva, whose magic is extraordinary, and to Jane Christie, who taught me to believe in fairies.

'Knowing another is endless. The thing to be known grows with the knowing'

NAN SHEPHERD

Contents

Introduction

One evening, in the late dusk, I am walking home. The shapes of the houses slope away from the road, which is full of a darkly honeyed light. The sun has gone, but it has left behind its glow. Quiet, in soft shoes, I move like a shadow past the neatly kept gardens. I am there, but almost not there.

Something trots along behind me and I turn, presuming that it's a small dog, and that behind it will be the owner. The street is empty of people, though, and what is running along behind me, close enough that I could reach down and touch it, is a little fox. It might be unwell. Hungry. It is certainly behaving strangely, even for a city fox: none of the usual bent-nose wariness in its gait. But it looks well enough, coat glossy, tail full, ears whole.

I keep my pace, and it keeps its pace. I am a little frightened that it will bite me, but it's so pretty, and the whole thing is so unusual, that I move past that fear, just. In a low voice, I speak: ask it how it is, what it is doing, is it off to the park that lies behind my house, has it brought me a message – no, of course not – has it had a good day? The sort of questions, largely, that you might ask a colleague, or someone you found yourself sitting next to on a train. It doesn't reply, but keeps to the shadow of the wall, just behind my heels. It isn't hurrying me up, but it isn't letting me slow down, either.

When I turn into my street, we turn together. I wonder if it comes this way to reach the railway bridge? Surely, it could just slip through the park fence instead. It is lovely, and in the low light it seems to glow, feral and strange. It looks as if it has stepped out of a story, but of course the streets belong to it as much as me, and it is no myth, all burnished fur and elegant nose. I reach my house, and half expect it to come down the path toward me, to be let in for supper. But it doesn't. It sits at my gate and looks at me, until I unlock my door. I won't be able to see it once I'm inside, but I can still feel its attention through the front door. I stand behind the door's reassuring solidity for a moment, and breathe. I have been scared, I realise – I am not used to encountering foxes that want to be close to me. Outside, everything on the street is quiet.

I ask everyone about this. Is this a regular thing? Have other people seen this fox? Nobody else has. Evenings for the next few weeks are spent looking to see if the fox is local, if he's loitering in the park or by the station. Of course, I never see him again. I tell someone at my office, who looks at me over their coffee cup. 'You know why these things happen to you, don't you?' he asks me. 'It's because you're a witch.' Just like that, matter-of-fact, casually, before he turns back to his work. He's being entirely serious, no hint of a wind-up, and I'm so flabbergasted that my mouth won't work to form a witty response. I am twenty-one years old, and this is the first time anyone has ever called me a witch.

This is the first time anyone has noticed. And it isn't a slur, it isn't an accusation, it isn't even a question. Just an observation:

the idea of me that makes the most sense to him. He's right, as well. I am a witch. Or rather, I'm *something*, at this point. Witch-adjacent.

Back then, I composed elaborate rituals in scraps of London forest. I found myself muttering little spell-rhymes, or whatever they were, when I felt vulnerable walking along. My cupboard was full of strange things that my housemates regarded with suspicion, especially if I offered them help with their problems – cloves for protection, oak leaves for wisdom – and I composed things into bunches, and hung them about the house. There were lots of other words for what I was, other than witch: eccentric, a bit of a hippy, maybe, though at the time I had a corporate London job. I didn't have a coven, or any velvet robes. I didn't have an altar, or much sense of a goddess, or any idea at all about what I was doing with any of it – or even, really, what 'it' was. Certainly, I assumed that most of my behaviours were fairly normal, for people who grew up with Buffy and Harry Potter – didn't we all just . . . implicitly believe in magic? Wasn't all of this just a sort of extended playing, a refusal to put aside childish things?

That colleague left the company shortly after his remark, about a year before I did. We weren't particularly friendly, and I doubt he'd remember what he'd said. But I took it entirely to heart, went home and thought about it, lying in bed. That was what I was, I realised. Or at least, that was one name for something that I felt, a set of things I was doing, the way I wanted to be in the world. Not only was there a name for it, but I could use it, if I wanted. It was a gift, that comment: the complex gift of someone else perceiving in us something we have not yet perceived ourselves. It felt shocking, or maybe a bit exposing, but it was something I hadn't known I needed to hear.

Men accusing women of being witches is, historically, a pretty bad situation, and I felt a bit embarrassed that I hadn't hit on what I was by myself. But the important thing, really, is not where the idea came from, it's that it came at all; that I realised something about myself, some way of talking about what I did and believed, that made sense.

So perhaps you are here, holding this book, because you are a witch, either newly, or of many years' practice. Perhaps you aren't. Perhaps you aren't sure, yet. Maybe you played at witch-craft when you were younger, and believed that the world would listen to you if you spoke. It might be the case that you keep finding yourself drawn to the sea, again, or desperate to go among the hills. Perhaps you sit in the park and look at the daisies, hopeless and ragged among the grass, and you some-times want to cry. Or you don't, until you see that there's sunset as well, all red-fingered, turning the plane trees into beacons of gold, and the whole world feels good, and big, and right up against you, threatening to engulf and overwhelm you entirely. Equally, perhaps that never happens. The world continues along, in all of its constant, outrageous beauty, and you largely nod, and go back to what you were doing, like an uninterested uncle being shown flowers by a young ward. But then, perhaps, you'd like to feel a different set of things instead. A little bit of magic. To go out into the world and maybe find it to be different from what you'd expected. To, possibly, look at it askew, askance, curiously.

Witchcraft starts happening when our bodies come right up to the edge of their sensory and linguistic abilities and life keeps going anyway. It happens when we realise that we cannot, truly, describe the way the flowers smelled one night on our holiday, but that we can hold the scent inside us, can conjure it back. When we try to describe the way geranium petals hold the light of the day inside them until the last second of dusk, seem somehow lambent in their redness, as if they could, single-handed, stop the night from happening, and realise that we can't. Not even if we were biologists, and could describe the mechanism; or poets, and could wax lyrical; or photographers, with extraordinary lenses, we could never actually, properly, fully and entirely convey to anyone else the experience that we had watching it happen. The edges of language are sharp, and pervert our meanings sideways. What the edges tell us, if we listen to them, is that there are experiences we can have that we cannot talk about using normal means, or at least not satisfactorily. These are experiences not just of our single personhood, but also of relation. They are experiences of the world, in the world; they are experiences where flowers reach their light right out into our eyes. They are experiences where we feel as if we are full of holes, as if the world can come not only close against us, but can actually enter right into us, so that we are as shot through with it as if we were Saint Sebastian, and the world arrows. The world does this: demonstrates, occasionally, that it isn't just connected to us, isn't a network in which we are one distant, autonomous node. Rather, it *is* us. We are, then, overpowered by it, entered by it and transformed. And in the same way, we enter the world, daily, and transform it, for better or for worse. Every time we act, every time we think, even, we are shaping the world and it is shaping us, and there is no escape from either. Understanding those encounters is the job of witchcraft. Learning how to enter into them, how to court them, how to cause them: that is magic.

Magic happens in all those moments when the world and you aren't separated any longer by any sort of barrier, be it the brain or the body. Magic, for me, is comparable to the strange phenomenon of blood-temperature weather: when, in summer, the air is the same temperature as the blood inside your body (37 degrees Celsius). Being from the UK, this is a comparatively rare experience, and so loses none of its strangeness in repetition. You probably know what I mean. This temperature gives you the feeling, when you leave whatever building you are in and step outside, that the edges of your skin have evaporated. The air is still, and the temperature – well, the temperature is exactly the same as the temperature that you are, there is no perceptible difference at all. It feels as if you've simply gone out without your skin on. As if the world is right there, entering right into you, and you into it, entirely. Magic is, for me, the equivalent of that feeling. It is the practice of removing any barriers that exist between myself and the absolute, total apprehension of the world through my body. That kind of weather makes me feel alive, excited, as if I could lift my heels off the pavement and just fly away. They are wonderful days, those days, when I feel weightless, but entirely comfortable. No resistance, nothing pressing against me, reminding me of my body. Just . . . potential. I am made of energy, of the networked big wide world.

And when I do magic, it is the same. It is a stepping into awareness of connection, a tuning into that same feeling. There's nothing stranger, or more lovely. As such, magic is a difficult thing to talk about. Witchcraft is, among other things, a good container for trying to communicate these difficult-to-talk-about experiences. We aren't sure how else to articulate them, so we use metaphor, metaphysics, magic. And I truly believe they are magic, that magic is exactly those experiences. By showing other people how to have them, we can all experience this magic, can learn how to control it, and can enter into the world on these terms. Witchcraft is, I believe, the practice of entering into relation with the world, of exerting your will in it and among it, and learning how to work with it in ways that are fruitful for yourself and the world.

What follows, then, is an account of one year attempting to do this. I am a long-standing practitioner of magic – mostly of this wild, strange kind. I am also a keen forager, and maker of all sorts of what my mum would fondly term 'nonsense', from tinctures and syrups to herbal preparations for use in spells. I also love the natural world, and have an academic background in the relationship between words and the environment. These various practices come together to be what I would call 'witchcraft', which for me is practical, spiritual, academic, magical and intuitive, all bundled up in one. Using the months of the year as a starting point, I want to share the curious magic of the world, the way it shimmers and changes if you walk through it as a witch, with your eyes open. And of course, that cannot happen in isolation. I am fascinated by everyone who has attempted, deliberately, to lead similar lives before, from magic practitioners to nature writers, from gardeners to philosophers. There is magic everywhere, and finding it in unusual places is vital, because it makes me feel that, under all the ordinariness of the world, there are bright constellations of people who understand, who see the world in all its vivid detail.

It is also important, I think, that we listen to the voices of those who were aligned with, or engaged in, witchcraft practices throughout history: from the accused witches who were victims of the European and American witch trials, which took place from around 1329–1750, and the austere occultists of the Renaissance, to more recent practitioners such as the Wiccan revivalists of the 1940–50s, and the free-love witches of the 1960s and 1970s. It is only by examining their writings and lives that we can get a sense of who we are as witches in this contemporary era, when we can walk into shops and buy scrying mirrors and nobody will bat an eye. When we can ask about star signs and telephone mediums, and have beautiful occult symbols tattooed on ourselves. This freedom is hard-won and grudgingly afforded, and it deserves celebration.

But magic also, in all its beguiling aesthetic aspects, needs to be tempered by a little knowledge, by the cultivation of something deeper than the occasional coloured candle and the occasional broad-brimmed, fetching black hat. Because witchcraft is a way of thinking with the planet, it is a way of thinking into the world, in order to change it. It harnesses all of the deep, good, vital parts of yourself. Witchcraft has been used in political action, to stand against systems of power, to protect rainforests and fight for women's rights. It has been used to attempt to overthrow dictators, and to stem ecological disaster. It has power, and practical application. It is also, straightforwardly, pleasurable. There is nothing lovelier than the little nudge in your worldview that pulls you toward witchcraft, that opens the world up to you, and you up to it. It's hard to love a world you're closed off from, and maintaining distance is often easier than embracing radical, extraordinary care for all that surrounds us. Witches are dwellers in the world as it is, but it can be a challenge to train ourselves to see it. We'd like to do our magic in beautiful places: in green fields, by clear rivers, in lovely cottages, all stone and roses round the door. But the world is full of municipal buses, and drying greens, and scrubby grass that's been kicked up by football boots. It's full of squirrels eating spring bulbs, and broken bottles on pavements, and uncollected Christmas trees, and dog shit. It's full of seagulls, and crumbling flats, and expensive heating, and friends we love being fucked over for jobs, or getting ill. It is full of precarity, and worry, fascist governments, continents catching fire, and the long shadow of global pandemic. The world is very hard, and it can feel impossible to walk out into it, to open up the body, to recognise that it is in fact already open, entirely permeable, and to let the world leak in.

This book is an attempt to walk through the year doing just that. Letting the world in, and seeing what happens. There are spells and recipes after every month, and together they make a sort of magical pattern to guide your year. There are sections that deal with what magic is, and why it exists in its current form. I wanted to excavate magic, to hold it up to the light. I wanted to take myself and my spells out of their quiet, dark privacy, and journey out into the wide world. I wanted to find magic everywhere, and see what it was like: I hope that you will enjoy the journey too. Perhaps you are a witch. Perhaps you aren't sure yet. Come and bring yourself into the wild – you already have everything you could need, and all the world is waiting.

A Note on the Spells and Other Magical Conduct

This book is not a grimoire, a book of shadows, a spell book. These are all useful things, but this book is different. There are spells included at the end of every month: sometimes these look more like recipes and sometimes they are more typical spells involving ritual language and objects. The reason that this isn't a spell book per se is that I work from two main principles. The first is that nobody can write another person's spells, and the second is that magic relies on the development and use of a personal symbolic register – spells are a means of structuring those symbols.

So what does it mean to suggest that nobody can write another person's spells? Doesn't it make the spells I include here a little superfluous? Well, not quite. I believe that we can borrow aspects from spells: their form, the equipment used, perhaps the words, but we shouldn't try to replicate whole spells exactly. Performing someone else's spell is not only challenging, it is also not the most effective way to do magic. If magic is the alteration of self and world through exercise of will and attention, then every spell, every magical endeavour, is necessarily entirely personal. Even if we do try to replicate other people's spells, we can't ever fully recreate another person's energy, the time or place or environmental factors that influenced their casting. It is the same as never quite being able to recreate someone else's experience of living.

Spells in Western magic are as varied as anything else, and have a complex history. However, they often appear similar to one another at first glance. This is because they can hold in common certain rituals based on shared roots, like calling the four elements. These are traces of High Magical practice of the sort laid out in the Gardnerian or Alexandrian magical traditions.[1] Many of the spells in commonly available magical books follow the rituals set out in these traditions, though they come to us through a number of diverse routes.

The second point is that magic is a practice of working with symbols. Symbols are how we systematise and understand magic in the world. Magical practice is often built on the understanding that certain sets of things (objects, colours, scents, moon phases) can stand in symbolically for, or be linked with, ideas, concepts or desired outcomes (wealth, luck, happiness). People enjoy symbols: English is a deeply metaphorical language. We often use words and images to evoke, link to or mean something else. Many of these symbols are broadly agreed upon, or even obvious, and not much considered: for example, that the moon symbolises night, and the sun symbolises day. There are cultural symbols we simply take for granted – a card with a picture of a four-leaf clover on it that says 'good luck in your new job' doesn't need any explanation to a British person, but may well seem bizarre to someone from another culture. Four-leaf clovers have been considered lucky in Western culture since at least the middle ages, for a murky set of reasons that might pertain to their being comparatively unusual, a genetic variant of a trifoliate plant; it might also be a remnant of Celtic and Druid ideas that carrying clover would ward off bad luck, and perhaps let the wearer see into the fairy-realm. None of that detailed cultural knowledge is possessed by most people: we just understand and accept that a four-leaf clover is a good luck symbol, because that's how commonly held symbols work.

Why is this important? I believe that successful magical practice depends on understanding, inventing and marshalling a vocabulary of symbols that is personal to you, which can be set into configurations, whether in speech or ritual, to help direct your will. Traditionally, practitioners of High Magic, such as the English occultist Aleister Crowley (1875–1947), borrowed symbols from various world cultures and co-opted them into Western magical practices. These symbols often came from religions and practices considered mystical by Westerners, such as Kabbalah, or from Egyptian hiero-glyphs, alchemy and other symbolic alphabets or systems. This uprooting of symbols from their cultural contexts and their insertion into Western magic is a fairly colonial and imperialist approach that marks the complex religious and spiritual practices of other cultures as less valuable than the occult needs of Western practitioners. However, many of these symbols are now so embedded in witchcraft culture that they come up frequently. It's easier, especially when getting started with magic, to pay attention to the symbols already used, rather than creating your own straight away, because the creating is the tricky bit! Symbolism is a vast topic, and one that can be approached from so many different angles. Because of my own magical practice and writing life,

I tend to approach symbols as if they were language: as if they were metaphors.

Magical symbols work in a similar way to metaphors. A metaphor works on the understanding that the reader will know what both the object and the thing it is being compared to are like, and so be able to assign the attributes of one to the other. Imagine that you wanted to do a spell to send peace to someone who was having a difficult time. What sort of things would you use? What sort of objects might you gather in front of you? Certain traditional cultural influences might permeate: soft colours are often considered soothing, so you might find something in a pastel shade. You might want an object, scent or word that represented the person in question: anything from their name, to a photograph, an item of clothing or a lock of their hair. You might want to evoke peace through smells, and aromatherapy considers lavender to be a soothing scent. Once you had arranged everything, what might you do? You might talk to a goddess or divine being, if you believed in them. You might focus on feeling your energy and directing it toward your friend. You might repeat certain words over and over until the spell felt finished. You might make an offering, or write down your intention and burn it, or bury it, or seal it. You might close your eyes and meditate on an image of your friend, well and happy. You might draw the peace sign on something. These all seem fairly natural things because we have absorbed huge amounts of cultural knowledge about witchcraft without even knowing it.

However, you might want to do none of those things. The person you're sending peace to might find their peace with their back pressed to thumping speakers in a club at four in the morning. You might know that their favourite colour is orange, or that you text each other a certain emoji to let each other know you're home safe, so you might want to draw a huge pineapple emoji and meditate on that. You might imagine them surrounded not by calming breezes but by great invigorating gusts of wind, because they love the roar, or because you do. Those symbols might not work for anyone else, but they would work for you. The spell would have no less efficacy just because it deviated from traditional symbolism. In fact, I would argue it might have more, because you would have decided on every element.

It is vital, then, to have a dictionary of symbols on which to draw: your own and those you find and adopt. And when you create your altar, it is useful to cover it in objects that are not necessarily overtly magical, but hold power for you. The potency of symbols often means that using your old baby cup as an offering vessel may hold more power than a perfect china cup inscribed with arcane symbols. All magic is deeply personal, even when it is executed collectively, and so only you will be able to find the right forms and symbols to communicate your will to the world.

This also gets around a pervasive difficulty in magic: the equipment problem. Like anything else, magical practice involves material objects, and people want to sell you them. For lots of people, magical practice comes with a heavily aestheticised 'feel' and while I've no desire to counsel against that (and am not immune to beautiful things), there are ethical ways of consuming, and almost none of that purchasing is necessary. Money is not a necessary component of magic: magic must be available to anyone.

What I hope the rituals in this book teach is that magical practice is a process of self-knowledge and development. It is also a process of high seriousness, and high silliness. It is difficult to imagine how much of an idiot it is possible to feel realising that the upper deck of a double-decker bus can see you doing an early morning ritual naked in your living room until you've done it, but trust me. It is also difficult to understand how transformative spells can feel, how strange it can be to enter into relation with symbols, to feel your will.

The spells in this book try to be non-prescriptive, because they will require adaptation. You might notice a certain looseness to them – an arguably sacrilegious lack of specificity as to moon phase, as to colour. This isn't sloppiness or accident: I cannot see the moon very often from my flat. We are mostly city witches, our climate strange, our horizons small, our sunsets great bursts of pink pollution light.

The same is true of spells that require walking, or outdoor space: I try to give alternatives to those less able to go out into the wild, or even into the city. I have also not included many spells for ritual bathing – not many of us have baths, either, and some people aren't able to use baths, anyway. Almost all ritual magic done in the bath can be broadly achieved with a basin of water or a shower, and I try to show everywhere how that can be done. I use a lot of herbs in my magic, and I forage for the majority of them. This is a privilege of my geography, my bodily abilities, my time. The spells I include here mostly don't call for large quantities of herbs, or anything esoteric. I also don't use poisons in this book, although I do in my magic. This is because what is safe and sane for me to do, as someone who is confident in their own abilities, it is not necessarily ethical for me to recommend. I do not want to be responsible for a spate of poisonings, for all that might make me feel like a glamorous wealthy widow with secrets.

Magic relies on our discipline, our commitment, our interest. It feeds on our intuition, on our learning, on our vital joys and sadnesses. Magic is in us always, regardless of where we are. It is about tapping into something, connecting, making real the ways we understand the world to work, the ways we want to change it. Magic does not, and witchcraft does not, rely on material objects. We bring things into relation with ourselves, to help us practise effectively, but those things can be, well, almost anything. Empty pizza boxes, our child's crayons, what-ever we have to hand. Witches are pragmatists. We are interested in effect, not in the minute and careful construction of rituals, however brilliant and fun that might be. We make magic as best we can, with what we have, acknowledging that everything in the world, from the most beautiful thing to the least, exists in relation to us.

SEPTEMBER

Foraging

It isn't until I have friends arrive to stay in my flat while I'm away that I start to worry about the jars on my shelves. Most of them are the usual herbs and spices and other substances: turmeric, thyme, several tins of treacle that I don't remember buying, coriander, etc. But toward the back of the shelves, things become stranger. Oak leaves, dogwood thorns, hawthorn berries. There are dried sloes and juniper. There are long, folded stems of yarrow, and viciously poisonous slips of yew. There are packets of valerian and broom, and rose petals in such abundance you'd think I was planning a honeymoon. It looks like an apothecary's pantry. But, I reassure myself, everything is labelled. Or rather: everything is labelled sufficiently for me to navigate it. It is, perhaps, not labelled entirely coherently, or properly, especially if you are a guest trying to find the mixed herbs for pasta sauce. Places and dates of gathering are noted, I realise with a jolt, but not edibility. I mean, I won't poison myself – I know the difference between the dried chanterelle I gathered earlier this year and the sections of bracket fungus I have kept. I know them, but others may not.

After a panicked phone call, they agree not to use anything they aren't certain about, and when I get home, I update my labels. My collection now sits, nicely demystified, and I wonder, as I look at it, exactly how it is that I became like this, with my strange strands of knowledge about plants and their uses. Still an amateur, of course, but keen. Keen on gathering beech-mast, on shining conkers for my altar, on labelling my pinecones, filling them with wax and aromatics and saving them for bonfire magics, where they crackle and smoke. When they leave, my friend writes a thank-you note. 'Thank you', she says, 'for letting us stay in your witch-house.' It makes me think of Baba Yaga, all alone in her chicken-leg dwelling, gathering things from the edges of the forest, iron-toothed and wicked. I might be a far cosier witch, all chilli flakes and whole cloves and dried daisies, but still. Guests in my house are all too aware, these days, of the strangeness.

I use these gatherings. I make teas, and balms; I make spells wrapped in cloth for the altar, for under my pillow, to send to friends. I use the materials I've collected in workshops and with groups of people who are learning about magic. They sit cosy in my house, but of course, I gathered them from outside. Foraging trips, from the planned to the fortuitous – walks up hills, trips to the sea. There are always scissors in my bag, and plastic bags. I am never, really, off duty in my search for green things to gather. It is part of why, and how, I love being outdoors. September is, for me, perhaps the most important month of the year for gathering plants: it is the time of later harvest, when jam is made and the second harvest of blackberries is gathered, when apples are ready and the days are still long. We begin our journey through the year in September, as if we are going back to school.

Pencils sharp, days still long, mushrooms waiting for us in the woods. Off we go.

Much is said about nature cures, in our increasingly indoor, urban world. And much of it is very well said: the world, and access to its green, living parts, heals us, gives us respite from our busy lives.[1] Or rather, it can do. Statistics about nature's curative properties are difficult, because there is almost no way of conducting studies that doesn't result in people accidentally equating access to nature with a number of other intersecting socioeconomic factors: access to transport; recreation time; a degree of financial independence that allows for opportunities for outdoor activities; being able-bodied, and feeling safe in nature in the first place, in terms of gender, sexuality or other minority identity.

Nature is, as an idea, as something we can access, only intermittently or complexly curative. And so, too, are the things that are in it. We are loath, often, to talk about nature's bounty as anything other than benign. The resurgence of interest in foraging in the UK is evidence of this. Newspapers and magazines give endless tips about the harvests that await us just outside our doors – often with very little thought to the numbers of people they are inviting to forage, the effect on delicately balanced ecosystems, and on the welfare of animals that need those wild-growing fruits and berries far more than we do. Often, there are blanket warnings: 'If you aren't sure what something is, don't eat it! Positive identification only please!' – but what does this mean, in practice? Who is going to come and tell you why this leaf, which looks like it should be entirely benign, is in fact bitter and sickness-inducing, or worse? There are expensive courses, of course – and some very good accessible ones – but generally the answer is careful study, knowledgeable friends, and a small degree of risk. There are things in the woods that can cure you, yes, but there are things in the woods that can kill you, and those are essential to know about, too.

Apples, however, are easy. We can all identify them, and my freezer is empty of last year's crop, so we go out to forage. The day we go and look for apples in the orchard is bright, and the trees are beginning to curl yellow at the edges. The woods are noisy with dogs and people, with shifting light. It has been a bad year for apples, and the harvest is slight, and I am so very cross about it. This year, we are looking for something that doesn't exist. The apple harvest is my favourite thing, and I feel robbed. Robbed of stewed apples, jam and vinegars.

The apple orchard we have come to is in the grounds of Craig House in Edinburgh. It lies in the centre of broad parkland, flanked by hills on one side and the gentle slope of the city on the other. It was bought, in the nineteenth century, by the Royal Edinburgh Hospital, and developed as Craig House Hospital, a psychiatric inpatient unit. Colloquially, it is still known as the 'Craiglockhart' asylum. There are ghost stories told about it, of course, and it seems to court them, rising as it does out of the green, a series of elegant, Gothic buildings with great staring windows.

Craig House has loomed above Edinburgh for a long time – or parts of it have. The central building, Old Craig House, dates from 1565, although it has been speculated that the site is far older. When a historian lived there during the 1850s, he described it as 'ghost haunted'. In 1600, John Kincaid, the owner, kidnapped the widowed Isabel Hutcheon for nefarious reasons, and trapped her in the house until King James VI, who was riding nearby, sent someone to him to demand her release. There are tales, too, of another lady, dressed all in green, who moves through the house and stands at the windows. Indeed, this Green Lady is sufficiently famous that the Edinburgh Dungeon, a schlocky tourist attraction, installed her as an exhibit in 2015. She was called Elizabeth Pittendale, and in around 1715 she married Sir Thomas Elphinstone, who was far older than she, and together they lived at Old Craig House. But her heart was young, her husband old, and she fell in love with his fair son, John. On finding this out, Elphinstone flew into a rage and killed her in the house itself, and her ghost was trapped there. She looks out of the windows, it is said, waiting for John to come to her, until her remains are united with his. It isn't noted why she is dressed in green, but I like to think that it is because she, in her heartsick longing, wandered the woods and hills that surrounded her house, robed in the rich colours of the forest, and the deep scrub of the hills. I think you can feel her, a little, and I always speak to her when we are out there, wandering. I do not look into the windows of Old Craig House, even though it stands empty, and you can approach it. It doesn't feel respectful, really.

Old Craig House stands, now, in the middle of the much larger complex of the psychiatric hospital, which had personalised villas for its inhabitants dotted around the grounds, the very cutting edge of rehabilitation for the well-to-do. It is understood that Wilfred Owen, the war poet, was a patient there, and Siegfried Sassoon was a longer-term resident, though there is some confusion about which specific building. No matter: we know that they were there, and that is enough. It feels, always, like a sad, heavy place, all wet grass and bowed trees. There are letters from Owen to Sassoon that refer to conversations about poetry in those buildings, and even to skirt near them is to be buried deep in the interlocking lives and considerations of the patients they housed.

Pooling in front of these buildings, across a gentle incline, is the Craig House orchard, planted by, and for, the residents. All sorts of apples grow here: cooking apples and eating apples, in a dazzle of varieties. The apples grow hard and sweet, usually, and in abundance. Despite their open situation, the general public are often wary of taking them, presuming that they belong to someone. But the hospital is all shut up, the patients gone, and the apples will, if left, all go to rot. They are ours: a gift from those who planted them and tended them. Each year, I fill my rucksack and bags with them. Ridiculous, as ever, gently shaking the branches of trees I'm too short and inflexible to climb, gathering windfalls. The previous year, I'd taken over five kilos.

This year, though, when we arrive, Craig House is in flux. The buildings that made up the psychiatric hospital are, like the plot of a big-budget horror movie, being converted into over a hundred luxury apartments, and everything is disappearing behind fences. The birdsong blurs with the noise of heavy machinery, and there are large posters advertising the flats as they will eventually look: spotless, luxurious and anonymous. They will hold very little of the original sense of the place: and perhaps that is preferable, given that many will have suffered in the psychiatric units. But it feels wrong that a place long dedicated to rehabilitation will fall to luxury property. There is also a question, heavy in the cold air, about whether or not the developers have artificially tampered with the apple harvest to discourage the great unwashed from tramping about at the edges of their manicured, expensive show flat. I cannot help but hope that the show flats start to smell a little: over-sweet, over-ripe, a subtle waft of rotting apples that drives the customers out. Something from the land, soaked with other people's anguish. I cannot help but hope that the Green Lady haunts the show flat, smelling of bright blood and rotting apples. I doubt it, though.

So we go out together, looking for apples, carrying Owen and Sassoon's poetry with us to read round the trees: a little light re-enchantment, we hope, and then home for pie. But what is there to do, when the trees are not laden with harvest, and our bags stay empty of all but the littlest things? The foragers sulk a little, thwarted. We fill our pockets instead with haws and hips and late blackberry leaves, which are almost certainly too bitter to make tea. I am not pleased. I feel I have let myself down, have failed some unarticulated test. A bad hedge-witch, her cupboard bare. And then, a friend spots them. Growing, sluggish and strange, out of treebark, as if they were the product of a wound. They pool like oozing liquid, as if the insides of the forest are escaping. But the trees are not leaking, of course. They are simply gracious hosts. This is *Tremella mesenterica*, known as yellow brain fungus, or, sometimes, 'witches' butter'. It blossoms up out of rotting wood, yellow and bulging and rubbery to the touch. It is vivid and hideous and entrancing, and I immediately poke it, as if I am a child. We cannot gather it, however. Nobody forages for witches' butter fungus. It cannot be eaten: or, more specifically, is ranked to be of dubious edibility, and to have no culinary value, because it is so meagre and slight. It isn't nice to touch, it isn't good to taste. You can't sell it. It isn't used in magic, or rather, you will not find it in most conventional lists of herbs, plants and mushrooms and their associated magical properties. It is an overlooked, edge-thing.

There isn't much written about the magical uses of common fungus, and they are broadly ignored by witches of my acquaintance and, as far as I can tell, have been by witches throughout history. However, people have long associated fungus (and indeed, poisonous or inedible items of all kinds) with witches. Witches' butter is a good example: from the name you can tell that the slime of it, the strangeness, is associated with witches and their unhomely fringe operations. Because witches existed outside societal norms, they were believed to somehow be able to convert the worst, most useless bits of the forest into strange, unnatural food. These sorts of names are evidence that witches and their vittels have long been considered semi-unreal, somehow mythical, beyond the requirements of normal human nourishment. They are, in this analysis, taking and producing something grotesque, something unnatural. Not butter churned from milk, but butter made from the scraps of rot that litter the forest floor: inedible, rubbery, a mockery of the thing it resembles. And yet, compelling. Something, by its very nature, bewitching.

We spend the rest of the afternoon looking for fungi, for the growths and protrusions other people don't trouble with. Gelatinous fungi, hard brackets, soft, rotting half-things, lichenous flowers stitched onto rocks. Touching them, and then washing our hands with sanitising gel because half the things we poke are poisonous. We find wood ear fungus (*Auricularia auricula-judae*), which sprouts out of rotting bark with such similarity to real ears, pricked in attention, that we feel the woods are listening to us. This fungus is used in Eastern medicine to help prevent heart disease and to thin the blood, but we don't pick it, not confident enough in its uses to take it home. The interest doesn't lie in picking the fungus, anyway, only in finding it, discovering the little brown curls that we would usually overlook. Most joyfully of all, toward the end of our afternoon, we find a collared earthstar (*Geastrum triplex*), which is inedible, and hugs so close to the ground it's easy to walk past it. It begins its life looking like a puffball, and then opens out like a star, and when it is mature, its spores puff out of the apical hole at the top of its central brown sphere, particularly when rain or wind buffet it. The effect is that of lazy smoke climbing up from a chimney. It's a beautiful, strange object, rather like the newly uncurled face of an alien ship, sending its little creatures out across the planet. When it appears in view, leather and strange, panting its dark spores out of its mouthpiece, we all crowd round to gape and squeeze. The apples aren't forgotten, our rucksacks light and empty, but we are doing something different, something that feels similarly lovely.

There are so many types of foraging, and this, though perhaps better described as a 'nature walk', surely fits into the broader definition of gathering from nature. We were just picking up different, less tangible things: touches and smells and information, and the thrill of looking closely at places our eyes would usually pass over. There is magic in discovering, in gathering up and taking in those things which the world does not deem important, which cannot be used and so are often ignored. Witches' butter fungus, ghost stories of half-forgotten women, the precious fruit trees planted by people experiencing crises in mental health. All of these edge-things, wrought slightly strange, falling into our notice. Fungus belongs to witches both in name and in character, because it seems strange, unnatural, similarly on the fringes of what might be acceptable. It is an edge-object, a little unpleasant and uncanny, and we aren't quite sure of its power. I found it intoxicating. It felt like a ghost story, like coming face to face with something unknown, and trying to understand its shape, size and relation to the world. We picked nothing truly edible, beyond a little clutch of puffballs, which I fried up in real, actual butter and ate, triumphant, for breakfast the next day.

Foraging, historically, was a vital means of gaining plants for food and medicine. But industrialisation and easy access to food and medicine caused it to become, over time, more of a recreational pursuit. These days, when it is always far easier to go to the supermarket and buy perfect blackberries than it is to pillage the dog-pissed hedgerows of your local park, foraging is no longer a survival activity for most people. It still, however, carries with it a pressure to harvest, to make sure you've got enough to do something with, to show your skill through glossy Instagram pictures of baskets – always pretty, wicker baskets – of shining berries. How much jam did you manage to make? Did you drive to a good unspoilt woodland simply bristling with things you could identify? There is a sense that foraging has been adopted by the middle classes in an attempt to promote reconnection with nature. It has been – as far as a free activity can be – somewhat capitalised on, given an aesthetic, sold back to the general public in the form of equipment, books and classes. If you are not someone whose participation in foraging looks like this, it is easy to feel like a failure. Certainly I have felt that, without access to 'unspoilt' nature, I'm somehow failing at foraging, failing at all of the 'back to the land' rhetoric espoused by both foraging and witchcraft books.

My 'unspoilt' nature is quite the opposite: it is, in the main, small parks and riverside cycle-paths, where voracious early foragers with longer arms than I have will hoover up every blackberry in sight. And it is even harder to gather herbs for ritual and medicinal use: there are so many warnings about car exhaust fumes and hedgerow plants, but when all you have are the shoulders of busy roads, and cracked pavements grubby with footprints and dog-marks, what are you supposed to do? Instead, I am increasingly interested in the lives of urban witches: where we go to get our supplies, what we are able to gather, and how it impacts our magic practice.

For me, one of the most important things here is learning to recognise and value that which is usually overlooked by other people. To source plants for cures, foods and rituals from what we can find around us, and not find ourselves wanting because we do not all live by fields and forests. To understand that the smell of hot tarmac shares with the smell of warm hay qualities of place, intoxication, delight. One is not better than the other: they are just different. The same is true of a bag of apples and a day spent looking at fungus. If we are reliant on neither to live, then why is one ranked above the other? Yes, nobody wants to see the fungus underneath a pretty Instagram filter, really, but there's still something wonderful about it, in all its glistening strangeness. I am trying to relearn foraging, let it truly be a part of my witchcraft practice, and that means being practical, valuing what I am able to find, and learning to work magic with things as they are, not things as I wish them to be.

Plants collected from cities are different from rurally gathered plants. Our atmospheric pollution levels are different, for a start. For another, urban plants have close foot traffic: dogs, people, shoes that track all sorts of germs and debris. All the advice is to collect plants from wild, empty places, especially if you are going to cook and eat them. But actually, you can find things to gather on pavements and round grass verges, in parks and along canals. You just have to treat them slightly differently. One thing people never tell you in books, for fear that you'll eat something obviously dirty and make yourself ill, is that most plants are fairly robust, and can be cleaned. You can rinse with cold water, or soak, or scald with boiling water, depending on what you plan to do with them. You can even wash plants with a tiny splash of vinegar in the water, to further disinfect them: just rinse them well after that. Yes, plants grown away from harsh chemicals, including exhaust fumes, are preferable, but we work with what we have. Attempt to be mindful of things grown at dog-pissing height or in popular dog-walking spots, but remember that plants can be washed thoroughly before use, and will not lose their potency, especially if they are being used for non-edible purposes. You do not have to grasp things with your hands, either. You can wear gardening gloves to pick plants. If you're bringing home, for example, pretty fallen leaves for your altar, it doesn't matter if they're a bit muddy. A delicate wash, and they'll be fine. We are very panicked about getting ill, as a society, and about pollutants. Not to be a doomsayer, but there are tiny microplastics in our blood, now. We are complexly related to, and already contain, all sorts of forms of pollution. Which is not to say we should give up trying to avoid them, but a certain degree of squeamishness can be dispensed with. Nothing is as pure as we would like to think it is, because purity is a nonsense concept.

So many books on witchcraft – hedge-witchcraft and foraging specifically – imply that we are able to radically alter our circumstances and ourselves simply by mystically communing in some way or another with the natural world. My argument is that the opposite actually occurs. We are made of the same things as the natural world: we are not only altered by it, we also alter it, every time we interact with it. It returns us to ourselves, by reminding us that we are networked into it – that we are not alone in many of the ways we fear we are. But our interactions with it are always double – we leave as much of a trace as it does. And the natural world can 'heal' us only as much as we seek to heal it. This is the trick. One must be a steward, one must give service, however small. It is enough to go and be in a forest: perhaps, try not to ask it to give you anything. You wouldn't walk into a room full of strangers and ask them for gifts, and this is the same. Relationships built on mutual care feel strange when applied to nature, but it needs the same care that we do. This is why the idea that one must visit pristine landscape to commune with nature is so faulty. You have a far better relationship with your houseplants than you do with trees you've never met, in many ways. You have raised and cared for them: they may not be ancient, but even the smallest window box, that hosts bees and grows herbs, can be such an enormously valuable source of happiness and usefulness. They help to show us, slowly, how similar we are – needing light, heat, nutrition in order to live – but they are also genuinely good companions that grow and change, that ask us to look closely and think deeply about things, and that ask us to relate ourselves back out into the world in an undemanding, but deeply rewarding way. Every living thing is part of the same network: there is no opting out, but there are so very many ways to opt in.

Foraging, to complete beginners, can seem complicated, bewildering, and potentially life-threatening. It is best to start with something you know, something that is fairly unmistakeable. It is best also to start with something that is in plentiful supply, something that you can take quite a bit of, if you need to, leaving enough for others, and for the ecosystem. One easy, bountiful and almost entirely unmistakeable plant you can easily forage for is nettle.

Nettles grow from spring into autumn, so will be easy to locate in September and throughout autumn, though they are at their most delicious in spring. You almost certainly know what they look like, but if you don't, they're easily identifiable:

they have strong serrated leaves and grow vigorously, to about two metres tall in places. They also sting: and the sting, because it is irritating but not dangerous, is an excellent way to identify nettles if you're unsure about them. The new growth is the most tender: that's usually the first little sprig of leaves. Unfortunately, the sting means nettles can also be off-putting to harvest, but grasp the nettle's stalk firmly to avoid stings, and you'll escape the worst of it. The other approach is to wear gardening gloves (Marigolds can be worn, equally, though be careful not to tear them), and this makes the job pleasant. Be sure your limbs are covered, though, when approaching a nettle patch.

Nettles are native to the UK and much of Europe, and in Britain they are among the first edible greens to appear in the spring. They were traditionally a marker of spring's arrival, and a welcome nutritional addition to winter food stocks. They are rich in vitamin C and are an excellent blood purifier (because of this, people who take certain medications may be best advised not to eat too many nettles – if in doubt, ask a doctor). In Scotland, a soup called nettle kail was eaten on Shrove Tuesday, to bring in the spring. It is still a lovely thing to make, and very easy. The tips of the nettles can also be saved and dried for tea, and were an ingredient used in beer-making, too. Nettles are an excellent foraging staple because you can find them almost anywhere, and because they need to be cooked before they can be eaten: nettle salad might be the sort of dish a Roald Dahl villain would serve their enemies, but you do not want to try it. Instead, nettles need to be wilted with boiling water in order to denature their sting. This means that you can clean them really thoroughly in warm water, with vinegar, and then rinse them before cooking, if you need to. Nettles, because they grow tall, are usually fairly clean anyway, because you only pick the tops. But still, it is comforting to know you can safely wash them before then cooking them in boiling water.

There are so many plants that are inedible that we can harvest, too. There is a joy in rediscovering the bringing home of things. I think that, as children, this is often encouraged: we used to bring home conkers and their spiky cases, we used to bring home interesting shells, rocks and sticks. The edge of my parents' car-parking space still has an inches-deep collection of 'very precious things', which we would be asked to turn out of our pockets before we were allowed back into the house. A lot of the parents I know have little 'nature table' spaces in their homes, which they decorate seasonally, and enjoy going out into the woods or parks in the city and finding objects to decorate them with. Most people grow out of it: I haven't. My pockets are always full. Leaves and twigs and little bright stones, berries and chips of sea glass. To go out and walk through nature and bring home (or photograph) things you see around you is such a lovely way of engaging with the world.

I bring home things for my altar. Broom, with its crackly black seed heads, is a particular favourite as it looks beautiful dried in a vase, and I use it for making sweeping brooms at Samhain. It is a vigorous plant, with bright yellow vanilla-scented flowers, and it keeps its green colour all year. I use it in spells to help banish the worst effects of the winter. It is also medicinal, although not for amateur use, being a halluci-nogenic. The hallucinogenic compound found in broom is sparteine, which is used in contemporary medicine to treat heart and circulatory disorders. Oil extracted from the green woody stems can produce a disinfectant compound that helps remove parasites from the skin, and this means that broom has long been associated with purity. It can also be used to induce vomiting, and thus has an association with cleansing. Its hallucinogenic properties have led to the association between broom and the supposition that witches fly around on broomsticks. Broom thrives on exposed ground and provides good, hardy cover, so is planted in many parks. It is vigorous and flourishes across the UK, so you are safe to pick some: you will need secateurs or scissors, and you do not have to wear gloves. There's no need to worry about broom being clean, as you aren't going to eat it. It's a lovely thing to gather, and perfect for building up foraging confidence.

In September, there is a wealth of things to gather. The rosehips are coming into the hedgerows, ripe for syrups and cordials, jams and teas. They are full of vitamin C, and have a lovely, round, citrus taste. The seeds are covered in tiny irritant hairs, however, so they must be strained through muslin after they've been boiled. There are blackberries, which people love to gather, and which in their first picking are wonderful − but please, if you are gathering them, be mindful. Other people will inevitably want to gather them too, unless you're taking them from your garden, and the birds also need some, especially as other food sources dwindle in the autumn. This is not a stricture against making jams and crumbles, but be kind in your taking, and the thorns will be kinder to you, I am certain. There are elderberries, dark and rank eaten raw, but yielding and rich once boiled with sugar for syrup. There are haws, the fruit of the hawthorn tree, which can be added into hedgerow jam. In September, when the light blushes golden through the sky and the days still trail long, there is nothing more joyous than foraging for lovely, ripe, glistening berries. They are a treat: a reward for the end of the summer; a bulwark against the dark. They can be found in cities, too, dusty with gravel from the cycle-paths, ramming their way over the pavement like bullies, spilling into supermarket car parks. You can find them: just keep your eyes open.

To discover something, pick it, take it home and make something beautiful out of it, jam to glisten on shelves through winter, is the most elementary form of magic. You are providing for yourself, bottling summer to see you through the darkest times. You are trapping sunlight in with the sugar, to unscrew when the days are hung rain and biting wind. You are affirming a belief that you deserve sweet things, and that sweet things are worth working for. You are putting effort into that production, into making something wonderful for yourself and those you love.

Foraging isn't easy, but by doing this, this little slice of time and effort, you are affirming that you will find pleasure in the hard work of life. Making food is magic, transforming berries to jam a form of unparalleled alchemy. September is a month for picking up final freckles and scratching your arms in hedge-rows. It is the month that asks you to bottle all the best bits of the bright high sun, and keep them for yourself until you need them.

Beyond the jam and the triumph, there are other reasons to go outside, to pick and learn and look. Lots of people say that foraging, and indeed just being out in landscape, lifts the mood, and helps us to feel more connected. The writer Emma Mitchell, for example, writes in her book *The Wild Remedy: How Nature Mends Us* of the 'phytoncides', the volatile compounds and oils that emerge from plants, and that, when inhaled, have a positive effect on our immune and nervous systems.[2] Handling leaves, and bringing things home, increases exposure to these helpful compounds. Of course, this is sound science, and it is another example of how humans and plants interact, and how beneficial the green and growing world can be. It is, of course, also a salient reminder of the preciousness and precarity of that green world, and the extent to which we are bound not just to participate in its attractive aspects, but also to help safeguard all of it.

Of course, smelling the phytoncides and immersing ourselves in the sharp green scents of the outdoors aren't the only obvious benefits to going outside. There is the sense of adventure and discovery these activities cultivate; the exercise undertaken when we go out into the world; the camaraderie of group expeditions, or even of dog walks or solo trips. Mitchell's focus isn't on magic, so she overlooks the magical aspects of time in the world among plants and creatures. Being out in the world connects us, bodily and truly, with the more-than-human world, and lets us regard ourselves as part of it, rather than estranged from it, or in a position of domination over it. We are able to understand our relationship with the world – as it truly is, not as we would wish it to be – most acutely when we are in it. It is magical, to understand the world around us: what this plant is, which streams and rivers run under our city. It is magical because magic is the act of putting ourselves out into the world, actively, receptively. When we learn about the world – what grows, and where – then we are paying attention, exerting our will to know and understand. And when we attend, the world attends back at us, and brings with that attention all of its complexity and energy.

There is much evidence that active participation in landscapes rich in vegetation and wildlife have positive effects on our well-being. Indeed, much of that work indicates that this cannot be replicated by cityscapes, which can have an adverse effect.[3] This is a shame: most of us live in cities now, and cannot easily escape them. It also overlooks the fact that cities have lovely semi-wild green spaces: from dog-walking parks to canal towpaths, from botanic gardens to playing fields. Cities hold green places within themselves like jewels, you just have to hunt them down. It doesn't do to write off urban living as doomed to misery, as existing in sharp contrast with healthy, happy rural folk. This also elides stark rural poverty, and many other issues of countryside land management: our countryside appears one way on casual walks, quite another if you live in it and tend it. My argument, however, is that stepping outside, even for a little time, even in cities, can still help things: going outside during the day exposes us to Vitamin D, which we are all chronically short of in Britain. It brings us into contact with unexpected things. These things don't need to be beautiful pastoral vistas: they can be seagulls, great squabbling squalls of them, and although they aren't the shy herds of deer we might wish, or the beautiful, diverse butterflies or insects one can spot in the country, they are still brimming with life and aliveness and wonder. (I do not suggest, however, trying to bring one home for your nature table.) You might pat dogs, see squirrels nicking stuff out of bins. You might see trees growing out of abandoned buildings, or daisies emerging from small scrapes of soil, or weeds pushing up through gravel. Above you, sitting on power lines, the chatter of starlings, the bouncing squawk of crows. There might not be rabbits, or wide horizons, but there is life: bustling and extraordinary. The countryside has enormous value, and I would not ever suggest otherwise. But the key is finding places that work for you, that meet you where you are. The key is not presuming you cannot do magic unless you are sky-clad on a mountaintop, in full view of the stars. You can do magic on street corners, between the news-agent and the parked cars. And the truth is that cities often have far better infrastructure, and the parks are easier to get to, and more accessible when you arrive. The woods are lovely, dark and deep, of course – but we do not need to privilege them as magical spaces. We witches know that our magic comes from the act of attending to the world, from drawing it into relation with us, regardless of which bit of the world we turn our attention to.

Much has been written, usually at length and in deeply strange, imprecise language, about what happens when we commune with the natural world. This is what Wiccan practitioner Silver RavenWolf calls 'secret shifting', which, she argues, moves your mind from inside yourself to 'the source'.[4] RavenWolf believes that this shift will allow you to commune with nature, at the source of its power, and truly alter your reality. What Raven Wolf is aiming at, I think, is a sense of interconnectedness with the world at large, and a knowledge of our place in nature, and that these can empower us to make changes in our own lives, and to work magic. When we turn our attention toward the more-than-human world, when we do our very best to notice it, then something happens. This could be on the level of the compound oils that help our immune system; it could be blood flow; it could be the smugness of having been out for a walk. It could be all of these things, but for witches, there is something more. Drawing things into relation with each other, drawing ourselves into relation with them, gives us an understanding of the way we are all, each of us, every thing, capable of filling up space, capable of energy, possessed of a solidity and reality and capable of producing reciprocal forms of attention. In *The Lord of the Rings*, the hobbits stumble into a forest full of Ents: animate trees. They listen to the forest and it, indisputably, listens back. Well, our plants listen back, too; they just use different means.

Evening primrose (*Oenothera drummondii*) can sense vibrations from something as small as the wings of a bee. Not only can it sense them, it can respond. As one report noted: 'Within minutes of sensing the sound waves of nearby bee wings through flower petals, the concentration of the sugar in the plant's nectar was increased by an average of twenty per cent'.[5] This makes the primrose more attractive to the bee, and in turn increases the plant's chance of pollination. It is a clever adaptation: but it is more than that. There are easy, anthropomorphising comparisons to be made with girls in Regency novels pinching their cheeks to make them red before the soldiers come in, making themselves pretty, hoping to catch their eyes. But even beyond such facetious comparisons, there is the sense that the plant is attending to, and responding to, its environment, just as we do, all the time. People say that singing and talking to one's plants is helpful for their growth, that it mimics the vibrations, perhaps. We can communicate directly with more-than-human aspects of the world, simply through proximity. Not only that, but they can communicate with each other, via vast fungal networks. The 'wood wide web', as it has been coined, is a mycorrhizal network of fungi that links plants and trees across an area. It is known that 'around ninety per cent of land plants are in mutually beneficial relationships with fungi' and that this relationship helps plants soak up water, and boosts their immune systems, because fungi colonising root systems 'triggers the production of defence-related chemicals' in the trees, so they are better able to defend themselves in future.[6] Scientist Suzanne Simard has found that carbon can be transferred, via the mycorrhizal network, between species of tree, and over considerable distances.[7] Indeed, this resource-sharing seems to indicate, Simard argues, that 'in fact they are interacting with each other, trying to help each other survive'.[8] This is, I think, what we have long suspected. The trees are helping one another, invested in the survival of the forest overall. They are acting in their own best interests, of course, but they are also achieving what is best for a group, not just for themselves. Things are very connected: so connected that they actively communicate. The forest does know things: it talks, it shares, it raises its defences at the same time. Trees are vastly more complex than we once assumed – and they

are kinder, too, or at least that is how we, as humans, interpret those acts.

If these complex negotiations and communications are
taking place around us, then we are not separate from them: we
too can build relationships with the more-than-human world
that surrounds us, and can transform it through an ethics of care
and attention. The fungus that we found in the woods, so often
overlooked, passed by, discarded for its ugliness and inedibility,
is in fact one of the most important things in there. It is the
linking web, the mechanism by which the growth and decay
cycles are made possible. We were right to pay it that attention,
to spend our time becoming as intimately acquainted with it as
we could. Witches do not overlook even what is ugly, even what
seems useless: often, it reveals itself to be anything but.

That, I think, is where the possibility is held, where the
reality of our connectedness allows us to start doing magic.
This feeling is somewhat like vertigo. The nearest comparison
I have is that of thinking very hard about the infinite nature
of the universe, something we cannot really imagine. The way
that thought pushes at the edge of your brain, makes you dizzy.
The way it is a process-thought, which cannot be accurately
completed. The bodily sensation that it feels closest to, for me,
is that body-alive surge that comes in high places. It is like
catching a glimpse of the ground far beneath you as you walk
over a glass floor in an office block, or look out of the top
window of a church tower. The reorientation of your reality:
you truly are that high, you truly can see the world laid out.
If you fell, you truly would die. Physics, in those moments,
reasserts itself. They are moments of heightened awareness.
On the Eiffel Tower, in even a gentle breeze, you are suddenly,

terrifyingly aware that you are standing on a collection of beautifully balanced metal, and so much air. That your trust has been placed in a structure that, unless you are an engineer, it is difficult to fully comprehend as solid, safe, stable.

That rush of awareness, that slightly altered, heightened state, comes with practice. It comes with going outside, looking around, and feeling enfranchised, among all of the beauty and chaos and pollution and wonder of the world. There is no shift that I can describe, beyond the shift from inside your house to outside it, from aloneness to being surrounded by the busyness of the whole living world. Sometimes, the feeling is of harmony: of place, among these things, of being one small part of a vast, live web. Sometimes, the feeling is of overwhelm, in bad weather, heavy traffic – a feeling of connection that is too much, as if the car headlights didn't just blind us but buzzed into our blood. Sometimes, it makes us cry. When I have stood in the park, the frost picking up its feet and disappearing from the grass, I have cried. Partly, that's because I'm a foolish, sentimental creature, whose life is spent thinking carefully about my place in the great web of the world. But mostly, it is because it becomes impossible, for me, in that morning stillness, to feel anything other than entirely certain of the intricate, intimate connections that exist between the big world and me. My footprints, melting the frost. My exhalations, breath made visible, dragoning out over the wide expanses of grass. My body, moving through this space, while above me tree branches move, and around me insects; under my feet, small creatures burrowed and sleeping. We are made of the same things as everything else, and here we are, able to talk to it all. That fact is the confidence and knowledge that lets me do magic. Witch Rae

Beth calls the magic of the natural world 'an enacted nature poem' and this feels like an excellent metaphor. Just as in a nature poem, nature is writ large and made vivid, every word attended to with deep care, so in these moments of awareness, the world seems to step into itself, reveal its true detail.[9]

This is how that connection feels for me. Rae Beth has called this connection the vast web of 'the self-repairing body' and while this isn't entirely true – especially not in the face of human damage – there is a truth in it.[10] Nature does tend to correct, and, when left alone, to evolve without our intervention. And that, perhaps, is why it is nourishing, healing, magical: because it carries us along with it, but does not need us. Because it reminds us that we are guests here for the short blink of our lives. And one of the ways that I feel most connected is by foraging. By taking a little of what nature has produced, and using it to work magic. To walk as a witch walks: to pay attention to what is overlooked. I wish to forage for knowledge, and details, and stories, because they are as much a part of magic as jam or the bubbling of homemade beer. I wish to treasure the objects that are most commonly missed; the apparently unmagical things: so often, they richly reward our looking.

A Herbal Soda for Fever and Heat

You will probably have stepped over it, not seen it. Pineappleweed (*Matricaria discoidea*) pushes up between the cracks in city pavements, blossoms round the bottom of lamp posts, blooms in neglected, poor soil. Pineappleweed is easy to identify: it grows no higher than about eight inches, and has feathery leaves. The flower, which is what we are interested in, is a little cone shape. It is green and then greenish yellow, and it blooms in summer. When crushed, the flower has the distinct smell of pineapples. It is a relative of the chamomile plant, and the leaves and flowers are both edible. However, by the time the flowers are blooming, the leaves are a little bitter. It is commonly used in herbal remedies, having the soothing properties of chamomile. It also has uses in bringing down fever, and dealing with upset stomachs. Eaten in excess, it can cause adverse reactions, and some people have a skin allergy to the leaves, so do bear this in mind.

One of the easiest ways to use pineappleweed is in a natural soda, which is refreshing and captures its calming properties.

For this recipe, the flowers are best picked fresh. You only want the flowers here: the leaves will embitter the mixture. Because you are most likely to harvest pineappleweed in cities, all of the usual warnings apply. Wash the flowers gently but thoroughly under cold running water.

You will need:

- *Three or four good handfuls of flowers per 1-litre container*
- *A 1-litre jar, or two 500ml jars*
- *Honey (in this instance, cheap synthetic honey actually works better, as organic honey is antibacterial and will kill the natural yeast of the pineappleweed flowers)*

Clean a glass jar with hot soapy water. Rinse well and leave it to dry. Once dry, add the flowers. These should form a scant third or less of the jar. Fill the jar with cold tap water, leaving an inch or so of clearance at the top, and add the honey. A tablespoon or two will be fine – the aim is not to make this overly sweet, just to give the natural yeast something to eat. You could equally well use brown sugar. Shake the jar until the honey has dissipated a little. Leave this in the fridge for two to three days (but no longer). The natural yeasts in the pineappleweed will cause the beginnings of the fermentation process. You'll be left with a beautiful, slightly effervescent soda, which is deliciously pineapple-tasting. Strain it out, and drink with ice. Once opened, consume over the next couple of days, and store in the fridge. It is particularly nice to wind down, to lessen stress, and it is excellent for soothing over-heated frazzled days.

OCTOBER

Samhain and Talking to the Dead

I don't talk very often to the dead. Or rather, they don't speak to me. Out in that grey place, in that ill-defined beyond, I do not think that they are clamouring for my attention. Some people hear from them all the time: the newly bereaved particularly. The dead are always sending messages, they tell me, and I, in my extraordinary luck (long may it continue), have lost comparatively few people who were close. None, apparently, who wish to speak, to whisper things, send certain songs on the radio. But then, I don't go looking for the dead. Don't dig them up, unrumple them from rest and ask them things.

At Samhain, the Celtic celebration that we know now more commonly as Hallowe'en, the evening before the liturgical celebration of All Saints, the time that the dead traditionally come calling, I feel a little ashamed of this. My ancestors, whom I seek to honour, I largely have no relationship with. They aren't near me, either: we were farmers and weavers a long time, confined to rural Aberdeenshire and to the Yorkshire moors, and I'm content to let them gather there. This feels like a failing in a witch, but not one I know how to rectify.

I have tried to cultivate a relationship with the dead before. I went, once, with my grandma, to see the house where she was born. It sits, hunched under the broad sky, high up on a Yorkshire moor, the wind scouring the short grass. Her brothers and sisters, all now gone, were not gathered there, or not that I could feel. Instead, there was just the empty noise of the wind, its motion giving body to the air, so that we felt we weren't standing so much as leaning on it. Even my grandma failed to cry: like clean-picked bones, the house held nothing of its former residents. We drove home, quite untroubled by any trace of them. My great-grandmother had the sight, it is said: my father a little too, sometimes. Births, deaths, marriages, sometimes illness. So I think if we had been going to see them, one of us would have felt something, had some signal tele-graphed. Instead, we had a nice pub lunch, and my grandma told us stories about walking to school in her wellington boots, snow falling in down the tops.

Some people are fascinated by their past, about the shape of those who came before, their lives and experiences. As a family, that is not how we are made. I feel guilty, sometimes, that the dead do not come calling for me – but then, perhaps I have never shown quite enough interest. At Samhain, I decide that I am going to have to do something about it. However, I am not sure at first how to learn about my forebears. After all, nobody in my family has collected stories. I ask friends who know their family histories well, and a lot of them reply with details of uncles who have 'done' the family tree, and of exciting results from those services that analyse your origins based on DNA sampling. Sadly, I do not have such an uncle, and I find that I do not want to give my DNA to those strange, intrusive schemes that tell you where you come from. They are too interested in revealing, with the callousness of undifferentiated data, secret adoptions, concealed infidelities, and the identities of criminals who thought they'd got away with it. I know where

I come from, more or less, and am as ethnically uninteresting as it is possible to be. If there are surprises – propensities to disease or forms of madness, raised likelihood of dementia or cancer – then I do not particularly want to know them. Nor have I any interest in being the one who climbs my family tree.

I have a friend whose ancestor was infamously tried as a witch; others who can trace themselves to kings and ancient nobles. They talk about their ancestors all the time: visit their gravesites, tell people at parties. I think that those sorts of ancestors might be easier to communicate with, because they live on in public consciousness. Not, I might add, that those are the only sorts of dead worth talking to, but on the other hand, if they speak, there's a sense that you've got something to brag about. I envy my friends who go to their forebears for advice, for succour. I do not envy them their losses, you understand, but I am perhaps jealous, a little, that my great-great-great-antecedents have never twitched the veil to chat to me. I fear we, in my family, lack even troubled secrets, desperate to be imparted. All our ancestors' faults were, as far as it is possible to tell, just as ordinary as their lives. And so, at Hallowe'en, when the veil between the worlds is at its thinnest, and witches of all types commune with their dead, my notifications are quiet.

Most other cultures are far less squeamish about their dead than we are. I've always envied that – easy conversations, and the maintenance of good relationships with ancestors. Many global cultures include ancestor-worship as part of their spiritual and religious practices. In Korean culture, for example, it is common to perform rites and give offerings to ancestors up to four generations above one's parents, and differentiations are made – by way of how the person died – between good and malevolent ancestor spirits.[1] In Mexico, Día de Muertos, celebrated on 2 November, sees shrines set up to departed relatives, and offerings made in the form of food, money, cigars, and little sugar or clay skulls vividly decorated. Possessions belonging to the deceased, or that they might want, are placed on that person's grave. The dead are acknowledged still to have preferences, to have needs, to require conversation and gifts. Buddhist traditions across Asia involve pious acts of remembrance to ancestors, again centring around the active remembrance of past family members through domestic shrines. In Japan, particularly, remembering ancestors is a part of both Buddhist practice and Shintoism, because the spirits of departed people are thought to be part of the animate fabric of the world. Europe, too, has a long history of ancestor-worship, but this receded with the advent of Christianity. The active inclusion of our dead in our daily lives and in our houses has ceased to be customary, and so our dead appear differently – they are not recognised as ancestor spirits so much as ghosts. And there are, commonly anyway, fewer ghosts than there used to be. It isn't really seemly to be haunted.

This is not to say I am entirely bereft of ghosts, mind you, even if I am not related to the ones who visit me. Around Samhain, I'm always made more aware of the ghosts we share our space with, whom I have known since I was born. For although we do not talk much with our ancestors, my family home has always felt haunted, by ghosts who were there long before we arrived. They are pleasant ghosts, and don't deter visitors. There is the man whose photograph my mother owns – but only that, no name, no anything. He likes, someone once told my mother firmly, to be near the piano, because he enjoys hearing my father play. If his photograph is moved out of the room it seems that he makes a fuss, casts piano music through the house from the still keys, to indicate he feels he's missing out. It's an easy enough request to keep and so there he lives, his kind, inquisitive face in its art-deco frame, while my father plays the blues. We keep him in the right room, now.

There is one other ghost, at least. Our family house is one of seven in a row, which were lived in by the tradesmen who built them, and she is, I think, the daughter of the man who helped to build our house. She lived in it all her life, and didn't die young. Almost a hundred years in that house, so no wonder she cares so tenderly for it. She caught me once, when I was a toddler and about to fall down the stairs. Instead of falling – I absolutely swear it – I bumped down the stairs gently, as if held gently by unseen hands. My childminder at the time also witnessed it, and I remember her face, all frozen in shock, as I floated down the stairs towards her. I couldn't have been more than three, and so, of course, in the way of these things, my childminder was long gone by the time I grew up, and there was nobody else to ask about it. The ghost remains present in the house, though, and I feel her most often at the bottom of the stairs.

Halfway up the stairs are wind chimes, and we ring them

when we climb the stairs. I am not sure how it started, but I like to think it lets the ghosts know where we are, so that we don't surprise them. It's a courtesy, as much as anything, although they are all friendly. They've never given messages, or not that I'm aware of, beyond the sorts of messages old houses give up like gifts. Spidery hand underneath old wallpaper that dates the last time it was changed, with signatures. My dad once, desperate for a pencil while redoing the bathroom floor, found one underneath the floorboards. A proper Victorian joiner's pencil, flat-sided, lead still good. He put it back under the last floorboard when he was finished with it. The house holds its gifts, and we respect them, let them reappear for the next person who needs them. We've added to them too, joined with the tradition, written our names on the plaster walls with our dates. My sister and I drew round our little child's hands: one day, we will be someone's ghosts, beneath the lining paper, shining back out at them from the past. We've left notes in the sealed-up chimneys too, because, well, when people unfold all that old newspaper, wonder at the news, we want them to know that we were there, that we lived through it, that we have left our trace. We are housemates, rather than friends, with our ghosts. I don't trouble them too much. It isn't polite, after all, to trouble ghosts. Except, perhaps, on Hallowe'en, when they are abroad.

Our family home, on Hallowe'en night, is brightly lit. There are candles in the windows and down the garden, marking the path home for the good dead who wish to visit, marking a boundary to keep away those we do not welcome. Our next-door neighbours have beautifully carved pumpkin lanterns flickering eerily on their wall. We can hear the children shrieking as they run past them. My mother remembers carving turnip lanterns when she was a child, the grim difficulty of sending a spoon down through that unyielding flesh, and the hideous, unsettling results. Pumpkins, which we carve nowadays, are softer, more amenable to being emptied out. One of my difficulties with modern Hallowe'en pumpkins is that they are bred to be carved, not to be eaten: the flesh is watery and tasteless. Better, however, than ruining all your best spoons and sending yourself to A&E in search of authenticity.

But if you've never seen a turnip lantern, I'd urge you to find pictures: there is something truly uncanny about their menacing faces. And there should be: after all, their name, jack-o'-lantern, is held in common with other supernatural creatures who conjure dread. The first is the jack-o'-lantern or Will-o-the-Wisp, those cruel, strange lights that hover misleadingly over bogs and marshes, trying to lure travellers to their doom. They are also linked with the Irish story of Jack of the Lantern, a drunk man who struck a deal with the devil that meant he would never end up in hell. Finding, on his death, that he was disbarred from heaven too, Jack was forced to walk the world unresting, carrying in his hand a turnip with a glowing ember in it, which marked him as a denizen of the netherworld. In both stories, the eerie lights signal something to the observer. They warn us, tell us that the supernatural world has entered our own space, somehow, and that we should be wary of it. By an act that is entirely in keeping with the principles of sympathetic magic, jack-o'-lanterns do the opposite in our own homes, actively guarding against the incursion of unwanted supernatural intruders. Or that, at least, is the hope.

Scotland likes to think it invented Hallowe'en: it certainly did etymologically speaking. Hallowe'en is the Scottish term for All Hallows' Eve, the night before All Hallows' Day – *hallow* is an Old English word for holy or sacred, and it came to mean 'saint'. But even before Hallowe'en was incorporated into Christianity and the liturgical year, I'd argue that we had some claim over it. Samhain, the Celtic celebration of the end of harvest and the beginning of winter, has very deep roots here, as it does in Ireland, and on the Isle of Man. Samhain, which is thought to mean literally 'the end of summer', is the mirror, or echo, to Beltane: if the Beltane fires are to draw the year back to life, to celebrate the living, then the bonfires of Samhain are their shadow, honouring the dead and the passing of the fruiting months. These celebrations were a time when the *Aos Sí*, or nature-spirits of Irish mythology, were most likely to slip out from their realm and tread into ours, which is where we get our notions of the 'thin veil' of Hallowe'en.

Many of the traditions of Samhain can be divided into two strands: those designed for honouring the dead, and those that help with keeping unwanted supernatural forces at bay. Scottish traditions are quite particular, and, spurred by the current folk and witchcraft revival, many of the more esoteric ones are coming back into fashion. There has been, for example, an upturn in turnip jack-o'-lanterns, and from my friends with children I hear there has been a return to guising. Guising is among the most interesting of Samhain traditions, because it carries magic within it. It is guising from which the American trick or treating is devised, a tradition that has been imported wholesale back into Britain. Guising is very different, however. Guisers dress up (to dis*guise* themselves from walking spirits), and go door-to-door performing songs and rhymes for their neighbours. In return for these performances – which brought luck to the neighbours – guisers were historically given objects to ward off bad luck. There were no requirements for the houses to give money or sweets to guisers simply for turning up. Instead, the guisers had to do a 'turn' in order for the mutual exchange of luck to be complete. I can still remember my turns from childhood. One year, my sister and I learned the witches' speech from *Macbeth*, and another year we learned William Allingham's poem 'The Fairies'. I can only imagine how we looked – appearing, small and seriously painted, to recite: 'Up the airy mountain, / Down the rushy glen, / We daren't go a-hunting / For fear of little men.' There is, I think, of all the strange magic in the world, nothing quite so focused, quite so serious, as the poetic recitation of two little girls who believe, wholeheartedly, in fairies. There is something deeply magical about Hallowe'en, about working on learning these poems by heart for the week prior and choosing our costumes to match. Guising is where my interest in the occult began. It felt like a summoning, some sort of joyous pact with another realm: we would become practitioners for one night, weave our strange magic and get given clementines and Freddos for our efforts. It was, as potential satanic pacts go, an extremely good deal, and it gave us, early on, a sense of Hallowe'en as a festival of protection, of luck.

Our turns were always themed for the supernatural and now, whenever I go home to help with the guising in my parents' street, the children who come to their door have learned turns

too, by and large. Although the 'trick or treat' refrain, ubiquitous in America, is more commonly heard in Scotland than it
used to be, it is still looked on with a degree of suspicion. I
feel, from a ritual point of view, that it misses out the magic;
instead, 'trick or treat' renders the performance a demand for
recompense. After all, the magic doesn't lie in the costumes,
per se, nor in the sweets, but in the mutual exchanging of luck
and protection. Hallowe'en is a festival that marks a point of
change in the year, the significant movement downwards, away
from the light and toward winter, away from plenty and toward
scarcity. The evil that walks abroad on All Hallows' Eve is both
fictive and seasonal, both superstitious and entirely natural.
Bringing good cheer to our neighbours, even if it is tinged with
eeriness, is a way of marking the change.

The tradition of guising is similar to another curious folk
tradition that places uncanny beings on the doorsteps of unwit-
ting inhabitants – that of the Mari Lwyd. This Welsh tradition,
which has been revived after near-extinction, sees a sinister
decorated horse skull paraded round the houses of a village.
The horse-creature must be greeted with open arms, and the
invitation of shelter, refreshments and revelry extended to those
who walk with her. If properly welcomed, she brings luck to
the house, and wards off evil. If unwelcomed, she may bring
it. The Mari Lwyd sits at the intersection of two pagan British
traditions: the hooded-animal tradition, where a person wearing
the disguise of an animal would go from house to house
demanding entrance, and wassailing, where a group of revellers
would visit houses demanding entrance and gifts in exchange
for money. The Mari Lwyd's Irish cousin, the White Mare or
Láir Bhán, was a Samhain-specific visitor who came visiting

houses at Hallowe'en, asking for money or food in exchange for songs. Guising is a Scottish variant of these traditions (another one is the Scottish Hogmanay tradition of 'first-footing', in which the first person through the door of one's house at New Year brings gifts of coal, bread and salt, to bring prosperity throughout the year). Guising is also sometimes called mumming, or souling, which comes from the fact that Samhain coincides with and formed the foundation of the Christian feast of All Souls' Day, when the dead are solemnly remembered.

Another Hallowe'en tradition with much older roots is dooking for apples, as we call it in Scotland – elsewhere it is also known as bobbing. Dooking for apples is reputedly a very ancient ritual game, dating from the period of the Roman invasion of Britain (the Romans brought apples with them). At certain times of year, apples would be hung on strings or placed in rivers and bitten for by unmarried young people – a sort of stressfully mouth-based equivalent of Pooh sticks – as part of a festival celebrating the apple tree in all its profusion. There is possibly a conflation of two separate festivals in this enmeshed tradition, but there is certainly something delightful about playing games with the last of the apple harvest. There is something magical about apples, after all. They are richly symbolic, of course, but they are also biologically interesting: like all seeded fruit, they carry the promise of next spring inside them. And apples are, for many, important divinatory and ritual tools, precisely because of how these seeds can be revealed.

Tony Locke, a practising Druid, describes the apple as important to Hallowe'en partly because of the symbol it bears within
it, arguing that 'the practice of cutting open an apple to reveal
that most potent symbol within – that of the pentagram – is
still carried on today, particularly at Samhain and Halloween'.[2]
The pentagram, or five-pointed star, which figures large in
witchcraft symbolism, lives within the apple like a secret,
holding all of the seeds. The apple has, here, replaced the
pomegranate in popular imaginings of Persephone, the Greek
goddess of the underworld. In her maiden aspect – that is,
before Hades kidnapped her – she is often referred to not as
Persephone, but as Kore. This name – which is also associated
with Ceres, the Roman goddess of grain and plenty – encapsulates her role as a goddess of harvest. As a result there is a
link, albeit a thread-thin one, that links dooking for apples
with mirroring and paying tribute to Persephone/Kore's descent
into the underworld. Her role as harvest goddess is over, and
she has other business to attend to. Armed with her five pips
– only one fewer than the pomegranate seeds she ate –
Persephone readies herself to descend, and we, lipstick-smeared
and cold-faced, chase her down into the liquid dark by plunging
our faces into the dooking bowl, and seeing what we can catch.

Catching an apple in your mouth may not determine who
among you will be next to marry, as it did in the Roman period,
but there is something delicious in the promise of the seasons'
turn, clamped between our wet lips. Apple magic demonstrates
how witchcraft has been practised through and adapted into
social games that have a ritual purpose. We may think of magic
as being solemn, solitary, serious work, but play is a huge part
of magic. After all, playing allows us to explore metaphors with

our bodies, to learn myths through pastimes that amuse us, to take part in social activities that have an embedded ritual function. Hallowe'en is amongst the most visibly social of our secular holidays, with its high number of traditional games. Dooking is a brutal game, especially for anyone who doesn't like having their head submerged in a tub of cold water that has been dribbled in by multiple other people. I remember at parties even as a child, kids with elaborate face paint would resist the allure of the dooking basin. After all, the reward of an apple perhaps feels less than glamorous amid all the other, far more tempting party food. I have always loved dooking, buoyed by my ability to hold my breath for a long time, and my delight in lording things over others. It was always my favourite Hallowe'en game, and I would sit at the basin fishing for the last apples, long after anyone else was interested in playing.

Guising and dooking are both excellent games, but there are other activities that traditionally take place on 31 October that are more complicated communal activities. Just as Beltane has its fires, so Samhain also has a strong fire tradition. Historically, Samhain fires were lit using what is known as force-fire, or need-fire. These are words that appear, in various manifestations, across Old Norse and Germanic languages, and refer to a ritual that was, until reasonably recently, performed across the Highlands of Scotland, and is in many places seeing a resurgence. It is a ritual that carries with it ideas of the complicated, purifying nature of flames. Need-fire and force-fire refer to how the fire is lit: the fire is literally forced into being through friction and was commonly, according to Scottish folk-lorist and anthropologist James Frazer, created in the open air: 'the proper places for performing the rite seem to have been knolls or small islands in rivers.'[3] This friction can be a rope rubbed against wood until fire is made, or two sticks rubbed together. Samhain fires were traditionally kindled using this method, which has a wide number of subsidiary superstitions attached to it: it was thought to be able to rid livestock of disease – particularly murrain and foot-and-mouth disease – if they were driven through it, especially if all other fires around were fully extinguished. There are reports of need-fires being lit against cattle disease as late as 1830. The ritual use of need-fire was similar: everyone extinguished their old fire, cleaned, and then kindled in their hearths new fires for the year, made from the communal Samhain need-fire. This way, the turning of the season was ushered in with clean, new flame, to rid the house of any pollution. It is very difficult to light a need-fire, and they were only lit in times, as the name suggests, of need. Samhain, then, is a time for communal warding: for getting rid of the potential for infection, and for looking forward to keeping everything safe for the winter. Almost all of these rituals are against harm, against the evil forces – embodied by the supernatural – that are often metaphors for the terror of facing a long winter ahead.

These days, there are perhaps fewer reasons to be concerned about the shifting seasons, but this does not mean that there is nothing unsettling about Samhain and its attendant spirits.

On Hallowe'en, while I do not worry about Will-o-the-Wisps, or about ghosts, I do worry, a little superstitiously, about the witching hour. For that is when the veil is thinnest, and is when all of Samhain's strangeness might appear before us. The witching hour is, traditionally, between 3 a.m. and 4 a.m. A lot of horror films have scenes that take place during this time – odd tapping noises lure sleepers from their beds, or a car pulls ominously up a gravel driveway. That small time, in the deep night, when your body longs so strongly to be asleep that it shifts between reality and dream. The hour when, in the crystalline, leaf-flapping nights of October, we are still stunned by the lack of light, we are still holding September's golden kindness to us, and wondering where it has gone. The witching hour is half-temptation, too: it is the way that we want to think about ghosts, unspooling into formlessness, touching against the edge of our exhaustion, when we aren't sure what we've seen. The witching hour is not, in fact, the traditional hour of actual witches' Sabbats, which take place at midnight, that liminal hour between the days when magic is afoot. Sabbats will be explained more fully later on in the book, but they are the main festivals that witches celebrate. Most witches I know, it must be said, are lucky if they even get to midnight, and certainly by the time 3 a.m. comes, we are all safely tucked into our beds.

But come Hallowe'en, I make an effort to be awake. I want to know if the witching hour will offer me help, if the veil does feel thinner at this time. This year, in particular, I am keen to talk to those who have walked before me. I wrap up warmly and sit by my altar with a little candle. Let the dead know that I am here, waiting. Make a circle of protection. Relight the turnip lanterns, which have guttered out with the late night, just to keep anything bad away.

I am tempted to use a scrying-glass, those beautiful glossy black polished stones that claim to help us see beyond the limits of our world, but I am nervous of them, too, and afraid that any shapes I might catch in the small hours of Samhain might be less than kind. Scrying is, really, any divinatory procedure that involves discerning shapes in an object: crystal balls, flames' shadows, dark mirrors. Because of its striking aesthetic, scrying, or divination, has often been a regular feature in depictions of witchcraft and occult activity. Divination, in the classical world, was something practised extremely regularly, simply part of the pattern of people's daily existence. 'It's likely that in antiquity most people practised or witnessed some form of divination at least once every few days,' historian Sarah Iles Johnston writes.[4] It seems strange to me that we do not do it anymore, although it does linger, transmuted into other things: horoscopes, scratch cards, prize draws. One thinks of the witch bent over her crystal ball or magic mirror, eyes wide with fear or wonder. This image of the witch performing divination is part of the stable of images most commonly associated with the occult, and most commonly laughed at. Scrying is associated with Victorian séances, in all their table-rapping, ectoplasm-coughing trickery. But laughing at divination is not new: people love to mock attempts to see into the future or into the beyond, even as they use them. Indeed, even Shakespeare's *Hamlet* contains teasing about the unstable nature of divination:

HAMLET: Do you see yonder cloud that's almost in shape of a camel?
POLONIUS: By th' mass, and 'tis like a camel indeed.
H: Methinks it is like a weasel.
P: It is backed like a weasel.
H: Or like a whale.
P: Very like a whale.

I am not a frequent user of divination, partly because I am extraordinarily suggestible; I see shapes where there are none, and imagine things instead of perceiving them. The mirror has its tricks, and I am a poor player, glimpsing myself and taking fright, moving my hands over it as if to seek assurance of my own continuing corporeality, firmly on this side of the veil.

On Hallowe'en night, I am all body, all fidgets in my chair and itches across my face. Nothing comes. I am frustrated and exhausted, and wonder if my magic is false, useless. Am I, perhaps, not a witch? Am I just a fool, who sits in the quiet darkness, waiting for something that will not come? I am taken, then, by a longing. Not often do I wish I had a coven, as I am mostly happy with the friends I practise magic with, on the rare occasions that we work together. Firm in my belief that all objects, all plants, all creatures and places can be called into relation simply through my sustained and open attention, I've often felt that negated the need for other, formalised, human co-practitioners. If the whole world is enmeshed, there is no need to don dark velvet and chant together. Tonight, though, I worry I have been snobbish. I worry that attempting to do magic based only on what I have, on my own understanding of the world and my research, is vain and conceited. I feel I have failed.

For Samhain is the time of the dead. Its traditional associations are with the goddesses who help us pass from this life to the next, and particularly, in Scotland and Ireland, the Cailleach, or crone. The Cailleach dates back as far as folklore, and is thought to significantly pre-date her first mention in writing, in the ninth-century Irish poem 'The Lament of the Old Woman of Beare'.[5] The Cailleach takes up her mantle at Samhain, and sits on her mountain to rule over the dark part of the year. While she might not be welcomed, as such, she is nevertheless venerated, and is honoured in poems and song, in blue clothing and pilgrimages to her sacred sites. On Samhain, as I sit alone, I think of her, looming in the shadows. I think of her with fear, and a little longing. She is ancient, definite as rock, and she has all of her power at her fingertips. She is the old woman aspect of the triple-faced goddess, and her name means 'the one who is veiled'. The Cailleach is a strange goddess, because she carries in her so many of the functions that are often separated out between different deities. In this, she is one of the overarching goddesses, or forces, responsible for shaping the land and overseeing humans and their condition. She is neither easy nor kind. She is a mother goddess, it is true, and a creator of life, but she also makes the weather, brings snow and storm and scouring wind. She is related to, and sometimes known as, Beira, the Queen of Winter, in Scottish folklore, although they are not quite the same. Because the Cailleach has come to signify 'old woman', she has been associated with a broad number of Celtic deities, and the word can also mean 'witch', 'wise woman', or even 'nun' in Irish and Scots Gaelic.

The Cailleach has many powers. She is a terraforming goddess, with a magical hammer that strikes shapes into the ground: wherever the terrain is harsh and wild, her hammer has been at work. She makes mountains, too, by walking the land with her wicker basket and dropping rocks as she strides. In Celtic mythology, lots of giants and deities drop peats and stones as they walk, making mountains and islands, and the Cailleach is part of that long tradition. She made Loch Tay in Perthshire by forgetting to put the flagstone lid back on a magical spring, which bubbled up until it filled the valley and flowed over at both ends. She is often associated with water: the Corryvreckan whirlpool off the west coast of Scotland is rumoured to be where she washes her filthy plaid come Samhain. The washing takes three days. At the end of it, her plaid is beautiful once more, and pure white. She settles it gently over the land, a delicate fluttering, and Scotland is wreathed with snow. No friend of summer, the Cailleach clips the new green shoots in spring until she is too tired to continue, for she hopes that by extending winter, she can extend her reign. Spring is when beautiful, youthful Bride, or Bridget, has rule of the land with Angus, her lover. Like so many ancient pre-Christian gods and goddesses, Bridget and the Cailleach are subject to ceaseless regional variation – in character, power and aspect. In some places they are at war, and in others they are the same person, only in two very different forms. Indeed, sometimes they become embedded fully in the landscape, becoming vibrations, traces among the very rocks themselves: the Cailleach was believed in some places to turn to stone over the summer months, and only to come back into her goddess form on Samhain, to rule over the winter. She is also, understandably, connected to death: bringing starvation, bringing storms. Unlike other death-goddesses, she does not have particular care of the dead. Rather, she is responsible for death in its most banal and physical aspect – she is the bringer about of its conditions.

On Samhain night, I want to appeal directly to the Cailleach. Magic has not, for me, ever felt particularly focused toward named deities, but Cailleach, in all her ancientness and multiplicity, seems more like the landscape itself than a goddess. She lives in places I go, in the grey stone and grey skies and the iron-grey sea of my country. She is cliff face and scree slope, she is freezing wind and sharp-sided hail. To appeal to her and her mysteries, to attempt to find her dwelling place, where all is dead and cold and still, feels like the best proper tribute. If I am to seriously think about Samhain, about the role of the dead in my life, then it is perhaps with her that I ought to start. None of us take the big questions of life lightly: one does not casually approach death, nor power. Instead, you prepare. The same is true when we approach the deities that represent such things. The idea that deities are masks for aspects of life that it is difficult to understand is one that resonates for me. Deities are practical, they are the faces we can talk to when we want to talk to parts of the human experience that don't have easy personifications. And this time, I have a question. I want to understand the relationship between magic and the dead better, and I want to know what I am doing wrong. Not that I think she will answer me, and not that it feels especially safe to ask such questions of a terrifying goddess, but she has always appealed to me. There is, I think, a kindness under her sternness. I think this, because I have secret knowledge. I know, for a fact, where the Cailleach lives, and how she tends her dwelling.

The Cailleach lives with her husband and seven children – though the number varies – in a little cottage, right up at the top of Glen Lyon in Perthshire, just as any other respectable crofter might. Like that of the rest of the glen's one hundred or so inhabitants, the Cailleach's roof needs turfed every few years, the sides of her house shored up against damage. In the summer months, she sits outside her home, blessing the bright-green wildness of that place, ensuring that the farmland stays fertile. She and her family soak up the soft summer rain, and the low, sweet winds, and gaze down the glen, toward the silver of the river. In the winter months, they retire indoors, from where the Cailleach emerges in spirit to wreak the havoc of winter onto the world. They are, all in all, a very ordinary family: except, perhaps, that they are made of stone. For the Cailleach who lives at Tigh nam Bodach, or 'the house of the old man, or ghost', is part, archaeologists and folklorists believe, of an ancient pre-Christian system of idol-worship. Her wee house hidden away up the glen may be the oldest site of continuous pre-Christian worship in Europe. She is looked after, and has been for hundreds of years, by the community she dwells in. Until his death, head stalker Bob Bissett, of the Invermearan estate, on whose land she lives, maintained the stones. They are still tended, although we do not know by whom; people are not in the habit of disclosing such things. The ceremonies – of inviting her out of her house, and putting her back in – are deeply private. And this respect, this continuous worship, gives us a sense of her being at home in Glen Lyon.

There she has her family. As the folklorist Dr Anne Ross tells it, the Cailleach and her husband, the Bodach – the 'old man', a trickster or bogeyman figure – arrived in the glen in deepest winter, and were warmly made welcome. She writes that they came 'in an unusually fierce snowstorm', which was perhaps the inhabitants' first clue that this pair were not mortal.[6] The second clue was the scale of the couple – they were 'an unnaturally large man and woman', who 'were seen coming down the mountain-side of the upper glen'.[7] The female figure was, it seemed, heavily pregnant, and so when they asked for help, for food and shelter against the storm, these were gladly given to them, and so delighted were they by the welcome that 'they took up residence in the glen when the inhabitants had built a thatched house large enough to accommodate them'.[8] Before they left, they instructed the residents to build a wee house, resembling their own, and to keep to the traditions and customs that they had developed. If they did this, no harm would come to them. And this explains why the *tigh* is cared for as it is, and why the inhabitants of the glen worship them still.

Like so many intimidating things, the Cailleach can be seen differently in a domestic context. She is no longer the one-eyed, blue-faced destroyer, who brings down storms and freezes the ground so hard that spring can barely peep through. In exchange for the kindness she found in the glen, she keeps the fields beautiful and fertile. And if her storms scour across Scotland come winter, well, who can blame her? She is, after all, only doing what she is supposed to. There is something there, I think, to do with acceptance. So often, we do not want the stranger to come among us. It is almost always easier to turn away people who ask for things, who require sheltering and feeding when our own resources are already stretched. Especially when they are different, when we suspect them of threatening the status quo in some way. But rather than turn her away, the Cailleach and her strange husband were welcomed, even if her true nature was suspected. Who wants a terrifying goddess for a neighbour? But in their kindness, the people of the glen found themselves rewarded. This is the moral of so much Celtic mythology. Welcome the strange stranger, treat them with courtesy. Stretch what little you have to meet their mouths, too, and you will not go hungry in turn. For a goddess of death, the Cailleach seems awfully kind and soft, here. But I think it's vital to remember that the point of the Cailleach, and of all deities of death and destruction, is that they cannot be stopped, or mollified. They cannot be altered or tamed. They can only be welcomed, with the full knowledge of what they are, and treated as well as possible. They can only be given courtesy, and this may allow them to look mercifully upon the giver.

We are able, I think, to recontextualise the Cailleach through this little dwelling. We all wish to be welcomed, and looked after. We all wish for good neighbours, who will shore up our house and spend time with us when it is appropriate. She also becomes a vital lesson in terms of how magic operates.

When I talk about drawing things into relation, about looking at things as they are, and working with them as they are and not as I would have them be, then this is what I am trying to grasp towards. So much of the world is polluted, endangered, subject to unimaginable destruction and violence.

We cannot work with the world as we wish it to be. We cannot do magic only when the air is clear, only on the tops of remote hills, only with the purest herbs. We must instead work in the world; do our magic among pizza boxes and microplastics. We must welcome the world in as it is, valuing every strange, broken scrap of it. We must house the world inside ourselves, as the glen houses the Cailleach, aware of its terrible nature, but kind anyway. And from that, from that loving, continued attention, we can do our magic, build habits that give back to the world, that take care of it, that work to alter and mend the parts that are not working, or that are destructive. But, crucially, we can only do this when we embrace and use the parts we do not like. The blue-faced hag is a blessing and a curse: were she not one, she could not be the other. The Cailleach is a complicated goddess, and so she forms a perfect way into understanding our complicated world, and how the magic we do can exist with it, and enhance it. We do magic in the world, yes. But the world also does magic in us.

It is a long way to the Cailleach. Many miles up the glen by car, and then a hard walk in by foot, along boggy tracks. My body, at the time, was in the throes of the relapse of my chronic condition, and that much walking was significantly beyond me. There was no way to go and see the Cailleach in her house. So instead, I went to the steep slopes that line the River Lyon as it rushes down the glen, walked as far as I could, and sat. The river – and the glen – are believed to be named for Lugh, the sun god. It is a lovely thought, that the sun god and the goddess of winter are neighbours. There was no storm, but the late October sky hung heavy, as if its belly grazed along the glen.

I sat in the cold, the wind slipping wicked fingers through my jacket, and I listened.

Nature writers will tell you, at great length, about what emerges from the world around you, if you will only sit and wait. And they are right. Deer across the hill, moving slow, seemingly oblivious to me. Birds of prey, cautious, then hovering again, as if I were a rock. The grass, moving in the wind. Spiders, small insects. The sound of the wind over rock. These things were beautiful, and I was glad of them. Sometimes, though, we ask more of an encounter. We are ready to receive resonance. We want the earth to speak to us with a voice, not in its usual series of indifferent, gracious signs. I wanted the Cailleach to descend from her shieling and speak with me. I wanted to know about the dead. An hour or so I sat. Until I was cold, and the light was slipping off the hillside, and nothing came. Sometimes, the answers we want do not come in the shape that we want, and that is alright. I took my gifts, and listened to the wind howling, and she did not come and speak with me. The Cailleach stayed quiet as a rock, quiet as a turf-roofed house.

It wasn't until I was walking home that I saw it, kicked to the side of the road. It was small, and broken: hardly a perfect specimen. It wasn't beautiful, or precious, or even necessarily a gift. But it was mine: I had seen it, bent to pick it up. The partial skull of a small bird: a blackbird, perhaps. Just the curve of its skull, over the top, the dip where the beak would have sat. It felt like nothing in my hand, curved and white and beautiful. What it looked like, on first glance, was part of an Airfix kit: the hooded cockpit of an aeroplane, some miniature. When I turned it over, it was considerably less clean. There was what I presumed was decomposing brain matter on the inside, grey and claggy. It had caught, was clinging, to the clean skull. It made me recoil, and drop it back onto the ground, check my hands to see if they were wet. It wasn't nice, this remnant of a dead thing. It wasn't pretty, or satisfying, or collectible. Instead, it was disgusting and strange. I started off back down the path.

Of course, I picked it up again, this time inside a handkerchief. I took it and rinsed it in the stream outside my godmother's house, where I was staying. My godmother lives close by the bottom of Glen Lyon, and is the Cailleach's neighbour. I didn't want to rinse it in her kitchen, grubby as it was. I had to slip the brains off the curve of the skull with a little sharp stick. What a gift. This little chip of skull, decaying, actively going back to ground. The Cailleach doesn't give easy lessons, I wouldn't say. She didn't show me my dead. Instead, she showed me, the world showed me, some incomplete moral, some not-quite-story, about how the dead are drawn back to the earth, clutter up roadsides and walk down rivers, are sucked by trees and howl with the wind. I wanted something neat. I wanted something I could point to – like distinct shapes in a scrying glass – and say, look, here, it is magic. Look, Samhain is here, and the dead are coming back again, out of the tidy boxes of the past we have trapped them in. Look.

But death doesn't work like that, and nor does magic. None of it is easy. The dead do not have to talk to me. Or perhaps they talk all the time, in skull-shards and strange winds and the way that spiders nest outside my bedroom window every year, and breed into dreadful profusion. Perhaps they do not talk at all. Perhaps the Cailleach, up there in her high home, wanted to tell me that death is a little shard of nothing, held in the hand, that it's all reabsorbed, that life is so complicated that death is striated through it, like soil levels, like rock strata, like pixels in a photograph. Perhaps she was out that afternoon, visiting friends, doing the big shop, swelling up storms in the North Sea.

Magic is patience. Magic is waiting, and seeing, and trying. Magic is asking, and listening even if all that is said is something that can't quite be worded, about the way death holds itself, viscerally physical, and offers itself to you. Ghosts that stand by the stairs, ghosts that want to use the rooms we live in. Perhaps the majority of the dead are busy, drawn back into the fabric of things. I hope that is true. That night, safely in bed in my godmother's house, a storm brews, and the wind clips the chimney pots. The dead, whatever they are up to, do not trouble us, and the Cailleach whips across the glen that welcomed her, wreaking havoc. We awake to bent trees and pitched power lines. Still, what do we expect? It is getting to be winter. I take the skull-shard home with me, and put it on my altar when I want to ask advice from whoever it might be – my family line, anyone who is listening, those who, in the great grey beyond, keep an ear out.

Witches wait for answers, hone our questions, work out how to clear the throat of the world, to hear its answer. I am still working on it. To be a witch is, perhaps, to listen in to the hum of the world, to try to pick out voices, and changes, to try to be of service. If the dead want to talk to me, I tell myself, then they know very well where I am.

Blessing a New Altar

*U*nlike many other activities associated with witchcraft – foraging, divination – I have found that seeking to commune with the dead requires a slightly more formal set-up, as do a number of other ritual activities. To this end, an altar is extremely useful. Any space dedicated to a particular purpose helps us to fulfil that purpose. A good kitchen helps us cook well. A clean, well-equipped bathroom means we can be happily scrubbed and hygienic. An altar is the same.

People are funny about altars, though. It's one of those boundary lines. Altars shock people. It's ok to theoretically know that an acquaintance is witchily inclined: it is quite another to be confronted by a room full of pentagrams and a table draped in midnight velvet when you pop round for tea. There is a prudishness among the general populace, especially in Western organised religion where, while religious art and artefacts might be present in houses, full-blown altars are usually reserved for places of communal worship.

Altars are, of course, nothing to be ashamed of. Your witch-craft practice is to be celebrated, and there is a horrible reverberation through history every time a witch hurriedly dismantles something to avoid detection. Indeed, witchcraft is still illegal in various countries: it is our job to be proud public witches where we can be, to show that witchcraft is a benign and wonderful thing. However, everyone's circumstances are different. I live in a house I do not own, and as a result, my altar is small, and tucked away in one corner of the room. It is also decorated with few immediately recognisable magical items.

What is on your altar is up to you. It will vary hugely depending on what tradition you follow, which gods – if any – you develop an affinity for, and what space and circumstance permit. The most useful things for me are detailed here. I use something to draw my focus – I have a representation of the tree of life. The tree of life appears in many cultures: it sits in the midst of the Garden of Eden; it is Yggdrasil, the Norse tree of life; it is part of the ceramic tradition of Mexican religious art, and also appears in Celtic, Hindu and Buddhist traditions, among others. The tree represents as many things as you might imagine, but for me it is a helpful way of thinking about life. The roots represent the unconscious, as well as our ancestors, or whatever afterlife tradition you relate to. The middle of the tree represents the sphere of the living, our earthly concerns, the bustle of daily life. The top of the tree is a space of dreaming: it is knowledge, transcendence, heaven. The tree is an exercise in symbolic thinking. I keep two candles on my altar, because I think of them as pillars on a gate. When I light them, the gate swings open, and the sacred space comes alive. Representations of things I hold dear have space on there: a little blue ceramic house, and usually one or two visual markers for the season. I also keep a hard surface to burn things on, so that the wood of my altar is not damaged. I wash and re-dress my altar once a month, or slightly more frequently if it's a busy month for magic, and I have a supply of altar cloths in seasonal colours.

Dressing the altar always feels a lot like playing: arranging everything neatly, deciding what fabrics go together. And there is an extent to which the aesthetic of the altar can feel like an indulgence, a frippery. It isn't, I don't think. Beautiful spaces inspire reactions in us, from gardens to opulent interiors, to small spaces of beauty in our homes. Nothing is going to compel you toward doing magic on a messy, disorganised altar. Luxuriate in the space. Make it somewhere you want to spend time. If you need to keep your altar hidden, I'd suggest a shoebox: you can set it up inside, and simply undo the lid when you want to access the altar. For years, as a child, I kept a secret altar this way.

Once you have set up your altar, you will need to bless it. In fact, I bless my altar every time I clean it, so I'm going to give suggestions for both. Cleaning the altar is easy: remove everything from it, and dust or wipe down as required. Get rid of any residue from offerings, and if you can, let the objects you use on your altar moonbathe or sunbathe for a few hours, to get rid of any lingering magic they've been exposed to. My altar is on top of a polished wooden table, so I wipe it down gently with water and add an essential oil for a good scent. Usually, I use something mildly disinfectant: tea tree or rosemary or lemongrass essential oil does the trick nicely. You can wipe down any non-porous objects with it as well, but do be careful that the essential oils have dried or evaporated before they touch silk or wood.

Then, carefully rearrange everything as you would wish it: one way I make my altar feel new each time I clean it is by incorporating aspects of the natural world. I like to bring in rowan berries, tufts of wild grass, birch leaves. Most child-free homes don't contain a nature table, but I loved making them in primary school, and always wish to bring seasonal flora into the house when I can. Even a single pretty red leaf in autumn can help you to feel that the outside world and your living space are in dialogue.

I give these small tokens of the outside world as offerings, as part of the blessing. The blessing begins with me lighting the candles (I use matches, because I find a struck flame to be more resonant) and then usually by lighting incense. I 'wash' the altar with the smoke from the incense, by wafting it over the objects three times, then I 'wash' myself. You could equally do this with moon-washed water or river water, or with sound. This is an idiosyncrasy and not necessary: indeed, I'm not sure where I learned it. One of the things it is good to learn quickly as a witch is that some things feel sensible, and they are often good impulses to attend to. As I do it, I make my incantations – these are very personal but broadly they follow an invocation of the spirits of the three parts of the life-tree, whom I ask to attend and protect my altar, and speak with me through it.

After I've 'washed' the altar and myself, I make an offering of the botanical objects. I do this by placing them on the altar and saying a few words. I usually name what I am offering, and why. I give birch a lot, because a birch tree was planted on my naming day, but I also give anything pretty. I find it useful to then speak to the altar, and the deities and spirits that I name as a way of giving shape to the world.

Blessing the altar gives time for prayer, which is a vital part of my personal witchcraft practice. This is a controversial belief: many of my friends who are witches only ever do spells, and don't commune with magic for conversation. I think this is a little bit like only attending church in order to be blessed, and never joining in with the collective worship. While technically fine, of course, it feels a little greedy to me. I like to chat, to tell my fears and joys, to believe that the forces I ask for favours, the world I assert my will in, know me. That they are familiar at least with the sound of my voice giving thanks, being grateful, and being in the world without my will extended. I do not visit my altar every day, but I try to stand at it several times a week. After all, I find when it is beautiful, candles lit, there is nowhere else in my house that I would rather be.

NOVEMBER

———◆———

Sex Magic

It happens, as it always does, after somebody has had a drink at a party. 'So you do witchy stuff?', and the bright eyes and the lean of the body mean I know what's coming next. 'So do you do . . . weird sex stuff, yeah?'

'Oh, yeah,' I reply, looking him straight in the eye. 'Really weird. It's harder to get goat's blood than it used to be, but I make it work.' And there is a brief, delicious moment where I know he cannot tell if I am joking, and his mouth falls open, halfway between disgust and admiration. I'm not sure exactly what he expected. Eventually, he smiles weakly, tells me how nice it was to meet me, and goes to speak to someone else.

It's understandable. Taboos all hold hands with each other in people's brains, and for so many people, witchcraft is still taboo, something to speak about in a hushed tone, something that conjures with it other forms of socially excluded behaviour. Ritual sacrifice, blasphemy, forbidden knowledge, weird sex. The sorts of things, perhaps, that make the average dinner party guest wish they were sitting next to a brisk accountant, or someone known for being an excellent baker. Witchcraft is neither a respectable job nor an acceptable hobby for many people, and worse than that: it actively seems to encourage the questions you'd never ask anyone else. 'Oh, sing in a choir, do you? Any weird sex stuff?'

I do wonder a little, though, what sort of thing might have made him happy, made him feel he'd got his money's worth. Did he want to know about my unbridled carnal lust? Long nights of orgies with my coven? Did he assume that my sort of witchcraft meant fucking myself with a shortened and specially carved 'broomstick' (which crime writer turned amateur occultist Michael Harrison has described luridly as a 'magical dildo') while hallucinating that I was flying?[1] I hope he did. I hope it all flitted through his head. I rather suspect, however, that he didn't even have those stereotypes to grasp at: I think he probably just thought about witches in popular culture – from Willow with her lesbianism in 1990s television series *Buffy the Vampire Slayer*, to the pretty, nose-wrinkling mischievous housewife witch in *Bewitched*. He probably heard 'witchcraft' and thought immediately of those ridiculous soft-porn B-movies of the seventies. I was, it must be said, a little sorry to disappoint.

Witches have always been characterised by – and demonised through – their association with 'unnatural' sexual appetites. Indeed, one of the most frequent confessions tortured out of accused witches during the medieval European witch trials was that they had sex with the devil. After all, sexual knowledge was the original biblical sin: it made sense that the worst corruptions of witches would be sexual, too. Notable among these characterisations is that found in the well-known *Malleus Maleficarum* (*The Hammer Of Witches*), produced in 1487 in Germany. This demonology proved so popular that, by 1669, thirty editions had been published. The *Malleus Maleficarum* contained information on, among other things, why women were particularly prone to satanic seduction. The answer, unsurprisingly, was their 'weak character and voracious sexual appetite', a misogynist, Church-sanctioned sentiment that echoed throughout the medieval witch-panics.[2] It described in no uncertain terms the excess of lust witches were thought to harbour: 'All witchcraft comes from carnal lust, which is in women insatiable . . . for the sake of fulfilling their lusts they consort even with devils'.[3] Often, the physical details of these demonic couplings would be pored over. The more lurid detail an accused witch could produce, the more sensational and widely reported the trial would be, and the more it would advance the project of religious adherence. Jeanette d'Abadie (born 1592), a French woman accused of witchcraft, described sex with the devil in minute detail in testimonies collected in 1609, including the information that his penis was scaly, and caused her great pain, and that 'what came from him', his semen, was 'cold', and therefore produced no pregnancy.[4] The devil was not only a sexual presence, he was a deeply strange one.

In anthropologist Margaret Murray's famous and often in-accurate anthropological history of witchcraft, *The Witch-Cult in Western Europe: A Study in Anthropology*, she suggests that women had sex with stone phalluses in magical rituals designed to aid conception, and that this had been going on since ancient times: the phallus was seen as a direct stand-in for the fertility god, and so the pain of it was tolerated. It was this, Murray argued, that led to the widespread assertion that 'The Devil was cold, and so was his seed'.[5] This is a detail that I've always enjoyed; it has a gossipy quality, a sense that throughout ancient history, women formed a consensus that the devil was charismatic, sure, but perhaps not a very good lay. Certainly a bit . . . well, weird. Indeed, the coldness and size of the devil's penis were much commented on throughout witch trials: a French woman, Sylvine de la Plaine, tried in 1616, confessed the devil's member was 'large like that of a horse . . . and cold like ice', and in 1662, a Scottish woman, Isobel Gowdie, said, 'His memberis ar exceiding great and long; no man's memberis ar so long & bigg as they ar'.[6] Extraordinary size and deeply unsettling sensation seem to be a commonality in encounters with the devil's dick, and he certainly doesn't seem to be more fun or more adept at pleasure than non-satanic partners. While Murray's theory has very little archaeological or textual evidence behind it, it is certainly appealing in its logic, although I rather suspect that after hundreds of years of unpleasant ritual sex with stone phalluses, someone might have come up with something more comfortable. Given that penises are usually warm, if not hot, in erection, these accounts may simply be a case of inverting biological norms to describe the devil's supernatural evil. Additionally, the medieval conception of hell was that it was freezing, so the devil's penis – being an extension of hell – might logically be considered cold. Besides which, in witch trials, the confessors wanted descriptions of demons and devils that matched those found in books such as *Malleus Maleficarum*, so these accounts quickly become similar.

So, the man who approached me at the party wasn't as far off base as he might have been – or, at least, he was drawing on stereotypes that have been around for literally hundreds of years. Magic contains a good deal of sex within it, and the 'weird sex stuff' is real, and arguably just as weird as he'd hoped it would be. And, because sex is such a taboo in Western culture, sex magic often places itself as a dangerous, exotic, secret form of revolution.

Surprisingly, though, the confessions of medieval women accused of having sex with the devil aren't considered to be sex magic. While the medieval witches consorting with the devil were committing adultery from a legal point of view, the focus in those contexts was not the sex, but the fact that it imbued the witches with magical power. The sex itself was merely a way to gain proximity with the devil: the magic was performed afterwards. Therefore, those satanic unions form a sort of background hum to the history of sex magic, but aren't usually directly included in it. A cynic might note that sex-as-magic, as deliberate practice, seems to spring from the pens and mouths of men. From outlandish rumours about the orgiastic masses of early Christian sects to the occultist Aleister Crowley's fascination with bodily fluids and their consumption, to Gerald Gardner, the father of Wicca, and his nudist frolics in the New Forest, sex magic has a reputation for glamour, intrigue and perversions that – still – strike fear into the hearts of the respectable mainstream. But, in fact, sex magic is, like anything else in witchcraft, as diverse as its practitioners. Sex and magic have lived alongside each other for as long as there have been either, and both have been crucibles through which issues of social control, religion, power and liberation have been melted and made anew.

I think about it, later, when I'm in bed. Wonder, idly, what he might have expected from me if we'd gone home together. What fantastical imaginings, what dark and extraordinary secrets he thought my body might know, that I might be able to teach him. Of course, I'm confident enough to think I've tricks up my sleeve, but perhaps not the sorts he imagines. When I think about the magic of sex – of pleasure – I wonder if the magic is inextricable. If it is, in fact, embedded in those grades of initiation into sex that come with development. There's such joy in discovery: I'm not certain everyone remembers their first orgasm, but it felt to me as if my body could make a shape or reach a note or speak a language that it hadn't previously even imagined. It felt a little like pain: a scald of hot water, or touching a lit stove. Intensely aware, suddenly, of being in my body, in among my blood and muscles and nerves. It was short and sharp and shocking. Bright, as if someone had filled me with electricity. As if I was emitting light. I wasn't sure about it, in the least: but I wanted to do it again.

Whatever I had just done, I hoped, naively, that other people had worked it out too, because was so interesting, and I wanted them to know there was this weird power that lived inside them that could make them feel strange and vivid and awake. I had, of course, invented masturbation. Pleasure has millions of creation myths: each of us discovers it, invents it, for ourselves. We keep reinventing it, too, throughout our lives, on our own and with other people. Adults say to kids, sometimes dismissively, that they didn't actually invent sex. But they did. We did. We all do. Over and over again.

Sex magic is, at its most basic, the practice of using the

energies and emotions of sex to work magical acts in the world. From highly disciplined spiritual practices such as tantra to the surrender to the libidinous drive suggested by Crowley, sex magic has been conceptualised very differently across eras, religions and parts of the world, but in almost all cases it can be understood as using sex to make things happen. As historian Hugh Urban puts it, 'sexual magic might be said to be the simplest, even quintessential form of "sympathetic magic"'.[7] By this, Urban means that sex is, in its historically understood form, an act that produces babies: an act of extraordinary biological magic. If sex does not produce babies, then there is still the sense that it carries with it a shadow of that productive potential, and that it can instead transfer that energy in other directions, giving rise instead to what he calls 'effects of a supernatural, magical, divine (or demonic) character'.[8] Whether or not it is helpful to characterise the product of sex magic as a sort of magical baby equivalent (and I suspect for most people, it is not), this feels very convincing. Sex is productive – and so using it to make something happen seems pretty obvious.

All magic uses energy, and so it's easy to see how you might reach the idea that sexual energy, given that it is fun to generate, should be directed toward ritual ends. This all sounds rather sensible – and, in fact, distinctly unsexy, which is one of the central paradoxes of sex magic. Once you get into the nitty gritty, it all feels rather like those school textbooks which referred to sex dispassionately and medically, as if to put us all off. However, unlike the sex information in our school textbooks, for many hundreds of years, sex magic was considered 'a lore of unspeakable danger to body and soul', and was available only to the highest initiates of whatever occult order offered it.[9] Even as late as the sexual revolution of the 1960s, sex magic was eschewed as dangerous and satanic. Nowadays, things have moved in the other direction, and sex magic is often cited as a way not to achieve magical effects, per se, but as a way to achieve longer orgasms and a more satisfying sex life. It has become a sort of pragmatic blend of tantra, the law of attraction and couples counselling, and while it is no longer shrouded in mystery, it suffers from the opposite problem – it has been tamed, diluted, made less appealing, and it still doesn't seem to address either sex or magic as they really exist in the world.

There's no denying that sex magic, when done joyfully and carefully, enhances both our sex and our magic. But the history of sex magic is like most of history: deeply patriarchal, written by those in power, and focused on heterosexual, cisgendered, white Western experience. Most of the definitive voices on sex magic from the eighteenth, nineteenth and twentieth centuries would argue that I can't even take part in sex magic. Some of them would say that, because I'm not a man, I can't truly harness the power of sex – the best I could manage, really, would be functioning as an instrument to help the man achieve power through sex. As Crowley put it in his writings on sex magic: 'Women are but a temporary expedient; a shrine indeed for the God, but not the God'.[10] Crowley's opinions on female participation in sex magic were far from abnormal for his day, and persisted for a long time. There is perhaps nothing less inviting than the idea of being one more tool on the altar of an occult man, no more or less helpful than a chalice or a scourge, or a nice set of altar candles. Nothing but a finely tuned practical instrument. How lucky for me, to be allowed to help out! What an irresistible proposal.

On the other hand, the overarching view given out by the founders of what we know as Wicca, occultist Gerald Gardner and those who came after him, is that I would be capable of sex magic, but only if it took place within a loving, heterosexual marriage.

For example, influential couple Stewart and Janet Farrar, who wrote on Wiccan practices from the 1960s onwards, are extremely emphatic that sex magic must be 'utterly heterosexual', and undertaken only by those for whom 'intercourse is a normal part of their relationship', with a stress on marriage being the best avenue for this.

Many contemporary witches still cling to outmoded interpretations of two opposing forces coming together to create energy or, as that is often called in witchcraft, 'polarity'. This is a common understanding of how magical power works in Wicca; Raymond Buckland, writer and high priest in both the Gardnerian and Seax-Wica traditions, wrote in the 1980s that 'we conceive of the Creative Power in the universe as manifesting through polarity – as masculine and feminine', and Buckland was drawing on older Wiccan practices.[11] One contemporary practitioner, Skye Alexander, writes in her book *Sex Magic for Beginners* that 'sexual polarity', most obvious in cisgender heterosexual couples, can also exist in same-sex couples, but only if fucking is sorted into categories of male or female: being fucked is feminine, and doing the fucking is masculine, which is, of course, ridiculous. Indeed, she actively encourages same-sex couples to engage in exaggerations of gender difference: 'You want to accentuate . . . the differences between you and your partner', she writes.[12] The message is clear: same-sex couples can participate in sex magic, but they must do so in what amounts to a form of drag, aping as best they can the differences presumed inherent in heterosexual anatomy, attitudes and traditional intercourse. The book was published in 2011. Shocking though this attitude is, it is in fact a significant advance in writings about sex magic, in that it includes at all, however clumsily, a token nod toward the idea of queer sex.

Sex magic makes me feel a great many things, but none of them is 'sexy'. There are increasingly few areas that actively discriminate against the LGBTQ+ community, but apparently, the world of witchcraft and magic is slow to change. It is strange to feel too queer for something as traditionally taboo as sex magic, too female, and simultaneously too wary of neat gender binaries. This is true for increasing numbers of people: our understanding of how we relate to gender, sex and sexuality is being expressed in more nuanced ways than ever before, and so too are our decisions about who and how we love. Sex magic has, in general, not really caught up, especially when it comes to partnered sex. There are, of course, lots of solo rituals you can do, but they are often described as preparatory, as if you're getting ready to finally do the 'proper' magic that can only happen between two bodies, or they feel compensatory, as if you're being told that what you are capable of doing in your own body is second best. And it is difficult to find evidence within traditional texts that helps to alter and refashion the harmful narratives they have put forward.

Sex magic has been taboo, secret and hidden away for years and, like so many secret, hidden things, it has been much speculated over and written about. While the source texts on sex magic are mostly sadly lacking in titillation, television, film and print media have put the sex very emphatically back into sex magic. In fact, media representations of witches have credited them with the power to do sex magic in a way that real practitioners of sex magic rarely grant. Witches who do sex magic either in terrifying ways, or titillating ways – or both – are a mainstay of witch depictions. As a result, most of the really positive understandings I have of sex magic – however problematic this might be – come more from the minds of script writers than from source texts themselves. Screen depictions of witches imbue them with allure, with magnetism. I remember the first time I watched Samantha Stephens wrinkle her nose charmingly: instantly enchanted, I wanted her glamorous 1950s suburban housewife life. Although she does not use sex magic as such, *Bewitched* is nevertheless a show where a witch's sexuality forms a central part of her magic. The ability to cause chaos but remain beloved because of one's allure is, I think, if not sex magic per se, then definitely one of the sexy things we think are magical. And the representations of sex magic we see on television and in film are, for me at least, really illuminating lenses for understanding the way we see sex and magic in culture – far more accessibly than those historic sources allow. By synthesising both, I think, we can really unlock and understand sex magic and its power.

The thing that is most frustrating about sex magic, from the perspective of a witchcraft practitioner or researcher, is its history of extraordinary secrecy and the way that it reinscribes society's prudishness around all things sexual, while claiming to overturn them. The beginnings of sex magic in the Western world take shape in ancient Rome, which probably comes as no surprise. The Roman historian Livy wrote of cults to Bacchus, the god of wine and revelry, in which 'men were mingled with women with all the licence of nocturnal orgies, there was no crime, no deed of shame, wanting'.[13] The orgies weren't only sexual, they were places of alleged criminal activity, and with the rise of Christianity, it was convenient for them to be characterised as wicked and lawless, so that they could be legislated against and eventually outlawed. When we think of outlandish sexual behaviour, we inevitably think of pre-Christian Rome as a hotbed of exotic sinfulness – brimming with mad emperors and violent orgies – and Livy's accounts are foundational to that idea. These sorts of accounts were attempts to suppress the outgoing pagan religion, and were extremely successful. The beginnings of sex magic are largely founded on accusation, supposition and rumour – there is evidence that Bacchic cults existed, but the actuality of their orgiastic rituals remains unevidenced.

The good news is that lots of occult thinkers were extremely invested in removing sex magic from the realm of the fantastical and into the realm of the very, very real. The bad news is that many of them did it in ways that, to a contemporary audience, feel horrifying. The mistake that many occult thinkers made was in taking bizarre accusations against religious cults as a good foundation on which to base their particular sex magic practice.

Infamous Victorian occultist Aleister Crowley, who was a contemporary of Freud, is someone whose writings on magic form the basis of much of what we consider contemporary witchcraft practice. Crowley was interested in pushing social and sexual taboos in his pursuit of power. He was rumoured to have committed all sorts of appalling acts, from murdering animals to cannibalism, and certainly confessed to all manner of sexual acts that were taboo – or illegal – in Victorian England. Crowley wrote extensively about having sex with other men, and particularly associated anal sex with 'encouraging demons'. He participated in sodomy believing that it was specifically deviant and evil, and so it would bring him great power. This is a fascinating attitude – at once inclusive and condemnatory of homosexual sex acts. Although he enjoyed them and openly took part in them, Crowley was never arguing that homosexual acts were natural. Quite the opposite: he specifically pursued them for their perceived abnormality and immorality. He equated homosexual sex with all of his other taboo acts, which included eating the faeces of his partner, Leah Hirsig, as a deviant Eucharist during one of his Gnostic masses. His practice of sex magic, which was transmitted to his students at various degrees of their initiations, moved through heterosexual sex, and upwards toward ever more extreme taboo-breaking, such as 'mentally meditating on his penis – masturbating – while thinking of gods and angels; consecrating talismans with combinations of semen, vaginal juices and menstrual blood; prolonging and intensifying sex through visualisation . . . beseeching gods for information, money and material possessions during sex'.[14] The central idea behind such extreme behaviours is that by breaking these taboos, one moves beyond the repressive social order and into a state of magical power, because what is sacred has been made profane, and everything has been upturned.

Hugh Urban argues that for Crowley, 'the most intense experience of transgression, the overstepping of conventional taboos, [was] a means to unleash an ecstatic, liberating power and thereby herald the dawn of a whole new era in human history'.[15] This power was two-fold – yes, it might unleash a new age of ecstasy and chaos – but it would also bring great personal power and control to the individuals who mastered it. Sex magic was not just about pleasure – indeed, much of what Crowley describes would be pleasurable only to a very limited number of people. Instead, there was a greater project at hand, one worth sacrificing individual qualms and scruples for: liberation. This ties in with a great deal of how we understand the era in which Crowley lived: he witnessed the birth of psychotherapy, and the dominant concerns of the era were very much those of plumbing the subconscious and breaking new ground – whether occult, scientific or otherwise.

The central problem with a great deal of Crowley's writing is its cruelty and disregard of the humanity of others. It is also not particularly helpful for most contemporary witches who might actually want to try sex magic. It is low on pleasure, big on effort, and preoccupied with taboo-breaking in a way that feels extremely characteristic of the nineteenth century. Crowley's is not a magic that promises small gains through private pleasures: it is magic that promises revolution at the cost of extraordinary, performative displays of extreme sexual behaviour.

Aleister Crowley is, of course, not the only man to found occult and esoteric teachings that use sex to gain power and control. Indeed, sex cults are a pervasive feature of contemporary society, though they might be a little less immediately shocking.

After Crowley, sex magic became more reserved again, but also gradually more mainstream. In the 1960s and 70s, and in the Wiccan movements that grew up around Gerald Gardner and Janet and Stewart Farrar, practitioners toned down Crowley's excesses considerably, although sexual coven initiations (having sex with an initiated member of the coven as a joining rite) were in some cases considered acceptable, as was having sex with a loving partner in a coven setting. While sex was supposed to be between married couples, sex with an audience of naked coven members watching was apparently fine, so some degree of freedom and experimentation was permitted. This is perhaps unsurprising: the Farrars had a long-term, successful polyfidelitous relationship with Gavin Bone, whom Janet officially married after Stuart's death in 2002.[16] So while the Farrars were far more accepting and open-minded about the complexities of love and sex than some of their contemporaries, they were still careful not to court additional controversy by making the arrangement the focal point of their books. Their most popular title, *A Witches' Bible*, which is still in print today, certainly knows its audience, however – although the contents might be far more thorough and less sensationalist than many might expect, there are lots of pictures of the Farrars and their coven, beautifully naked, adorned with ritual jewellery, and posed outdoors on mountain tops, or together in living rooms. Sex between non-couples might have been frowned on, but naked coven rites and the re-enactment of myths of fecundity and fertility both took place and gave an illicit, erotic edge to books such as *A Witches' Bible*.

This emphasis on sex magic as the preserve of established, heterosexual couples is absolutely at the heart of many books that still shape our witchcraft today. However, the media – even during the 1960s and 1970s – had very different ideas about magic, sex and witches. The 1970 film *Legend of the Witches* shows the workings of a coven and presents itself as a serious documentary, revealing hidden secrets of the occult. In it, a large number of coven members leap about in the forest, beguiling and naked. The scandalous artwork for the film – which shows the copious full-frontal nudity – clearly markets it as an erotic film rather than a serious work of documentary film-making. It is available online and worth watching for its fascinating mixture of the scandalous and the deeply tedious. The narrator spins tales of gods and goddesses, of ancient rituals, in a rather dry tone that even the nudity cannot offset. It's a lot like an early nature documentary but with more nude frolicking. It's rather sweet, really, though not sexy. I love the idea of it being shown in Soho sex cinemas, eagerly anticipated by men who ended up merely having a thorough lesson in Wiccan creation stories.

There are plenty of titillating B-movie films about witches, however. If *Legend of the Witches* is a little on the cerebral side, there's the 1973 American horror film *Season of the Witch*, which features masked satanic intruders, bored housewives, sex, drugs and a scene of female masturbation. It is campy, shocking and directly links witchcraft rituals practised by women to ensnare and enchant men with the fulfilment of female sexual desire. It's not a sexy film, perhaps, especially by the standards of pornography available today, but it is a film where sex and magic are both portrayed as corrupting, countercultural, and inextricably linked. Similarly, *Virgin Witch* (1972) is a British horror film that goes deeply into sexploitation territory, with a plot that revolves around the deflowering of two young sisters with magical power in ritual settings. Naturally, there is also evil lesbianism, and lush interiors, and white cotton knickers galore. I am quite fond of these films, despite their obvious issues, because they link witchcraft irrevocably with sexual freedom. The two become synonymous, and that offers a refreshing – if lurid – change from sex magic as a highly complex, detailed, often either boring or vile enterprise. These films, however distasteful, laid the foundations for contemporary depictions of witches and sexuality, like *Chilling Adventures of Sabrina* (2018) or *The Love Witch* (2016), which take the tropes established in these 1970s horror and sexploitation films and reshape them into media that centre women, and give them control. This is, after all, one of the prevailing features of modern Wicca – the High Priestess of the coven is in charge, and the priest is her second in command. As the Farrars write in *A Witches' Bible*: 'Wicca is matriarchal, and the High Priestess is leader of the coven'.[17] For the Farrars, and many of their era, the most vital animating force of the coven was the polarity between the two energies – the masculine and feminine, embodied in High Priest and Priestess.

In the 1960s and 1970s, Wiccan sex magic was written about in a serious, quasi-scientific way, invoking the body's responses and a loosely psychological approach to the process of sex. Raymond Buckland describes 'sex-magick' as working due to four different factors: he claims that extrasensory perception is heightened during sexual arousal; that orgasm makes the mind hypersensitive; and that 'peak sexual sensations' give access to 'the unconscious realms'. He also believes that an orgasm can throw a person out of time, and dissolve their ego.[18] This seems like a sound approach: using the altered state of consciousness that sex can bring to allow the mind to access power. Because sex can often be described in terms of build-up and then orgasm, we understand it as an accumulation and release of energy – and it is this, Buckland thinks, that allows sex magic to transport our intentions and desires out of ourselves so effectively, and into the world. There's nothing here to suggest that any of these physiological states require either a bond of marriage or an opposite-sex partner (or a partner at all). So this is, I believe, where sex magic offers opportunities for reclamation, and reintegration into contem-porary culture as an inclusive, welcoming practice.

Even when feminism met witchcraft in the 1960s, and women

upended much of what had gone before, female pleasure – and particularly queer pleasure – still stayed largely invisible. The feminist witchcraft revolution did not see a concomitant rise in books about sex magic by women. And this is perhaps unsurprising: quite rightly, the fomenting power of the revolution was not lust, after all, but anger with the way women in magic (and society) had been treated. Crowley's 'consorts' and 'scarlet women' spring to mind. Witchcraft was certainly due for a feminist overhaul, and from political activist groups such as W.I.T.C.H., who used magic as political power, to Zsuzsanna Budapest, the second-wave feminist activist, magic was thoroughly transformed. Budapest is credited with introducing Wiccan subcultures such as Dianic Wicca, which focused on Goddess-only worship, largely free from both male devotees and masculine deities.

The feminists who attempted to break down the traditional hierarchies that swamped witchcraft, and who carved out space for those (privileged) women's experience deserve thanks and praise. However, although the feminist reimagining of magic departed from the rigid masculine ritual magic that had gone before, it didn't dismantle its preoccupation with highly gendered worship and ritual. Creating women-only spaces certainly avoided the pitfalls and polarities of traditional Wicca, but it did so by excluding all masculine influence, rather than thinking about ways of breaking down the god–goddess binary and moving towards a more nuanced understanding of how magic, and binaries, operate. By excluding men altogether, it makes the boundaries between masculine and feminine influence in Wicca even clearer.

Luckily, times are changing. Have changed already. There are now more resources than ever available to help contemporary practitioners of magic to engage in sex magic – everyone from solo practitioners to members of the LGBTQ+ community. I was so delighted to find articles with cheerful names, things like 'Queer Sex Magic: You Can Do It Too!', and I clicked through, desperate for the secrets, the rationales, the theories behind how sex magic would work.[19] I was looking for bold new takes on polarity, I was looking for practical advice, and I was looking for revolution. And I almost had it. But most of the articles could be divided into two categories. The first was the rather weak, although well-meant, assertion that as queer people, any kind of sex we engaged with was, de facto, magical. This is, I think, an attitude that sets out to be comforting, but ends up being patronising. Why is the sex I might have with a cis straight man less magical than the sex I would have with someone of any other gender (hold your tongues in the back)? However, where these articles do brilliantly is in expanding the way we understand gender and magic. By decoupling gender from sex assigned at birth, these articles are able to reshape how we understand the scope and practice of sex magic.

In a *Vice* article on attracting a partner through candle magic (which involves, rather gloriously, fucking the candle), journalist Sophie Saint Thomas writes that although a phallic candle is helpful for insertion into the body, this doesn't mean you have to be looking for a partner with any particular genitals. After all, she writes, 'we all contain both feminine and masculine energies, which also do not need to correlate with genitals'.[20] In magic, this is still a much-needed, radical utterance. Saint Thomas confidently navigates the world of contemporary sex magic, talks about it with confidence, without reverence – an example of pragmatic, rather than spiritual, sex magic. She refers to the goddess Venus as 'a Hitachi wand – reliable, a sure orgasm, and has been around for a minute', which made me giggle. Saint Thomas' magic is cool – and her spells are straightforward, clear and results-oriented. She makes sex magic feel accessible, and queers it in a straightforward way. And that's great, but it feels a little too easy to me. In witchcraft, I always think it's a wonderful idea to understand why you're doing something: how each action fits together, and how it fits into a greater whole.

It's one of the things I like about the witches that I grew up with on TV. Willow from *Buffy* was beautiful, powerful, and her love of witchcraft grew from an interest in early internet technology. I fancied her so badly: she was clever and funny and, yes, geeky – but she still got to hang out with the cool kids. Other girls wanted to be Buffy, but what I wanted, what I craved, was Willow's introduction into the occult. I wouldn't have minded Oz, her werewolf boyfriend, either, but he disappeared, only to be replaced with – of all things – a fellow witch called Tara. Willow wasn't just in a relationship with Tara – which, for a young bisexual teenager, would have been enough – they were co-practitioners. They did spells together. They . . . well. I spent a lot of time thinking about all the ways sex and magic might interact between Willow and Tara when I was young. Far more time than it was given on screen – but they did kiss, and were obviously intimate, which was one of the very first female same-sex relationships on television, and certainly the most meaningful one I'd ever seen. I still know half of their lines off by heart, and for all that *Buffy* isn't a perfect show, it is one of the best depictions of queer witchcraft I've ever seen – it doesn't question how two women could do witchcraft together, it doesn't trouble itself with polarities – they love each other, they fuck, and they do magic. That's all there is to it.

If Joss Whedon and the *Buffy* writers can do it, then what's to stop us rewriting how sex magic works, making it into something we can engage in and enjoy? The first thing to do in order to achieve this, I think, is to bring everything back to pleasure. Suffering can be a significant part of magic, from ritual fasting to scourging (cleansing rituals that seem to move us into altered mindsets), but pleasure is, for most of us, much easier. The pleasure of getting turned on and getting off, whether by ourselves or with someone else, is something most of us are already familiar with, and so it is an easy thing to incorporate into our witchcraft. The theory behind all these states is the same: that altering our consciousness lets us experience states that we cannot usually experience. And pleasure opens so many wonderful doors: the slow way it washes through the body in desire; the urgency of its thrum as it moves us toward orgasm; the bright, still, bursting point of pleasure; the limb-stretched lethargy of post-orgasmic bliss, when everything floats, and time stretches. So much of witchcraft is concerned with using our bodies in the world: receiving the world's great, interconnected energy, which radiates from each thing, and from ourselves, and putting our energy into the world in the ways we think best benefit the world, each other, and ourselves. And my energy, the good, sweet, strong energy of my pleasure, is a way of being grateful, and alive, and present in the world. It is a form of communion, it is a form of taking in the vast brilliant power that crackles everywhere, and, at the same time, of radiating it back out. It makes sense to make pleasure part of worship.

We can dispense with traditional hierarchies of male and female energies because we can understand ourselves complexly as made of multiple, constantly overlapping energies. As Yvonne Aburrow writes in her 'Inclusive Wicca Manifesto', polarity does not need to be based on gender; it can refer to any sets of tensions or differences (she gives the example of morning or evening people) – and it can also be based just as well on the tension between self and world, between individual and everything, and can, in pleasure, come together and be resolved.[21] When I am at the point of coming, alone or with a partner, I do not feel myself to be made of male or female energy. I just feel myself to be deeply, vastly powerful, and made of stardust and light, and to be dissolving at the edges, into everything else. If we understand sex magic as being about dissolving and re-forming, about making ourselves edgeless against the world, then we have truly made sex magic a place where anyone, of any sexuality or gender, can be safe to participate.

We can use pleasure in spells that ask for things, that focus on what we'd like to achieve, while moving towards a place of pleasure. Focusing on making a new friend or feeling inspired while getting off though is not, I think, particularly sexy, and most sex-magic books are very vague as to what 'focusing on' something might actually mean while masturbating. I don't imagine the experience, per se. Instead, I assign it to an object, and incorporate that object into a pleasurable fantasy that I can get off thinking about. I always think of it rather like the objects in a memory-palace.[22] By putting all of my energy into imagining my wish for inspiration as the beautiful embroidered hangings of a four-poster bed at the beginning, I can then imagine whatever I like happening on that bed, and am seamlessly incorporating my desires into my pleasure, without forcing myself to split my brain between pleasure and the outcome I am trying to achieve. If you aren't someone who likes vivid fantasies, you could do the same with an actual object: focus all of your attention and will onto a sex toy you like, and then while you're using it, you can enjoy the sensations, confident in the knowledge that you're getting pleasure from the very ideas or outcomes you are trying to invoke.

Sex magic with ourselves is powerful: it isn't preparatory; it isn't a replacement for sex with a partner. Sex magic can be wonderful on solstices, especially if there are safe places where you can do it and feel connected to nature. In the summer solstice, it is tempting to go outside, to have pleasure amid the wide world in all its growing splendour. In winter, I recommend a bath. Solitary sex magic is a way of observing the energy of witches' Sabbats, and a way of participating in stories of change and alterations – seasonal, lunar, spiritual – without necessarily needing to engage with the narrative of (hetero)sexual generation that they are often based on.

Certainly, it is what happens during sex magic that seems most relevant. Aburrow identifies 'resonance' (the energy between two similar people – two people who love the same books, for example) and 'synergy', the energy created from working in groups. Anyone who has ever sung in a choir will have a great sense of how synergy works. And it's absolutely no stretch to incorporate these into sexual contexts, into having sex in ways that don't require us to engage along heteronormative lines. This also allows us to reinstate the witch as a powerful sexual presence – no longer are the men who write about sex magic its sole practitioners. Not vessels, not handmaidens, not lesser – witches are allowed to make the rules, to make sex magical and to have magical sex.

In sex, all acts are at once sacred and profane, magical and ordinary, transcendental and bodily. It is among the most complicated things we do – for all it is also an instinct – and to layer magic on top of it is both very powerful and very tricky. We have to negotiate the sex itself, but also all of society – and magic's – attitudes towards it. Sex is resonant with mutual understanding, if it is done well, and it is within that resonance that we can connect outward: with one another, with the world, and with the power that sweeps through and animates everything. Sex magic is the magic that lets us move from imagining union with the world to feeling it. It is an act that both is itself connection, and mimics and models other, broader connections that are harder to conceptualise. And it need not model them as procreative, or in ways that oppress one gender, or in ways that reinscribe gender binaries. Instead, it can model the vast, entangled, strange and unknowable magic of the world. If everything gives and receives energy, if the world is everything we know, then sex is a brilliant way to join ourselves to that energy. To feel it in our bodies. The world moves in ways that incorporate us, that we barely understand, and sex is a way of taking that energy for ourselves, for a second, passing it through the beauty of our pleasure, and releasing it again. Sex is one small fraction of the pleasure of the world, and we get to keep it for those moments. Sex magic is a way of understanding the world with our bodies. It is a way of making pleasure and unleashing it, in all its beauty, back out into the universe.

A Healing Ritual for
Winter Aches and Pains

*P*erhaps you thought I was going to give a sex-magic spell here. But I'm going to offer something else, related but tangential. Good body magic. There's nothing less sexy than feeling unwell, miserable, not in one's own body properly. So here's a spell for getting back to health – for feeling more in a position to do sex magic in the first place. Nice and gentle.

Magic and modern medicine are friends. They go together. The body and the mind need all sorts of care, throughout our lives, from exercise to education, from having our nappies changed to being tended to in our old age. I am an advocate for many things, but perhaps chief among them is appropriate medical care. The NHS is a life-saving miracle of a service and we are lucky to have it. All this is to say: if you are unwell, by all means use magic alongside medicine, but your priority always has to be accessing medical care. And take serious care, also. When you are unwell, your body is devoting all of its energy to healing, and there isn't much, really, left over for anything else.

So this ritual is extraordinarily low-key. It uses the idea of food-blessings, which are a staple part of many world religions and belief systems. Whether or not you say a grace at the table, we all of us feel grateful and lucky to have enough to eat, and these thoughts are especially prevalent around harvest time and other periods when we recognise that not everybody has the same privileges as us. Food is one of our most magical substances: it literally keeps us alive. It is never more vital than when we are unwell.

This ritual can be done in bed, or on a sofa, or anywhere where you're laid up. What you need is very simple. Your evening meal – for me, with a cold, it is almost always tomato soup – and a glass of water. You also, if you have one, should hold or have nearby a talisman that you identify with, so there is a little more magical power than you alone can muster.

Before you eat your supper, draw your hands over it three times clockwise, in a circle, saying quietly to yourself, *everything I eat will help me heal*. Repeat this three times further. As you eat your meal, think about the food turning into golden lights that move through the body, particularly targeting those parts of you that ache, or feel stuffed up or sore. Imagining the food actively helping you helps the magic to take root. Rest up, and repeat this for every meal you eat until you're better. At the end of your convalescence, give an offering to the altar, of a rich food. Marzipan is good for this, if you don't want to leave the more traditional cream or milk out on your altar. Thank the world, and all its magic, for nourishing you and helping you combat your illness. If you wish to give further thanks, a wonderful congruent action is to donate to a food bank.

DECEMBER

Midwinter and Magic in the Dark

December comes down hard on us all, this year. The sky is tight, leaden, and will not give in to snow. The dark days open like a throat, and we all file downwards, into winter's belly. We are so tired.

Politics lurches from farce to satire, and all the time there are people queuing at food banks, facing homelessness, suffering as the temperature drops. We face recession, and the ongoing tragedy of global pandemic. Everything feels bad. Even I have to admit, as I squint through my hands at the news, the morning after the general election, that everything feels pretty hopeless. This is not easy for me to do. I am an inveterately festive person. I love holly, I love carols, and I love the greenery and the frippery and the groaning tables and the beribboned parcels and the whole-body hope for snow. I am festive to my bones. What I like best is the grey margin of this most smudged holiday, half-pagan, half-Christian, each jostling together happily. The greenwood, the dayspring, the running of the deer, and the sky-rivening angels. It is, of course, possible to pick apart which aspects of these winter traditions come from pre-Christian religion and which are later additions: people like to do so in end-of-year interest articles and compendiums of Christmas facts. Part of the magic, though, for me, is the melding, all the traditions butting up against one another.

The most glorious of our winter traditions, I would argue, stem from Yule, the winter solstice. Solstice means 'sun-stop', and that is what it does. The sun stops. It disappears. It hides away, barely rising, seeming to sit still at the horizon line, rather than cresting the sky on its daily journey. Instead of sunrise, midday and evening, we have mostly variegated dark. As a response to these long days of darkness in the northern hemisphere, most of our winter traditions boil down to ways of coping with the lack of light, and ways of calling to the sun to get it going again: the spiritual equivalent of defibrillation. *Do not stop now*, we call. *We cannot do without you. Please come back to life.* We all become sorcerers of light, for this month. From decking the halls to burning Yule logs, our winter celebrations are, at heart, defences, measures we implement in the hope that, this time, the dark will not swallow the light entirely. This year, though, I am afraid it will.

It is December, after all, and December is about the light dying. It is about everything dying, really, and I keep telling people this, in apocalyptic tones. Frost has in its clutches almost everything that bloomed. It eats water to ice, it eats rosehips to rot, and it eats the round ball of the sun down to nothing, leaves us in the dark. December is the month the earth hangs still, the month the dark might swallow us, all hungry and cold and cruel. Rather than harvesting, instead the world asks us to feed it: with food bank appeals and sponsored Christmas places at hostels; with birdseed and fat-balls for hedgerow creatures, and hot pans on the pond to melt neat circles and make sure animals can access the water to drink. In December we are caregivers, guardians of life during the dark periods. Guardians of light, too. As the sun barely shows itself above the horizon, so we are called to trust that spring will come, that frost will thaw, that light will win, victorious, over darkness. It is hard, however, to believe that it will. In all the misery, in all the dark coldness, I itch to do something. To feel something. It is as if the darkness has settled over me, run through me, made me numb and strange. Nothing shifts it.

We have always feared that this winter would be the one that heralded eternal winter, that spring would not follow. Think of Narnia, held by the wicked White Witch in a state of perpetual winter, but never Christmas. This reality – no thaw, no light, and no ceremonies to invite the sun back – is the worst fate the Pevensie children can imagine. In Neolithic times, sacrifices were made to entreat the sun to return. Henges were built: Stonehenge, for example, sits on a sight line that aligns with the winter solstice. So does Maeshowe, on Orkney. Maeshowe is a chambered cairn, with a long entry corridor. Inside are stone-lined recesses, which would once have held the bones of the dead. It feels comfortable, the cairn: tall enough to stand in easily, and cosy. There is something womblike about it, of course, the round chamber and the long exit corridor, which must be walked through with bowed head, or at a crouch. And on the winter solstice, the sun reaches down the long stone passageway and illuminates the chambered cairn, bathing the back wall in concentrated light. Has the sun come to take the souls of the dead, or return them? Does the sun's entry into the cairn signify its own death, and rebirth? Of course, there is no written evidence of the intention behind Maeshowe's construction, so we cannot know for sure. What seems to occur, though, is a kind of capturing, of holding the sun close, trapping its rays in stone and space, and letting it find rest there, letting it be coaxed into staying. Maeshowe is a beautiful reminder that we literally build spaces for the sun's return, to make it feel comfortable. We wish so badly to know that the dark will cease that we have, throughout history, constructed myths, rituals and buildings around the vital importance of observing the winter solstice.

Aztec religions believed that the sun, Huitzilopochtli, died entirely on 20 December, and was reborn the following day. He battled his sister, the moon, and his brothers, the stars, constantly, to stop the world being condemned to eternal night. This is why he needed such frequent sacrifice: he had to remain well fed, and capable of taking on his four hundred star-brothers at any time, for he was always chasing them across the sky. Every fifty-two years, it was believed that the world would end: and Huitzilopochtli, if not given enough precious human blood, could not ward it off. It is a beautiful story, though deeply violent, and details the lengths we will go to to bring the light back securely. It is, after all, our most precious commodity. We all need nourishment, just like Huitzilopochtli, if we are to survive through the winter and fight the dark.

This year, however, I cannot seem to get any. I am well fed, yes, but my soul hurts, a strange numbness of cold and grief with the world. I do not know how to nourish myself, how to take up arms against night's forces. Of course, I am doing my best – but none of us, at this sun-still time, can fight off the darkness alone. And so a friend visits me, laden with gifts of preserved light. They bring mincemeat, brooding in its heavy jar. They made it last year, in early autumn, and so it has been ripening for over a year. For me, mincemeat is perhaps the single most festive comestible, and holds all good things within it. Raisins and dried fruit and more alcohol than any recipe needs, and candied peel, which tastes to me like a medieval feast day, and looks like light, crystallised so we can hold it. The mincemeat has deliquesced down into smooth, beautiful, dark richness, as if it held the dark of the winter and the light of spring inside it, and had turned both to velvet. They hand it over like contraband and I could cry to see it. Making mince-meat is expensive, and time-consuming. One year, my godmother and I made it with beef suet, and it was as potent and as deli-cious as anything I've ever eaten. Mincemeat is a form of pure kitchen magic: the gathering of the best things, things the sun has ripened at its peak. You take all of summer's good sweet-ness, bottle it against the dark, to let the mixture sit and sulk its way toward sweet potency. It is as much a promise as it is a gift: *we came from light,* whisper the contents of the jar, *and we will guide you back toward it.*

My friend and I make mince pies, and talk, and slowly, very slowly, I begin to thaw. We drink whisky, washing the amber light against the sides of glasses, tonguing it as if we could taste the sun. There are marzipan fruits, which hold for me almost the same fascination as the Turkish delight did for Edmund in Narnia. They nest in their dark paper, little gaudy facsimiles, keepsakes of summer, all bright ripeness. And each one is like a gift in the mouth, the sweet yield of almond and sugar. They look like summer and taste of Christmas, and the contrast lets the two live alongside each other. The sun and the dark. The cold, and the promise of future blossoming. Summer will come back, perhaps. The marzipan fruits and the mincemeat are food magics, kitchen spells that enchant and transform. But the best magic, of course, is that my friend sits with me. We light candles against the darkness, and we talk long into the night, turning thoughts inward, using the little light that is left to illuminate our darkest places.

It isn't surprising that humans quickly turn to introspection as the light fails. Just as plants show little external sign of life through the winter months, so humans, too, traditionally turn our attention indoors and inwards. If you're in the northern hemisphere, then these short, harsh days are traditionally a time of telling stories, telling one another how the world works, passing on wisdom and information. Winter gives us what we need, lets us prepare before going back out into the world when the light returns. Winter can be seen as a time of healing, regrouping, of doing work on ourselves rather than work in the world. It is easy to believe in this structure, but hard to enact it in contemporary society. Our rhythms are not those of rising with the late sun, working with what little light we have, and sleeping early – they are quite the opposite. I have worked for a lot of wonderful people, but not a single one, alas, would accept a sick note for six months of hibernation.

In the main, our daily routines don't change much from one season to the next. In spring, summer and autumn, perhaps that is ok, but in winter it is brutal – we rise in the dark, shower in the cold, spend time on buses with people sneezing into their hands. The darkness brings with it immense privation for so many people: those who cannot afford hot food and water, or to turn their heating on. It is also a time when, for millions, darkness brings seasonal depression, periods of illness and a pervasive feeling, for months, that we are just not quite awake. Modern life means we often work in the teeth of nature, against its cycles. This has been encouraged by alternative means of illumination. Who needs to heed the sun's rhythms when we have electric light? Electric lights and the light from screens mimic daylight in wattage and intensity, keeping our brains awake. But even before electricity, gas and candlelight extended the hours of daylight. We are perfectly capable of living in this false light, of conducting our business by simply ignoring the dark. What is difficult, however, are the effects of living against the rhythm of the day: it is exhausting, our bodies are prone to illness, and our brains to sadness – quite literally, in the sense of SAD, or seasonal affective disorder. The darkness highlights how dependent we are on the sun not just for light, but also for brain and body health.

But while those difficulties wouldn't necessarily be altered by living in a much smaller way through the winter months, it might be helpful to us all to try. If we were able to sleep more, to work from home more, we might find winter's bite less cruel. The festive season should be bright, with light and good cheer and bravery against winter, but there also, crucially, needs to be time dedicated to resting.

The same can also be said of our magical practice. The year rises and falls, and witches are no different. Our power waxes and wanes too. Magic is harder when everything is cold and wet and miserable. Magic is harder when there's no incentive to be outside, and when we feel apart from the world, barricaded into our homes by central heating, by double-glazing, by jumpers and blankets and heavy curtains. We have to find new ways to make magic during the winter, ways that often feel less than ideal. Nothing grows, so our spellwork relies on preserved plants, herbs, dried fruits, twigs and mushrooms. If we haven't been organised and gathered herbs throughout the year, this can feel disastrous, disappointing. What's more, there's often more call on our power during winter. People require comfort and healing. For many people, this is a time when all the bad things sharpen: bereavements and losses are felt more keenly, and people require more succour from one another as they can take less of it from being out in the world. Our bodies often feel different in winter, and they are harder to keep running. So what does it mean, in the midst of this, to treat this as a time of year for turning inwards? What does it mean to honour this often hostile time as a part of the year when true, good, expansive work can be done? What does it mean to do magic in the dark?

Firstly, it is useful to see nature with fresh eyes, to look again at that which seems so dead. This is a skill, and it isn't an easy one. It is hard enough to go outside to the supermarket in winter, let alone to spend time in cold, damp, raw-winded nature. But put your hat on, and, if you can, go out on your lunch break, or on a Saturday morning, and think about the world as not dead, but sleeping. Know that under the ground, roots are still bringing water to trees, and that although we cannot see them, things are still growing, and sleeping, in soil. Winter has some benefits, even, in terms of wildlife-spotting. In Britain, garden birds are often reliant on food set out for them in winter, and this means that humans can see and interact with them more. Even if you don't have a garden, you can often watch birds in parks – and can, if you are happy to revisit and refill them all winter, put up feeders on hedges or public footpaths. There are several around my area and I love watching what flocks to them. There is a pleasure in seeing a robin, or watching pigeons puff up from cold as they waddle under park benches. Some birds, like pink-footed geese and Canada geese, overwinter in Britain, and so our ponds are full of visitors to welcome with birdseed. You can hear them, often, honking overhead, a lovely sound in the clear winter air. Geese are always slightly surprising to me: their size, their noise, and their inquisitiveness. Near where I live, they gather in great numbers by the pond, filling the cold air with sound. These might seem very, very small things, but just making an effort to notice them can remind us that not everything is dead and ruined.

It can be useful to reframe your own, cold body – and your own magic – in the same way as we reframe winter. By not resisting the alterations that the dark months bring, but by seeking them out, and looking to gently investigate them, we can mitigate much of their possible discomfort. There is a practice known as 'non-judgemental attention', which has its diverse places but is commonly found in mindfulness. This, master of mindfulness Jon Kabat-Zinn argues, is 'paying attention in a particular way: on purpose, in the present moment, and without judgment'.[1] This can be very difficult, and takes practice, but it is an important principle, for me, for surviving winter. If you notice things, really attend to them, they are drawn into relation with you. Even if you do not 'like' these things, even if they are ugly, or frightening, or boring, drawing them into your attention is a way of connecting to them, to the broader world. By applying the principle of 'non-judgement' to our noticing, we are able to engage closely with the world even when it is not as we would wish it. By doing this, by engaging with ourselves, and our bodies, we are better able to see what it is our magic needs, and to provide it.

Simply noticing can reveal all kinds of things. For example, you may notice just how much like the plants and wildlife you are, in winter. You are still growing, just more slowly. You are still beautiful, but less showy, less vibrant, more covered-over. Like the landscape around you, you are undergoing slow, thoughtful change, whether it feels like it or not. Your brain is working on things that are inside. It is reflecting, taking stock. Your view is turning inward: try to follow it, to see where it leads, to see what it reveals to you. It can be a productive time to keep a dream journal, or even just a diary, tracing your thoughts and emotions through the winter season. It can be useful to celebrate these sleepy, slow-growing months, rather than hiding from them. Working with nature as much as is possible helps to alleviate the sense that winter is out to get us.

There are lots of practical things you can do to ensure that winter passes as pleasantly for you as it can, and that you undertake good work in that time. What my friend and I choose to do on a sunny Sunday afternoon is perhaps the least practical of them. We catch a bus to the beach, where the sand is biscuit-coloured and freezing. The last of the afternoon's meagre light hangs still and thin above the sea. Those people who are walking up and down the promenade are doing so quickly, to exercise dogs or get somewhere. Nobody lingers. Everyone wears hats, gloves and thick coats. In my bag, there is a towel. We aren't going to hide from winter: we are going to race it, run alongside its biting teeth – we are going to play with winter, and make ourselves giddy with the cold. So we slip onto the beach, take our clothes off, to much public consternation, and walk into the water. I go first, while behind me my friend yells down the beach about what an idiot I am, to ask them to do something so ridiculous. I go first because I feel brave, and because I'd suggested it. But more than anything, I walk into the lapping waves because for the first time in weeks, I feel something. Winter's settling numbness clears, for a second, replaced by the bright pain of warm feet on freezing sand, and the cold wrap of the wind. Then the water hits me, colder than shock. Colder than my body can find a nerve response for, at first. And in the absence of nerve response, just as the biting cold sets in like knives, there is a leap of elation inside me. I am, I realise, happy.

A lot has been written about wild swimming, in beautiful, lyrical prose, and I will not add my voice unduly to the pile. But there is something about being immersed in freezing water that alters the way you feel. Swimming in the sea and rivers is a wonderful experience in which the physiology of the body and the magic of the water come together. Scientifically and magically, being close to, and in, bodies of water is extremely good for you, when undertaken safely. We are used, as humans, to seeking out comfortable feelings and situations: the freezing sea is the opposite of that. Cold water is used to treat forms of depression, because it essentially administers shocks that break thought patterns, and bring temporary relief to sufferers:

certainly, it is very difficult to think when submerged in cold water[2]. Instead, you become concerned with only the immediacies of your situation. Shock is one valuable effect of cold water to the body and brain, but there are others: a recent survey found that hydrotherapy of various kinds '[is] widely used to improve immunity and for the management of pain, . . . chronic obstructive pulmonary diseases, asthma, . . . fatigue, anxiety, obesity, hypercholesterolemia, hyperthermia, [and] labour.[3]

Cold water is no cure-all, of course, but immersion in the December sea — albeit briefly — resets our brains, alters our central nervous systems, makes our skin tingle on exiting the water, makes us grateful when we can pull a proper lungful of air again, after gasping in the waves. Our feet go numb immediately, and it takes longer for our legs. We stand close to one another, in the water, faces up toward the last of the sun. We are giggling. We can't stop giggling. We hold hands, shove each other, threatening immersion. There is magic in the water, of course, and not just jangling cold. The swimming is a ritual, as much as it is a fun activity. When we run into the water, when we commit to doing something frightening and alluring, we are telling the world that we would like to commune with it, that we are seeking connection. Together, my friend and I cast a spell. This is a spell that says we will not let the other go under. This is a promise that we will brave the freezing cold for each other, to make the other one smile. Afterwards, our hands and feet feel alien, like blocks of wood, and we can't have been in the sea for more than three minutes. We sit in the sand and laugh. People walking past comment on our bravery, our whooping out across the cold water. We don't feel quite human, anymore. We could be wild birds, we could be fish. We shove our shoes back on, clumsily, our socks full of sand. The light is leaving the day, and we go to the pub. For weeks afterwards, every time I think of the cold water, my mood lifts and my body sings.

Walking into the sea in the coldest month of the year is certainly one way of keeping the dark's despair away, but there are also ways that leave you drier, happier and not quite so likely to die. One strategy is to celebrate the solstice, which falls on 21 December. The winter solstice is one of the eight Sabbats, or holy festivals witches celebrate annually. Midwinter, or Yule (from the Norse *Jólnir* , one of Odin's names), is a lesser Sabbat, which means it marks a lunar or solar event rather than an earth-based event (e.g. harvest). All eight Sabbats can be represented as eight spokes in a circle, forming a wheel that encapsulates the year. Because some of them are equinoxes or solstices, they fall within different dates each year, but are usually within two or three days of the given dates. They are:

- *Samhain: 31st of October to the evening of the 1st of November*
- *Yule: between the 20th and 23rd of December*
- *Imbolc: 1st of February to the 2nd of February*
- *Ostara: between the 20th and 23rd of March*
- *Beltane: the 1st of May*
- *Litha: between the 19th and the 26th of June*
- *Lughnasadh: the 1st of August*
- *Mabon: between the 20th and 23rd of September*

These dates apply to the northern hemisphere.

These are a mixture of solstices and other festivals, such as equinoxes or traditional named harvest days. Their names vary by region, but these are the most popular British names for the Sabbats. However, the idea of the eight Sabbats, and that they are all celebrated by witches, is a Neopagan innovation. There is no historical evidence, for example, that any particular culture or time period celebrated all of these, and certainly not under the names they go by. As contemporary witchcraft and nature-religions are syncretic traditions, the eight Sabbats have been adopted from a wide range of sources and turned into the idea of the 'wheel of the year'. It is up to each individual practitioner which of these, if any, they choose to celebrate. However, the four of these that are not earth-based but solar and lunar events (particularly the solstices), are easy to remember, and easy to mark, even just in small ways. Even if you do not feel moved toward Wiccan spirituality, even if you simply wish to acknowledge the points of most-light and most-darkness, the winter solstice may well feel important. It is, after all, the moment when the light returns, a holding-on point, a hopeful thing.

It can be easy to lose midwinter in the overwhelming run-up to Christmas, and the juxtaposition of the two can feel jarring, despite their close connection, but it is an excellent time of year to take stock. It is also the perfect opportunity to bring feelings of hope and joy back into winter, in a non-commercial, quiet way. Although it is one of the lesser Sabbats, winter solstice is perhaps the most important to me, personally. It was also, historically, the most important annual celebration across ancient cultures, from Roman Saturnalia to Germanic and

Egyptian celebrations. In many early calendars, it marked the new year. By creating a space for the solstice, you can also create space to explore its central ideas: the struggle between light and dark, and the ultimate return, or rebirth, of the light, the spring, the year. Horologically, the winter solstice is the day containing the fewest hours of light. Interestingly, our 24-hour clock is too neat for the turning of the earth. There is, every year, at least one newspaper article that myth-busts the idea of the shortest day. Essentially, it is all to do with the curvature of the earth and the way we measure time: unless you are in the Arctic, the solstice may contain the fewest hours of daylight in the year, but the sun will actually set slightly later than on the preceding days.[4] The solstice cannot be quite contained within our clock. This is, I think, an excellent reminder of the messiness of time, and our relation to the turning of the year. It is comforting to think that despite scientific advances, we still try to box things in too neatly. Light and darkness keep their own balance, and we simply try to catch up.

Midwinter and midsummer were historically marked, not only because they were environmentally unusual events, but also for more practical reasons. They helped provide points on a calendar, to measure time into organised blocks, which helped with resource distribution and survival. Winter months, especially in northern regions, were deadly, and winter could usher in starvation. Knowing when the midpoint of this season was helped early civilisations gauge supplies and plan accordingly. Structures were built that measured the progression of the year's light, with central architectural features illuminating at the solstitial points.

At midwinter the sun, which has been ebbing through the gathering darkness, is finally reborn after its longest absence. The rebirth of the solar deity, out of the gestation period of the longest night, presages spring and the growing season. There are traditions of feasting and celebration. In many early agrarian communities, the majority of non-breeding, feed-intensive livestock, such as cattle, would be slaughtered around midwinter to provide sustenance until spring. Midwinter was also a helpful point to mark from a food preservation point of view, as a number of foods could not be preserved all winter – the solstice marked a good time to use these up. Therefore, feasting often took place as a celebration of the last of the fresh meat until spring. *Jul*, the northern European pagan celebration of the solstice, lasted for twelve days of feasting – and offerings to the gods were made, in order to help seeds germinate in the coming year.

Similarly, fuel was an ongoing concern to early peoples (and, indeed, still is for many in contemporary society – fuel poverty remains endemic and costs lives every winter). However, in order to call back the sun from his absence, and petition the gods to provide more fuel, fires would be created: this mimetic invitation was thought to coax the sun back and shorten the winter. Ancient Celtic people seem to have believed that the sun stood still for twelve days in the middle of winter, and during this time a Yule log was lit, which was believed to bring luck. There are accounts of the log being the length of the house, and being slowly fed forwards, into the fire.

The Yule log brings blessings for future endeavours, and

future success. And it is easy to understand why its firelight was so important through the darkness – every day after 21 December gets a little bit lighter. It will not be so dark again for another year. The burning, the light, the feasting, have all pulled us through the most difficult part of the year. Although January and February can feel gloomy, those few minutes of light per day mount up. This change is incremental, but it is there – light is, quite literally, returning to the world. We are quick to make light and darkness metaphors, attaching them to good and evil, or to deities, from the pagan to the Christian. But these forces are powerful enough on their own. An absence of light slows growth, drops temperatures, freezes water, and enacts change over the whole earth. What can be more important than a celebration of its return? It is, even in the darkness of winter, a true hopefulness. Even without any attachment to gods or goddesses, spirituality or religion, the return of the light is vital, longed-for, and so should be celebrated.

Celebrating this Sabbat can be done in many ways: you do not need a vast tree to burn, nor do you require a henge to trap the light in. Instead, you can make your home a temporary shrine to light's return, to the perseverance of living things in darkness. I like to have specific decorations, different from those used for Christmas. I usually add my festive decorations for Christmas over the top of the solstice ones, it must be said, but at least I am aware of the difference. There are records of historic decorations for Yule in medieval carols, many of which document winter traditions that coexisted with Christian practices and probably pre-date them. The word 'carol' in English comes from the French *carole*, a dance accompanied by music, and traditionally carols were neither overtly religious in nature, necessarily, nor exclusively sung at Christmas: there were various carols for the different festivals of the year. The 'Boar's Head Carol', for example, first printed in 1521, although almost certainly significantly older, details bringing in an elaborately decorated boar's head to consume at the Yuletide feast:

> The boar's head in hand bear I
> Bedecked with bays and rosemary
> I pray you, my masters, be merry[5]

Although I'm not particularly recommending you seek out and serve the head of a boar during your midwinter celebrations, it is worth attending to the herbs with which the boar's head is bedecked: 'bays and rosemary'. Not only are these aromatics delicious when served with pork, they are also hardy evergreen herbs that can survive frost, and keep their leaves through winter. They are signifiers that even in the depths of winter, good things grow, and that, therefore, more growth will return. Bay and rosemary are symbolic as well as culinary, and the 'Boar's Head Carol' suggests, as many other winter carols do, that bringing greenery into the house and decorating with it is a way of celebrating life in winter.

Another medieval carol tradition is the focus on holly and ivy. These evergreens, which flourish in winter, have been made part of Christian iconography (the holly's berries are said to represent drops of Christ's blood, and the thorns of its leaves the crown of thorns). But prior to their adoption into Christian symbolism, they were a joyous part of Yuletide celebrations. You may be familiar with the popular carol 'The Holly and the

Ivy', but there are several more, including one credited to Henry VIII, which compares the constancy of love for a lady to the perpetual green of the holly and the ivy, even in winter. Anyone who knows their history knows that this is, perhaps, more poetic licence than political reality, but the carol itself is rather beautiful:

> *Green groweth the holly,*
> *So doth the ivy.*
> *Though winter blasts blow never so high,*
> *Green groweth the holly.*
> . . .
> *As the holly groweth green*
> *With ivy all alone*
> *When flowers cannot be seen*
> *And greenwood leaves be gone*[6]

Here, there is no Christian association with either the holly or the ivy: they are being used in the carol to symbolise longevity, resilience and persistent blooming even in adverse conditions. They are always grouped together because, in a forest in winter, they are usually the only two green things to be seen. The greenwood may be bare, but these two evergreens flourish. There is something lovely about the historic tradition of bringing greenery into the house – literally decking the halls – and every year, I try to do this to mark midwinter.

The area around my house is largely urban, although I am lucky to have two parks close by. Every year, ahead of the winter solstice, I make a series of forays into the darkness for greenery. These covert gatherings are not entirely neighbourly of me, but perhaps that is part of their thrill; it seems such a shame to buy holly, when there is a holly hedge so near to me, and ivy crowding the walls, glossy and green despite the cold. I have been known to take my secateurs for a walk in late evening, letting myself into the park with a click of the metal gate, and feeling my way down holly stems. While, of course, ethical gathering is paramount, and I'd never take so much as to deprive the birds of berries, it feels perfectly reasonable to snip a few stems to see me through the winter. After all, my meagre clippings pale in comparison with the harsh cutting back of the holly undertaken by the park wardens. Unfortunately, that other beautiful greenery of winter, the mistletoe, which was considered sacred to Druids, does not grow abundantly in Scotland. Even where it does grow, you may not have noticed it – it is a parasite, and grows high on trees, taking advantage of their root systems and nourishment. Its little round balls are difficult to reach without tall ladders and hooked gathering implements. It is abundant in East Anglia, and they used to sell it cheaply in the market in Cambridge come Christmas. The most mistletoe I have ever seen in one place was on the outskirts of Paris, between Charles de Gaulle airport and the city proper, where, from the highway, every tree seems crowded with it. But I buy mine for a slightly excruciating price in Waitrose, and I always have it hanging over a doorway so that people can kiss under it.

In fact, a beautiful traditional decoration that we don't commonly have in Scotland is the kissing bough, a willow or wire structure hung from the ceiling, decorated with greenery, including mistletoe, ribbons, and sometimes candles. This tradition, which also dates from the Middle Ages, has its origins in a year-round greenery installation thought to bring luck, and which was probably used to sweeten the air of dining areas. This evolved into a Yuletide tradition, and it prefigured the Christmas tree in Britain. Some florists offer kissing-bough building courses, although I am tempted to advise trial, error, and heavy-duty gloves for handling the holly. It is a beautiful, lucky, heavily symbolic addition to the house at midwinter. Hung over the dining table, or any communal space, it offers protection against illness, as well as bringing good luck, and kissing, into your house. I often add pine or fir to my midwinter branches – although the Christmas tree is a Germanic tradition originating in Yule, it feels ubiquitous now. I have a rather sad, small, plastic Christmas tree, because I am so rarely at home over the festive period. So, every year, I speak politely to the man who sells Christmas trees round the back of the pub, and he gives me offcuts. These are the branches lopped from the bottom of pine trees in order that other people can fit them into their cars, and they're usually cheap or free, because they'd just go to waste otherwise. This is enough to bring the green into my house, to fight off the darkness with resinous life, and to make a display of festive greenery that lasts until Twelfth Night. I find it easier, somehow, to do magic when I am surrounded by greenery. I decorate my altar, too, in holly and ivy, and altar cloths in festive colours.

Bringing flame into the house is traditional at the solstice, and so is nursing it through the night, to ward off darkness. My Swedish friend has gifted me some of her festive traditions surrounding fire, although I have not adopted them all. In Sweden, it is still fairly common to have live candles on the Christmas tree, in beautiful, decorated clip-on holders. This tradition appals the fire-safety warden in me, and I cannot in good conscience recommend it, unless you inhabit a mostly bare building made of stone: a medieval castle, perhaps. But, despite fearing that we will all burn alive whenever I am near her tree, I hugely admire its flickering beauty. The candle flame has a light that cannot be mimicked, even by the best substitutes, and the way the flames dance makes the tree seem entirely alive. A beautiful wood-god, brought in to protect us from the excesses of the dark, dressed in all the finery of the sun. I have managed to mimic the beautiful dancing lights, although not perfectly, with LED candles with moving lights. They aren't as beautiful, but nor are they as risky, and they mean that the symbolism is still present.

The other beautiful tradition she has introduced me to is Lucia Day, or St Lucy's Day, celebrated in Sweden – and across Europe – on 13 December. Saint Lucy, a fourth-century martyr, was killed for bringing aid and sustenance to Christians sheltering in Roman catacombs. Her hands were full of food and water, and so she lit her way with a candle crown, as she walked through the dark of the catacombs. Before the calendar reforms, St Lucy's Day coincided with the solstice, so it is no surprise that it is a festival of light: the name Lucy, of course, comes from the Latin for light. A young girl, dressed in white, is chosen to represent St Lucy, and she wears a crown of candles. Songs are sung and saffron buns are eaten, and the whole hope of the festival is that, like St Lucy, it provides enough light to live through the darkness with. It is a beautiful festival, and one which represents perfectly the complex dovetailing between Christian celebrations and their pagan precursors.

Tips for eating, drinking and decorating often sound rather flimsy and superficial. After all, we are so used to Christmas as a religious festival, that it can be difficult to think about the magic inherent in these practices. It can be difficult to shift our minds to acknowledge that it also has magical connotations, that its significance is always double. It can help to remember that practising witches do not in general have a collective sacred space. Churches are decorated seasonally, and people work hard behind the scenes to ensure there are flower displays, incense and objects to signal that one is in a sacred space. In the same way, our domestic spaces can be made conducive to witchcraft. These can be small things – no huge altars, or pseudo-Gothic beams. Indeed, many of the ways we make our spaces feel more sacred are intensely personal and relate directly to our practice. I often have herbs hung up, drying – which looks, I suppose, stereotypically 'witchy', but is in fact partially practical. I have lots of things I want to dry out properly, and high ceilings, so up they go. They represent the working life of the kitchen, the practical evidence of my practice, and that feels important. I remember, as a student in shared halls, feeling a little embarrassed about my collection of weird dried things – I don't, now. I rather like my kitchen resembling that of a traditional witch, that you might see in a children's book illustration. And the décor doesn't stop with dried things: on the windowsills I might

have candles, and in the windows I often hang charms, to keep
darkness at bay. A set of little golden suns, a prism containing
wildflowers, a metal skeleton in a bonnet, whose smile wards
off bad fortune. These things have accrued over time and have
felt useful and sensible. At no point have I intentionally decorated my house in a 'witchy' style – not that there is anything
wrong with that. There can, however, be a fine line between
an atmosphere conducive to magic and living inside a stage set
– the line will be different for everyone, and you can't know
where that line is, I don't think, without experimentation. My
rule of thumb is that I keep nothing that doesn't feel useful,
or that isn't beautiful: even then, however, I think my mother
despairs of my inability to leave a surface clear.

If you feel that you'd like to celebrate the winter solstice,
there are a number of things you can do during the day, before
the evening falls. On the afternoon of the solstice, perhaps set
aside time to reorganise your altar, and then prepare a meal.
The solstice is an excellent time for doing the winter work of
looking deep inside yourself, thinking about what you are
composed of: the good bits, and the bits you do not like so
much. It is an excellent time to consider what you would like
to leave in darkness, and what you would like to take forward
with you to the new year, and it is a time for working with the
returning sun to ask for help with the germination of projects.
The spellwork at the end of the chapter will offer suggestions
for how to do this. To prepare, perhaps decorate the altar in
bright colours that suggest warmth and life, and make sure you
have new candles, or trim the wicks of used ones so they 'feel'
new. Bring branches in, and perhaps use cinnamon or cloves
to scent the space. This can easily be achieved by doing what

I call 'false mulling'. Instead of making mulled wine, or cider (although feel free), you can simply heat a pan low on the stove with water, orange peel, cloves and cinnamon – your whole house will smell of Christmas. I would like to tell you that this is an ancient pagan tradition, but if we are being entirely honest, I first saw it on 1990s Channel 5 programme where a woman helped people whose houses wouldn't sell. The key, she said, was to fill the house with warm domestic smells – vanilla or festive scents – and this could be done cheaply and easily in this way. Witchcraft truly is syncretic, and although I am embarrassed about where the tip came from, I am a great believer in the delicious, welcoming, festive scent it brings.

Nothing takes the darkness except time. We gain just over a minute of daylight per day between 21 December and 21 June, the summer solstice. Slowly, the heat and life of the sun returns to our lives. We cannot hurry it. We cannot petition it. We cannot alter the course of the heavens or the wheel of the year in those ways. But we can celebrate the knowledge that the sun is coming back. We can tempt him with fine foods, with feasting and music and young girls with crowns full of candles. We can acknowledge the depths of the dark: the way it fills us with fear, the way it seems to snuff something vital out. We can live with the darkness in ways that feel easier on our minds and bodies, and we can distract ourselves from it, we can do things to counteract it, we can pay special attention to how the darkness makes us feel, and remember that the world's processes are not stopped, only slowed a little. We can eat mincemeat, and drink whisky, and tell stories. The best winter magic, for my spirit, was running into the sea, making the decision to enter winter's cold as wholly as I could rather than being afraid of it. To make a statement to the world about my willingness to be brave in the face of winter's teeth. And that is what Yule is all about: it is about revelry, and bravery, and refusing misery, even when the world tempts us to it. It is about finding hope in the very darkest part of the year, clinging on to it like a life raft, and letting it power us through until the spring.

Witches change things: we bring new perspectives, we bring hope and change and different modes of relation to the world. In winter, in the dark months, we have to make sure we bring it to ourselves, too. We have to be sorcerers of light. It is a vital task, and we are well equipped to do it.

A Spell for Hope in Darkness

Midwinter sees the departure and rebirth of the sun. In the Wiccan tradition, which worships the triune or triple goddess (Maiden–Mother–Crone), midwinter honours the Crone in her final stages, before she is reborn as the Maiden in spring. Symbolically, it is a good time to consider the wisdom you have gained during the year. Consider what serves you, and what you have learned that you can let go of. Consider also what you'd like to learn, what sorts of wisdom and experience you'd like to gain in the next year. It can be useful to make a list of things to let go of, and burn or bury it, and to sleep with the list of desires under your pillow. In terms of spellwork, it is an excellent time of year to perform magic for renewal, hope and change. The spell I have suggested is a spell for hope against darkness.

You will need:

- *An altar or sacred space*
- *A cushion*
- *Incense*
- *Four candles and matches*
- *A scarf or shawl*

- *Anointing oil (an essential oil of your choice)*
- *A bowl of water, preferably left for several hours to de-chlorinate, or spring water/sea water*

Light the candles and incense, and, as you do, call the elements. If you wish to make a circle, you can do so with drops of the water, or with salt or smoke. Once you have sanctified the space, take the bowl and position it in front of you, and place the scarf on the floor beside it. If possible, arrange the candles so their flames are reflected by the bowl of water. If you cannot, fix your eyes on a flame. If you can, fix your eyes on the dancing flames in the water. Ask the Crone, or the deities of winter, or simply the darkness and its stars, to guide you.

Some suggested words are:

In this long darkness, I ask [the Goddess as the Crone/the energy of the old year/those deities that bring winter's deep reflection] to guide me into hope. I give thanks for the year gone, and look to the year to come. Guide me toward you, and toward the light, that I may wear hope as a shawl, and walk forth into the new year so covered.

Then, allow yourself to fall into imagining. Imagine a dark forest, and round a bright fire sit winter and spring. They may look, to you, like the Crone and the Maiden, the Holly King and the Oak King, or like animals, or lights or colours. Imagine the cold air on your skin, and the sounds of the forest at night, the crackle of the fire. Approach their fire, and watch as, slowly, winter unwraps a mantle from around its shoulders, and hands it over to spring. The mantle might be made of fabric, or of light – it might be plain, or decorated. What do you see? Do any patterns emerge? Do any words pass between them? Is the handing over peaceful? Joyful? Violent? The scene slowly becomes lighter, as if dawn is breaking, until the pair are surrounded by glorious light.

It is important here to let yourself linger on this scene, taking in details, which you might later want to record. When the exchange is over, step back out of the trance. Open your eyes slowly. Sprinkle a few drops of the chosen essential oil into the bowl of water, letting them make ripples on the surface. This breaks the water's surface as a journeying space into the sacred realm, and brings us back to earth. Take the scarf you have beside you, and anoint it with three splashes of the oil and water, saying words such as:

As winter passes its mantle to spring, so that the light may return, so I wear this mantle as proof of light against darkness, to take me through hardship, to guide me toward the turning of the year, the triumph of the light.

Put the scarf around your shoulders, imagining it as the mantle you saw earlier. Once this is done, you may stay a while, or close the circle, and snuff the candles, giving thanks.

JANUARY

———◆———

Smelling the Weather

It is dark outside. It was dark on first waking. Now, as I crawl out of a Saturday nap to answer the phone, the stomach of the sky seems set on touching the ground, like a great grey cat stretching over the city. A day of little profit in going outside. But it is warmer after weeks of freezing, and the alteration is enough of a temptation. The ground has been wet since last night's frost wilted. It is like stepping out into a damp woollen glove.

It smells like rain. Not as if it has been raining, because it hasn't – none of that relieving petrichor. Instead it smells as if it is *going* to rain – not urgently – not for several hours – but the damp heavy sky will burst eventually.

I take the back lane down from my cul-de-sac – a little road called 'The Snakey', which sits on the waste ground where two final houses, which would have closed the cul-de-sac properly, were never built. The developer ran out of money, left a gaping hole the width of two town houses. And gradually, the path became a use-path, a desire line, saving the residents who live at the bottom of the hill, by the river, a much longer walk.

A strange little curve, slithering through the city, joining two parts. I have it all to myself – the wet metal bench, the red sandstone façade of the Victorian swimming pool, which seems to glow in the low light. The Snakey feels as if it has been there forever.

It wasn't always like this, safe and bedded-in. The residents had to fight for it – the land must be worth a fortune. And it's nothing special. Nondescript bushes – some bramble, some dense shrubbery of the type found in housing developments, some thin silver birches. A rowan tree which has berries of bright orange. The path is always studded along either side by dog shit, despite the signs, and it is constantly in use. It brings people along our street in a way it wouldn't otherwise. It appears to be the least magical of spaces. Dirty and busy, and everything grows despite, not because of, any sort of attention.

I love it. Almost every day something has changed in it – new leaves, new birds. The grass that has been ruined all winter springing green again. Since I don't have a garden, it's a good stand-in. I walk out across the bridge, and the river underneath is low for January, sluggish and cold. Through the long tunnel of holly and rhododendron that leads into the park, alongside the playing field where, in high winds, oystercatchers stalk as if the trees susurrate a sea for them.

There is a rugby game on the next playing field. People are crowded by the park wall to watch. I walk clockwise around the oval pond, which smells of swan shit and old bread, which ripples dully. They've got a local residents' group who dredge things out of it, keep the algae under control. At one end, they've created a marsh, with walkways and bulrushes. It is my one of my favourite places in every season except winter. In winter they cut the vegetation down, and nothing feels private. People stand at one end of it and throw white bread into the water.

The rain smell is getting heavier. I don't have long, if I am worried about getting wet. I wonder if anyone else can smell it. Telling the weather is multisensory – even someone with no sense of smell at all could see the banked January clouds and make a reasonable deduction.

Smelling the rain as it rolls in – the direction, the distance – isn't, per se, magic. It is just a form of sensory attunement, a slipping into noticing. Perhaps. On the other hand, it's a form of augury – of reading the signs and interpreting them. Any prediction, anything that anticipates the alteration of one state into another, is surely a form of magic. Reading the signs is exceptional knowledge, whether it's rainclouds or scattered bones. It is a small magic, a learnable skill to transform the way you know the world. It is a beginning of understanding how the body reaches out of itself and into the world, and how the world permeates the body.

I grew up close to the sea. Close enough that there were days the air was full of salt, like slipping your head under the water at the shoreline, and days when the wind took the sea-smell back out over the water – you wouldn't have known it was there. Then there was the smell of sea-fog, the haar that would bank and settle over my parents' house, even if, twenty minutes up the road, the sun was shining. Haar smells close, clogs the noise, feels like breathing in cold steam, and it carries smells inside it – salt, yes, but also fumes, or the unpleasantness of the sewage works near the house.

Haar holds smell, and wraps it round you. Nothing passes through it without being held. It hangs round houses like frozen shadows, as if it is coming to swallow everything you know, to alter it subtly and spit it back out.

I met a man from Uist on a cold January day who told me he could smell where the wind came from. Not its compass direction, exactly, although it is true that you can sometimes smell warmer winds from the west, colder winds from the east. But you can cheat, check with a compass, so that's a game that anyone can learn. He said to me, 'The other day, I smelled a cold wind, but it carried with it a warm place.' What a gift, to smell the wind's origin, what it had blown through. He didn't think of it as mystical, as anything other than a skill developed out of necessity, from living on a small island constantly scoured by wind. Having a keen nose for its vagaries let him assess how safe it might be to take a boat out, how likely he was to land a catch. I must have looked at him as if he'd just unveiled himself to be a wizard, and he laughed at me a little. 'It's just learning,' he said. While that is true, perhaps, it doesn't make it feel less revelatory.

Smelling the weather may not, perhaps, be a magical act, but it is often figured as a mystical one. Commonly, it is used as a literary trope to denote an intimate knowledge of land, and an embodied relationship with place. People who can smell the weather understand the weather – and so the world – as they might understand the body of a lover. It is an intimate form of knowing, built up over a long time.

It is also, often, perceived as a 'low' form of knowing. Scent is a secondary sense in our overwhelmingly visual culture, and so bodily sensing weather is often considered primitive, the preserve of people without recourse to science. Smelling the weather is set in opposition to dominant Western modes of scientific meteorological comprehension. This divide between the embodied and the scientific as regards weather is not new: Ptolemy observed the angles of sunlight's refraction, and in 1021, the Arabic mathematician Hasan Ibn al-Haytham recorded the beginning of twilight, as calculable based on the degrees of the sun below the horizon. His book, *Kitāb al-Manāzir* (*The Book of Optics*), was formative in situating sight as the primary perceptual sense. With the invention of the barometer and the thermometer in the sixteenth and seventeenth centuries, changes in atmosphere such as air pressure and temperature, which would help predict weather and which had historically been sensed by the body, became quantifiable through scientific instruments.

As with so much scientific change in the Early Modern period, however, the invention of the barometer was immediately met with enormous suspicion. Indeed, because he was working at the height of the European witch trials, in 1643, Evangelista Torricelli sought to make as small a barometer as he could, so he could conduct experiments within his own home, since his neighbours were beginning to suspect him of witchcraft.[1] Only a few years before Torricelli invented the barometer, Galileo had been accused of heresy by the Roman Catholic Inquisition for his support of heliocentrism. Tides turn, however, and after the successful establishment of the barometer as a scientific instrument, suspicion would eventually shift to fall on those who still used their bodies to sense atmospheric change, rather than keeping pace with scientific innovation.

There is something sympathetic, perhaps, in the cycles of suspicion and subsequent acceptance. Anything new and strange is hailed first as witchcraft, and then as science. It is first outlawed, dangerous, other, and then absorbed into society, which accepts it. And there is something deeply horrifying when that cycle does not happen. The Scientific Revolution might have brought suspicion down on certain learned men, but the European witchcraft trials that immediately preceded it killed an estimated 50,000 women. Women who, unlike Torricelli, did not possess the opportunity to revolutionise science, or fight for their innocence through networks of scholarly connection. Women whose version of exceptional knowledge most likely was bodily, connected to immediate haptic perception.

In contemporary depictions, it is often non-Western and colonised peoples who retain embodied weather-knowledge: First Nations peoples, rural trackers, shaman and tribal societies – these groups are often perceived as having an ability to sense and predict the weather, with their instincts figured as both strong and primitive. Indeed, these individuals are often depicted as animalistic – awareness of bodily sensations seems so other that it is attributed to different species altogether.

Perhaps the zenith of this is found in Kenneth Grahame's beautiful, strange children's novel, *The Wind in the Willows*. Its central characters, Rat and Mole, are at once anthropomorphised river creatures, a water-rat and a mole, and rural English gentlemen. Both have the acute sense of smell expected of their species. One evening, walking home, they both access scent-knowledge to discover their surroundings. Mole can suddenly smell his old home – a place he'd totally forgotten in favour of living with Rat – and the smell is so powerful he is physically drawn towards it. Meanwhile, Rat can smell something else – there is 'something suspiciously like snow' in the air, and he wishes to hurry Mole to safety. Mole is entirely focused on the smell of his home, a primal sensing of something of the self, something vital. Rat is not so easily distracted, and he can smell the weather coming, and quickly. Both are using their bodies to sense something vital, hugely important, and the two different scents relate the body both to where it belongs, in Mole's case literally in the earth, and also highlight the fragility of their bodies in relation to the elements.

In *The Wind in the Willows,* everything that exists in the world is held in constant interdependence, and nature is never figured as benign, or merciful. Knowledge of the patterns of the world is what keeps characters safe, and their bodily perception is a crucial aspect of their continued existence – it is the most useful and valuable type of knowledge within the book. Rat and Mole might be animals, but they are also conceived as the ideal residents of rural space. *The Wind in the Willows* argues for responsible stewardship of the rural environments, and this is achieved partially through intimate bodily relationships with that landscape.

The Wind in the Willows might not seem like a book much concerned with magic, but it carries in it some deeply strange, mystical moments of extraordinary magic. Kenneth Grahame was himself prone to moments of mysticism, and penned a book of essays called *Pagan Papers*, including an essay on Pan.[2] A book largely concerned with the lives of animals, *The Wind in the Willows* contains one rather uncharacteristic encounter –

the acutely observed animal characters meet the Greek god Pan on the river. The episode is hallucinatory – my mum skipped it when she read it to us as children because it made her feel strange, she said. Mole and Rat are out on the river and stumble across Pan, who is piping in the dawn, and who appears as both the genius loci of the riverbank and an almost benign protector of the land. However, his potency makes him dangerous, and coded into his song are words of forgetting, so that they can never clearly recall their encounter with his power. Pan is a strange, wild insertion in this idyllic English countryside, but he acts as the vector between biological and mystical under-standings of the natural world.

Pan's masculine virility hints at the unknowable strangeness and sensuality of the woods, the river – and at the more-than-human always lurking behind what can be superficially assimilated. We identify with Rat and Mole, aspire to their intuitive ways of knowing – and then we are shown that even though they have learned how to relate to invisible things, stranger forces again lurk behind what can be rationally appre-hended or bodily understood. Elsewhere, Grahame wrote of Pan that there were wild places left in England where he could still pipe with 'freest abandonment'.[3]

What seems strange is that Pan should inhabit England at all, let alone sit piping by its riverbanks. His magic is of a strange, mischievous kind; he seems an unusual god to borrow from the Greek pantheon. Pan is often understood as older than the Olympians, a god who emerged instead from nature-worship. He inhabits and represents wild Arcadia, its glens and forests, its places of hunting and fertility. In this, he shares lineage with Pushan, a god in the *Rigveda* who guides and guards, and whose etymology means 'to lead to thrive'[4]. They both, most probably, share a Proto-Indo-European origin, as a masculine fertility- and nature-god.

That's perhaps why the use of Pan here seems especially out of place when a number of wild gods, depicted as masculine, exist within Northern European and pagan pantheons, and clearly share Pan's lineage – Cernunnos, the Horned God; the Green Man – all perhaps more traditionally British manifest- ations of the masculine, wildwood energy Grahame captured in Pan.

However, Grahame's work forms part of an eighteenth- and nineteenth-century revival of interest in Pan in Britain, connected to a broader interest in Greek and Roman culture during the Romantic movement. There was a noticeable blos- soming of interest in Pan as a cipher for the wild, uncontrollable magic of place that sprang up in the literature of the early twentieth century. D. H. Lawrence's exploration of Pan is particularly detailed. Lawrence understands Pan as representing the force that joins man and the natural world together, and allows them to inter-penetrate: 'In the days before man got too much separated off from the universe, he *was* Pan, along with all the rest . . . the tree's life penetrates my life, and my life the tree's. We cannot live near one another, as we do, without affecting one another.'[5]

Both Lawrence and Grahame understand Pan as the link between the human and the more-than-human – Pan represents the process by which mankind may become wild again, may enter into and become part of the space around him. This is, of course, not without its difficulties. Firstly, and unsurprisingly, Pan addresses primarily masculine relations with nature.

Secondly, Pan's presence isn't place-specific. Lawrence and Grahame take an ancient Greek deity and introduce him into other countries' rural places – they are uprooting a set of culturally specific ideals of both pagan divinity and masculine virility and planting them in the leafy English countryside.[6]

Despite these difficulties, Pan is an alluring figure, and one that helps us to think through ideas of the mystic relations between body, environment and magic. Pan, for Grahame and Lawrence, is the means by which man might understand himself affected by the weather, the atmosphere, the land. He is the mechanism – he is the moment of changing one thing into another, of combining man and not-man to produce a third, wild thing. Pan, then, is magic itself. He is the transformative force. He is the moment of noticing nature, and being altered by it. Alchemical Pan, whose music enchants us, inducts us into the wild places.

Pan is both the weather and the ability to smell it – but more than that, he is the knowledge produced by understanding *what* you are smelling. He is arcane place-knowledge, albeit presented in a patriarchal, twentieth-century classical revival package that figures this knowledge as arcane, as ecstatic, as removed from the rational everyday nature of knowledge.

Of course, skills such as smelling the weather, understanding a place through the senses and recording that knowledge using myth and ritual are useful more than they are arcane or ecstatic. Sensing both local weather changes and oncoming storms, sensing when rainy season will come – these are forms of mystical knowledge that are highly prized and practical.

My being able to smell snow is neither here nor there – nobody cares, and I'll still check the BBC weather and feel vindicated if I'm right. But elsewhere, for example among remote agrarian communities such as the Kenyah Badeng farmers of Sarawak, Malaysia, sensing the weather is vital for farming. In this community, meteorological awareness has two levels – the magical and the practical – and these overlay in ways that chime with many Western witchcraft superstitions about weather.

The Kenyah Badeng people have a weatherman, whose job it is to preside over and interpret yearly rituals that seek to determine the coming weather – the long-range forecast. However, they are also a Christian society, and now no longer associate weather with place-based religion. Previously, bad weather was thought to directly associate with moral trespass. Practically, however, the Kenyah Badeng still use their bodies to foretell the weather, and these embodied skills include smelling the monsoon, and monitoring their own appetites, sleep patterns and aches in order to forecast what is happening in the atmosphere.[7]

Rather than weather-awareness being an isolated activity, it is a form of constant environmental monitoring, where the gaps between body and environment are broken down, treated equally. The Kenyah Badeng are using their traditional embodied knowledge to predict and monitor weather as they go about their daily activities. It is this continual checking-in, this continual noticing with all the bodily senses, that contemporary Western meteorological science neglects. We do not need to notice our environment in the same way, and so, most often, we simply don't.

That's why there's a feeling of strange mystery when we meet people who can smell storms coming, or can tell when it's going to rain, or what the sky is doing, or whose joints ache before damp weather. A sense that these people hold arcane knowledge, that their power is somehow uncommon and of unknown origin. If someone has a weather station and can predict the weather, they are doing amateur science. If they interpret those same signs through their body, they might be a witch, a mystic, acting in ways we can't quite see or understand.

These rejections of bodily knowledge in favour of scientific knowledge position humans as detached interpreters of data. And although the Kenyah Badeng have rejected superstitions that punish bad behaviour with bad weather, it is difficult not to believe in that just a little. Pathetic fallacy runs strong in Western culture, whether it's Shakespeare's 'foul and fair' weather in *Macbeth*, or the damp and obscuring mists that cloud vision in *The Great Gatsby*. Weather both influences and reflects mood, and we are endlessly wrapped in its shifting language. Weather, in all its inconstancy, somehow seems a reliable territory across which to map the human condition.

Increasingly, however, the weather proves itself erratic, its patterns coming loose, its swings more extreme. Climate change has scribbled its way across the map, and the days are both far fairer and far fouler than they should be. Dispensing with the idea that bad weather is caused by bad decisions seems dangerous in this current climate.

After all, what is environmental catastrophe if not bad weather caused by our bad behaviour? Not individually, perhaps – if I fail to recycle a plastic water bottle I know I'm not going to be struck by lightning. But collectively, our planetary destruction has caused the breakdown of seasons, of weather systems, of ecosystems and biodiversity. And now, of course, we can feel it in our bodies. It's in your body when you're exposed to too much UV radiation because there are holes in the ozone layer. Those red burns are our bodies responding to the weather, interpreting it, foretelling disaster as it blisters on our skin. Our bodies have not stopped feeling the weather coming. They haven't stopped getting tension headaches, or dry skin, dry mouths, feeling sleepier in periods of low pressure, or weepier as the moon waxes. What we have done, however, is tuned out. Our bodies have turned from one thing into another. We have become matter out of place in the world, moving through it as if it does not also move through us. Not entirely, of course – and as I said, it makes no odds to most Western civilisations, whether we can smell the weather or not. Or at least, it doesn't at the moment.

Which is an apocalyptic thing to say. But I think often about the apocalypse, and about what it would mean for our current modes of understanding the world. About what might change once oil runs out, once countries flood, once capitalism grinds to a shuddering, horrific halt. As Peter Grey says, in his book *Apocalyptic Witchcraft*, 'The wheel of the year has broken from the spokes of the season'.[8] Grey positions witchcraft as Lawrence and Grahame position Pan: as our means of accessing and understanding the world and our point of engagement with it. Witchcraft must change, adapt and fight back, he argues, now that the organisational principles of the world are in disarray. And if witches are to help resist and find alternatives to our current environmental catastrophe, then perhaps it is best to begin to tune our bodies back into the world, to learn to interpret these body-signs. And besides, come the apocalypse, I'd like us to trust our bodies. To look at the sky and know what we are seeing. To scent the air and understand what it smells of.

It is important, then, to bridge the gap between the detailed data that science provides and the rich, vital sensory information given to us by our own bodies while we still can. There is no sense in my sticking my head out of the flat window, breathing in and making declarations if I've no idea what I am doing or why. The science of smelling the weather is well-documented, particularly as regards the smell of the earth just before a storm, or the scent that presages rain, especially if the rain has already started out of view.

Petrichor, that word that sounds as if it rose up whole from a deep cave, has an etymology brimming with magic. It comes from the Greek *petra* (πέτρα), meaning stone, and *īkhōr* (ἰχώρ), which is the fluid that flows in the veins of the gods in Greek mythology. So, petrichor is stone-blood, the scent of a stone's true essence or self. You can conjure blood out of a stone, it seems, with rain. The stone's ichor is, in fact, geosmin, which means 'earth smell' and is a by-product of a prevalent soil-dwelling bacterium.[9] Humans are very sensitive to geosmin and can detect it at levels as low as five parts per trillion. It makes us feel happy – and it's been argued that this is because we are delighted in some part of our brains by a cessation of any periods of drought. Certainly, when I lived in Cambridge, dry for long spells, I craved rain. Became itchy for want of it. Would walk by the river just to smell something damp, even though the dampness was of the wrong kind. I used to stand out in the gardens in the rain, especially spring rain, to celebrate its joyful heaviness. Get soaked, and sated with the smell.

Geosmin is found in foods, too, foods that smell particularly earthy – beetroot is one of them. Lots of people love the smell but hate the 'muddy' taste, apparently, although if you are craving rain-smell, you can cut beetroot to smell, then later cook it with vinegar, which removes the muddy note. There are other notes, too, that go into making up the smell of petrichor, that render it subtly different from just geosmin. These include oils released by plants during drought to slow down germination so that its chances of survival are not reduced by dry weather. What we are smelling when it rains, then, is an entire connected network of plants, bacteria and soil, rocks and air. We are smelling the point at which things transform, the point at which networks of connection start up. We are smelling Pan, as Lawrence and Grahame conceive him. All relations suddenly become apparent, and we are exposed to and exchange with nature through our bodies. We are suddenly given sensory access to a series of complex connections that usually pass beneath our senses. We are given a form of under-standing.

Other chemical preponderances foretell different forms of encroaching weather. Snow, too, I can smell – that is, appar-ently, because the low pressure of snow clouds floods our atmosphere with ozone, which smells shimmery and sweet. It is also, meteorologists think, to do with the epithelial lining of the nose, which produces less mucus when the air drops to below freezing. When the air warms enough for snow to actually fall, the mucus production rises, and you can suddenly smell things more acutely.[10] This revivification of our noses we have come to associate with snow – a joyful re-exposure to smelling the world. Then there's the headachy, body-trapped feeling before storms. One summer in my early twenties in Tuscany, the whole family would start arguing, like clockwork, ten or fifteen minutes before an electric storm broke. Sheets of lightning would fill the air with static, and our dinner table, positioned under a walnut tree, would suddenly be raucously disrupted by unripe walnuts hailing off the tree into wine glasses and laps. But without rainfall, there was little let-up to that close, uneasy feeling. Headaches and lethargy and, for me, an inability to will things into being. I would stand outside, gazing at the slate sky, and will the pressure to burst into rain.

If we can, without trying particularly hard, sense rain, smell snow, foretell storms in the way our bodies act, then it is easy to understand how people who had acute abilities in this area might also be credited with controlling the weather. How these individuals might have been seen not only to understand, but also directly affect the weather themselves through magic.

And there are so many means of controlling the weather embedded in folklore. When societies were mostly agrarian, it appears that almost everyone, having a vested interest in the weather, would try to understand, foretell and even influence what was happening around them. Charms for good weather are many and various, and some carry more weight than others. Pine cones close up when there is moisture in the air, as does kelp on the seashore, and so can be a reliable way of foretelling rain. Cows, however, said to lie down when rain is coming, are not actually obliging weather-tellers, and tend to lie down when they feel like it. *Red sky at night, shepherd's delight / Red sky in the morning, shepherd's warning* is, in fact, a reasonably accurate rhyme – the red colour is caused by particles in the air that react to dry and wet conditions. These foretellings have entered popular superstition – they are forms of small weather augury, but they are not spells per se. They don't claim to control the weather, only to understand its movements. So what of spells for weather? They have, of course, a long and illustrious history.

I have always known weather spells; they have been handed down to me. My mother wouldn't call herself a witch. She certainly wouldn't say she was gifted in magic – she'd even deny doing much of it at all. But she does. One of the most potent magical acts my mother does is a spell for fair weather at parties. My father, whose love of festivals is great and who enjoys nothing more than hosting a huge fireworks party every year, would swear by Mum's ability to bring us fair weather every 5 November, even if it is only for an hour or so. The fireworks have, in my memory, never been rained off.

It is an easy spell, requiring no specialist equipment, no moon-phase, no cauldron or selection of herbs. Mum takes a broom and her gardening knife, sharp but a little rusty, chipped green paint around the edges, and plunges it into the group of plants beside the Japanese maple they planted for my sister's birth. In its branches, she balances the broom, upside down, the broom-head gently resting between the first bifurcation of the tree. I've never asked her if she asks for good weather aloud. I don't need to. The spell is clear as crystal, as powerful as if said in high ritual settings, echoed by fellow members of a coven: *a knife in the ground and a broom in the tree*. She tells people, too. 'Don't worry, it'll be fine weather. There's a knife in the ground and a broom in the tree.' People look at her blankly. My mother is not a particularly eccentric-seeming person, so I wonder if they often think they've misheard her. She's uncannily good at it, though, and whatever you believe, the sky above our street is clear enough for fireworks when it needs to be.

She learned the spell from an elderly woman who lived in Argyll, in a big stone house with a stream running through the middle of the house, under the floor, and spouting out of a wall at the front steps – ironically, to ward away witches. She was fiercely independent, living all alone at the end of a track. The road ends right after her house. She was of the highly practical school of being – she had been an army wife, and sent her boys to board in England while she lived in New Zealand with her husband. She didn't hold truck with nonsense. But she fed the fairies some evenings, probably once a week. Outside the back of her house was a green mound, low and rising in a nearby field. It was common knowledge that the fairies dwelt there. And it was common knowledge, too, that there was no harm in having fairies as your neighbours, provided you kept them sweet. She used to give them bowls of cream – beloved of brownies, and other supernatural helpers. She might have given them other things too, but when we stayed with her it was shallow bowls of white cream, carried carefully in my little hands up to the top of the mound, and left without a word. You didn't need to say anything – I think she would have been quite scathing if we had. The offering was enough. Enough to keep them out of her affairs, I think, enough to be neighbourly.

The fairies, in exchange, helped her with the garden, and left her alone. They weren't much interested in humans, but if treated properly, she told me, they would bring help and good weather. She didn't always leave the good weather up to them, however – she was a woman of direct action. And so on the nights before we took the boat out, we would join her in the garden, and she'd put a knife in the ground and a broom in the tree, somewhere in the orchard. Whether it was a special tree, I have no idea – but the next day, there was sun on our little rowing boat. A little benign weather magic, and we think of her as she was then in her Argyll garden, whenever we ask for clear skies.

However, not all weather magic has such benign or domestic consequence. For a long time, weather-knowledge was particularly dangerous if the wrong people heard about it. A perceived ability to control the weather has historically landed witches in a huge amount of trouble. Indeed, men and women have been killed for exactly this: for calling up storms. The North Berwick witch trials of 1590 saw Agnes Sampson and many other people – both women and men – put on trial for raising the vicious sea storms that almost drowned King James VI and his new wife, Anne of Denmark, as they sailed home to Scotland after their wedding. In Denmark, several individuals were put on trial for storm-raising and tortured for confession. Two were convicted of witchcraft and killed. On hearing this, King James ordered a similar trial to take place in Scotland. The brutal chapter of Scottish witch trials began with this sensational case of weather-raising.

North Berwick lies a short train ride out of Edinburgh,

twenty-five miles north-east of the capital. It has everything a seaside town could want: little stone houses curving right down to the shore; a salt-water swimming pool built on the beach from when it was optimistically considered the 'Biarritz of the North'; a seabird centre; a number of shops selling nautically inflected interior design; a family-run ice-cream parlour, so that children can stand shivering along the shoreline, licking cones in the freezing cold.

There is also a little green, tucked into a diamond of space by the sea. Exactly the sort of place one might picnic on a fine day. Or, as Agnes Sampson said, in front of a room of judges in 1590, the sort of green on which two hundred witches would gather together, to consort with the devil himself. They almost certainly did not: two hundred people would barely fit on the little green. But Agnes Sampson had been tortured horrendously at the king's command at the Old Tolbooth in Edinburgh. First, she was disfigured by the shaving of all of her body hair, and next she was placed in a torture device known as a branks, a scold's bridle or a witch's bridle. This iron headgear had four sharp prongs, which forced her mouth open and her tongue down. It was a humiliation tool, used to punish publicly women who were outspoken or nagged. It was considered a 'mirror punishment': a form of torture designed to poetically mirror the accused's crime. It was common in Scotland, and especially used on women on trial for witchcraft – the apex of outspoken womanhood. Additionally, Agnes Sampson was deprived of sleep and chained to a wall – she suffered a litany of damages and tortures. Then she was brought before the king himself, whose death she was accused of seeking, and made to confess.

Six thousand men and women (although the vast majority were women) are recorded as having been executed during the Scottish witch trials. Because of the way court records were kept, especially in the Highlands, those numbers may be higher. Many – and many more who were not executed – suffered torture. What is remarkable about the North Berwick witch trials is both the severity of the torture and the weather-crime. The crimes that Agnes and her peers were accused of were unusual, being both heretical and occult in nature. Plots against royalty were not uncommon, and there were many who were opposed to James's rule – he was the son of Mary Queen of Scots, a Catholic, and there were rumours and intrigues surrounding him. Most plots were straightforward treason. But James, obsessed by a fear of murder and the occult, was always suspicious of foul play and his enemies engaging witches to bring about his death.

It is perhaps strange that King James ordered the North Berwick witch trials, when two witches had already confessed and been burned in Denmark. After those accused of storm-raising were executed, why did James feel the need to accuse, try and kill further witches in Scotland? Such is the mystery of witchcraft: anyone, or no-one, could have raised the storm. More than a hundred witches were tried for this storm-raising. In Agnes Sampson's confession, the theatrics of storm-raising are laid bare. As the king sailed for home, Sampson said, the swell of witches

tooke a Cat and christened it, and afterward bound to each parte of that Cat, the cheefest partes of a dead man, and . . . saide Cat was conueied into the midst of the sea by all these witches.[11]

The high drama of this spell, as Sampson recounts it, is extraordinary. It is intensely physical, and deeply shocking. There is also a visceral imagery to the spellcraft, which delights in despoiling corpses and making a mockery of the Christian rite of baptism. The perversion of natural order – men denied burial, cats brought into the fold of the faithful and then drowned – is highly dramatic. Only such foul actions, under the instruction of the devil himself, could hope to overthrow someone as powerful as the king. Indeed, Sampson in her confession attributes the spell's failure to the king's faith. The strength of his holiness and the veracity of his divine appointment are being directly pitted against the power summoned by the witches, seeking to depose him through corrupting the natural order of things. Sampson's description of the satanically directed ritual chimes with many similar confessions extracted from accused witches under torture. It is a collection of vileness, a sort of collage of the worst things a person might be able to dream up, of folk superstitions about witches taking to the sea in sieves, perversions of burial, dismembering of corpses. A feast of unholy images. The spell is not particularly convincing, of course. It is outlandish, claims things that the speaker knows sound shocking, but cannot be evidenced. It shows no particular knowledge of weather or the occult beyond general profane imagery. This is, of course, because Agnes Sampson and her associates were victims of witchcraft hysteria and because no extraordinary, devilish storm was ever raised by a hundred witches at North Berwick, with the help of Satan himself.

What happened was that an unfortunate weather event, predicted by nobody, felt in nobody's body, detected on no instruments, almost drowned the king and his new bride. Such a portentous storm could not be understood to be mere accident, mere fluke of weather. Instead, it loomed large in the imaginations of both the Danish and Scottish courts. James was beset by paranoia about his security, and the storm took the shape of all of his worst fears – that people were plotting against him, employing whatever dark means they could to bring about his death.

Agnes Sampson and her confession are not evidence of occult plots or witchcraft. Indeed, there is no evidence that any of the individuals executed during the witch trials, were ever witches. There is no evidence that they did what we popularly understand magic to be, beyond perhaps a little herbal healing, and traditional knowledge in some cases. In most cases there is no evidence that they transgressed in any way: many were what we might now understand as disabled, or mentally unwell, widowed or disfigured or a little too outspoken. They were vulnerable women, or women who held too much power. Once witchcraft hysteria struck, it was straightforward to accuse one's neighbour, to realise that boundary disputes or long-running grudges could be solved by a quiet word about the victim of your ire in the right person's ear. This is, of course, part of the wider sociopolitical underpinning of witch trials. Persecution of suspected witches was far more concerned with politics, with fear of heresy and the state's oppression of women, than in discovering anything at all about magic.

The storm is recounted by King James in *Daeomonologie,* his 1597 philosophical treaty explaining and condemning various forms of occult activity. In it, he writes that witches 'can rayse stormes and tempestes in the aire, either upon sea or land',

and then the text moves on.[12] But the tempest sits there, threatening, on the page, a reminder of his voyage. The storm haunts his interest in witchcraft, fuels it, gives it shape. The storm is both pathetic fallacy and real event, it is a point where nature, in all its vivid interconnectedness, came too close to the body of a king. And because even kings, divinely appointed, cannot bend nature to their will, scapegoats had to be found, proxies for this misfortune. Agnes Sampson and her ilk, with their healing and their dancing, with confessions extracted under extraordinary torture, were perfect substitutes for a natural world that could not be called to account.

Agnes Sampson was executed on 16 January 1591 by garrotting and burning. She was executed for an imagined link to a natural weather event. She was simply in the wrong place, under the wrong bit of sky, holding the wrong bit of information. She had no demonstrable extraordinary knowledge – she was simply part of the structural oppression of women for perceived occult leanings. I think of her as I hurry home from the park, walking against the rain, which I smelled coming and which has arrived, a film of cold wetness soaking into the city's architecture. From where I am, I can see Castle Rock, the site of her execution, sitting above us. It is visible from almost every vista in the city, and all roads seem to lead to it. It hangs above us, a great spur of rock, the castle grey and foreboding. I cannot see smoke from the esplanade, rising its thin thread into the slate sky. I cannot, and yet I almost can.

She would have died in front of a packed crowd, head shaven, the signs of torture all over her body. She died for such a number of reasons, none of them really to do with magic, but as I look at the slate sky I hope, in some ways, that she did raise a storm, of one type or another. It would be a comfort to pretend she was not, in fact, just a woman accused of witchcraft, but in fact a vastly powerful being, able to bend elements, endanger kings, to dance with the devil and sail the sea in a sieve. I know the truth, though. That magic would not protect against torture and death. That Agnes Sampson's storm-raising was spurious, that she was an ordinary woman who was taken from her home and tortured and killed in service to a king's paranoia.

But perhaps she too foretold the weather, felt it in her body, looked out across the sea and smelled what was coming next. Perhaps she had favourite paths to the beach, felt sand on her feet, smelled the sea, lived among her neighbours and nodded to them, the way I do to mine. The Snakey is wet, smells of dead grass and dog shit, and there's a wind picking up. I think of storm-raising, weather magic, of all the extraordinary ways our bodies have of telling the world, and of all the ways the world has of disclosing itself, entering our bodies, interacting with us. Agnes Sampson died on a January day, much the same as the one I'm walking through. I will learn the weather, how it lives in my body, and any magic I do – intentional magic, magic that declares itself as such, whatever people think of it – I will do with her in my mind. Raising storms to kill kings by taking apart the bodies of men is an elaborate claim, but building barometers and smelling snow are too, to the wrong people. And everyone likes to think their method of letting the world in is best. I think back to the apocalypse again. I want to rouse our bodies into magic before the world ends. I wonder about what the end of the world will look like: a great storm, a wild sea, a cruel burning. I wonder where the witches

will be among all of that. Perhaps, I think, I will take to the
sea in a sieve and drown a king. More likely, perhaps, I will slip
down a path like the Snakey, turn out of the corner of someone
else's eye, and disappear.

A Spell for the Full Moon

*J*anuary is a month for new starts — and the joy of that is that it brings with it the first full moon of the year. If resolutions seem beyond you, if actually you're enjoying leftover Christmas cake and watching endless TV reruns, then one small new-year ritual can be to welcome in the first full moon of the year with joy and a little ceremony.

The full moon is a time of heightened spiritual and psychic energy. It is a time of general heightenedness, of boiling over, of waxing into uncontainable fullness. Blood clots more slowly, and people very sensitive to moon phases may have their sleep disrupted and notice considerable fluctuations in their energy levels. I flirt far better near a full moon, for some reason, and luxuriate in the idea that her shining face means that I am somehow, magically, wittier and more attractive. Generally, spells that pertain to blessing, larger magical acts and increase are best done around a full moon. Spells for new plans are benefitted by a new moon, and as the moon gets smaller, as it wanes, is the perfect time to eliminate from your life those things you no longer need.

The spell itself is easy. Do it on the night of the full moon if you can, but two days either side is equally fine. Take a jug of water (tap water is perfectly good, but let it stand overnight so the chlorine can evaporate). Light your altar, and then place the jug beside a cauldron. A cauldron, really, is any ceremonial vessel that will hold water: a saucepan will absolutely do. Then, slowly pour the water from the jug to the cauldron, saying something along these lines as you do:

Blessings of the full moon, which governs us and fills us up, bring health, increase and peace.

Once the water is in, let it settle, and move slowly, three times clockwise, around the cauldron. I like to hold a flame while doing this, to focus my energy, but it is not necessary. A wand, if you use one, would be just as good: failing that, keeping your hands outstretched so they are over the water is a good idea. If you cannot easily move around the cauldron, then you can just move your hands over it clockwise.

As you move around, speak to the moon, ask her to bless the water, and try to visualise a fine silver light moving from you into the water, until the water itself glistens and glints with silver. Once the water is charged, step forward to the cauldron.

The next three steps can be modified for accessibility or ease: all that is important is that three distinct actions take place with the water. One on the body, one in the body, and one in the world. For the first action, take water from the cauldron and sprinkle it over your head. Speak aloud, or in your head, some variation of:

I ask that this moon bless my body.

A Spell for the Full Moon

Secondly, fill your hand with the water and drink a few drops, as you say:

I ask that this moon fills me with energy.

And then finally, sprinkle a few drops over the altar, and say something like:

I ask that this moon bless what I have and hold dear.

This is also a good time to ask for things, to petition the deities you speak to – or the moon herself – for something. Traditionally, it is best to follow a two-part structure: asking for something for yourself, and something for someone else.

These can be simple requests: something you can envisage is always easier, and helps give potency to the request. For example:

Please give me confidence for my job interview on Saturday, and I ask too for good health for X, who is suffering with their chronic condition.

Speak these one at a time, slowly, and imagine both happening, suffused with a silvery light, as you ask. Remember to imagine that these things have already been granted, and so after you have asked, thank the moon. Thanking the deities immediately afterward is not only good manners, it also helps cement the idea that the thing you have asked for will happen.

After this, you are finished. Often the deities you work with will leave when the ritual is complete, but as a formality you can dismiss the deities by thanking them for their time and aid, and closing the altar, safely extinguishing any candles and releasing the protective circle, with a few words such as *you may safely go, the work is done*. The moon-filled water is good for watering plants, or for adding to your bath. It can also be made into a herbal tea if you use it immediately.

FEBRUARY

———

Fairies

It is February, and the weather is ruined. The BBC keeps jauntily announcing the hottest winter day ever recorded, 21 degrees in Kew Gardens, as if it calls for ice cream rather than weeping, as if it is a great fête day, and not the sort of weather that heralds the end of the world, the final drink-up bell before the bar catches fire.

From my window at Moniack Mhor, where I am on a writing retreat, I can see the moor across the valley burning. Saddleworth Moor in north-west England burns, too, and the gorse on Arthur's Seat in Edinburgh. All across Britain, great tracts of wild space are on fire, the dry winter and the fierce heat too much provocation. It is heartbreaking and unseasonal. Insects and small animals are at risk, and all the budding vegetation that will not now flower reduced to a season of ruined habitat. At lunch, at dinner, we talk about it in low tones.

The sunshine just keeps going, and we enjoy it, and then feel guilty. We don't know what stories to tell about what's happening. We sit in a cottage, high on the side of a hill, and watch the moors burn. Stationed like sentinels, each in our little cell-room, with its bed, desk, window. From a distance, we may look like a holy community, some fringe group seeking refuge on the moorland six miles north of Loch Ness. A motley crew of monks and nuns, rosaries the keyboards and notebooks under our hands, watching, bearing witness to this unseasonable burning.

The stretch of land our cottage sits in lies above Eskadale, up the River Beauly from the Beauly Firth, about an hour from Inverness. A lovely hilly stretch of highlands, mixed woodland edging around the cultivated pine, the land in places damp and deeply boggy. The fires aren't deadly, as far as we can ascertain. But they are like beacons, just one in a long line of unexpected moorland fires that move up the country from the Brecon Beacons to the far north of Scotland. Each a signal of damage: it is too dry, too hot, too early. The world is kindling, ready to spark.

On Arthur's Seat, the fire covered eight hundred metres, burning through the habitat of an extremely endangered insect, the bordered brown lacewing, which is found only there and in one other place in the UK. Because the fires were so unseasonable, the lacewings were still underground, hibernating. The same was true where the fires caught in other places, of course – Wales had over two thousand grass fires in 2018–2019, more than double the previous year's figures. The Welsh grasslands were described as a 'tinder box' by Professor Stefan Doerr, who likened them in their intense dryness to the African savannah.[1] Wildfires also intensified across Europe, particularly in Sweden.

Moorland fires are alarming, but there are far more dramatic indicators of climate catastrophe. Climate catastrophe is a sensationalist's dream, and new images to splash across front pages are almost always available – seahorses with their tails wrapped around straws instead of seaweed, turtles raw and tangled into incomprehensible shapes by plastic, whales whose meals have been plastic bag after plastic bag, until they starve to death. These images are shocking, of course, and often illustrative of particular moments of and extremes in habitat corruption.

Nothing tells the whole truth – not images, nor articles, nor any historically located moment. The whole truth is vast, impossible, and wears too many voices, and every voice speaks at once. The suffering of these creatures in nature photographs provokes a particular feeling for which a neologism has been coined – 'solastalgia', a melancholy provoked by engagement with the ecological destruction of environment. The word, coined by Glenn Albrecht, a professor at the School of Environmental and Life Sciences at the University of Newcastle, is derived from *solacium* – solace – with *nostos*, which means 'to return home', and *algos*, or 'pain'. He describes it as 'a homesickness you feel when you are still at home'. It is a perfect word for that melancholic situated-loss, rather than situatedness. We tend to believe we belong globally, to our planet, and so our sense of home can stretch to take in the gut-wrench of seeing an animal destroyed by forces not immediately apparent – an apex predator brought low and suffering. Solastalgia has a global element, but it is also suited to describing the hyperlocal experience of witnessing destruction in a place you love. Certainly, it was applicable to a group of people on a creative writing retreat, mutely separated by walls, watching the land burn.

What other purpose do we have, beyond impotently bearing witness? Nothing direct, that much is certain. Witnessing, however, is slippery, not always effectual. If witness accounts were all it took to wake the world up to injustice, to encourage people toward change, then there are far more startling accounts than ours readily available – those of the peoples of Micronesia, for example, whose island homes have disappeared beneath sea level, covering eight of the islands entirely, displacing their populations and erasing their history. The Solomon Islands in the Pacific Ocean have been acutely affected by these rises, owing to their high wave activity, and the fact that the average sea-level rise there has been particularly high.[2] These facts are not difficult to find, and yet despite that, despite witness accounts from displaced peoples, governments and corporations have largely resisted undertaking the drastic measures that would help prevent further harm.

Shocking images and witness accounts: neither seem to shake us into action, into demanding different futures for ourselves and our environment. These are, of course, reports at a distance. Even the immediacy of a photograph is still outside us, distant enough from us to feel deniable, to feel that it is all happening 'over there', that we can still drive and fly and use plastic and feel worried, perhaps, but not so worried that we do something mad, like leave our homes and camp outside Westminster demanding change. There must be other ways of understanding the world that will let us take better care of it, we all say over lunch. There must be forms of knowledge, types of intimacy that lead to working with the world, not working against it. We aren't sure. We wish we knew. The moorland fire keeps smoking over the hill. Lunch is over, and we go back to our rooms. But I can't work. Everything feels urgent and impotent. Then the rain drifts over, soft and low, the clouds covering the fire. I slip my jacket on, and leave.

I am standing in a forest in light rain, six miles from Loch Ness. It is mostly cultivated pine, grown and logged and sold. Around the edge, some birches straggle. The rain, when it reaches the floor of the forest, finds moss, pine needles, and little other vegetation. The soil smells like soggy pine, faintly astringent underfoot. The moss smells green, my brain supplies, and I can't find another way to say it.

The edge of the woods is interesting. First the road, then a black ditch, all wet peat, then a heathery rampart that needs crossed in a single jump, then the slope into the trees. Good trees: crop trees, mostly, although also a stand of Scots pines and some scrubby birch that can't quite flourish in the acid of the soil. The ground is boggy here and the trees keep falling, hauling their root-slabs up with them as they go down. The roots are ghastly, great round rips out of the ground. They are like biology cross-sections, like operations shown on television. Hidden things that are suddenly seen.

The forest clothes a low hill, slopes up and away. At the bottom, where the path begins, the ground is spongy and mossy. The four o'clock sun is low, signals an hour and a half or so until sundown, and that's the excuse I give myself for not venturing further in. Forests are sticky places, where fear accretes with every step, the way lichen accretes on bark. Each branch is bowed with Grimm's fairy tales and dire warnings, and I've no breadcrumbs in my pocket. The forest tries to draw me in like a hungry mouth. It beguiles, shows shadows in the trees that I cannot quite make out, birdsong I want to tread nearer to hear. Or perhaps I tempt myself. Perhaps the fear-pleasure shiver that runs down my back is just an instinct to walk to the heart of a green, damp place, clothe myself in quiet and the quarrelling of blackbirds. My brain likes to imagine that I throw my sensible waterproofs off, lie down, let the moss cover me like an abandoned statue. Not today. I remain peripheral, keep the low rise of the cottage just in view.

I sit with my back to a Scots pine tree, head tipped right up so I can see the long column of pink-red bark, lichen creeping across in places. Squinting into the light, I look at its umbrella of branches, which spiral to the top. Always, I think, I am looking for something extraordinary, and I find it in the way it makes my head spin. My eyes dazzle, and the tree seems to lean crazily. I am caught for a second by the opposite of vertigo, and bring my gaze back down. The sun glints off a carpet of spider web that traverses the long grasses and spins over the moss like a shawl. The spiders here are small, black and shiny – I keep snagging my gaze on them as they weave over the tussocks. Sitting on the soft ground and breathing in, suddenly I'm aware that under me, doubtless, are more spiders. Innumerable. There may even be a nest, though I have no idea if spiders of any kind nest underneath mossy knolls, like so many arthropod Barrow-wights. I am not good with them, particularly, although I am trying to learn in my adulthood to cope with insects, perhaps in the knowledge that squeamishness seems incompatible with magic. More than that, I am trying to acknowledge that they are as much part of this as I am, more so here in the forest. The least I can do is be kind to them. I am trying, but my skin crawls.

The sun is low enough to be blinding, steady and huge, warped a little by a corona of thin fog that is trapped on the hills opposite, on the other side of the valley. A lack of pollution here makes the sunset quiet, muted, a slash of salmon spinning into grey. The sun is angled so that I can barely see, so that my eyes water constantly, prickle and hurt. Sitting face into the sun is unpleasant, forces the eyes shut. The eyes close, and the breath follows into calmness, and I've tricked myself into sitting meditating in a forest.

There is almost no feeling more mundane than being somewhere magical. It is relaxing, lovely, the air clean, the birds loud, and it is fun to track the sounds around and behind me. But all my magic seems to leave when it might be most valuable, like a sort of stage fright. Now I'm really here, in a pristine place of the kind so advised by Wiccan practitioners. I am at the source, whatever that is, away from the much-derided urban spaces where apparently, magic cannot flourish. What if I can't do it, I think? What if it turns out there's no such thing, that I'm entirely flesh and blood and quantifiable neural firings, what if there is no network of living creatures? The spider web glints mutely in a reproachful way, but everything in the whole world feels like an accident, and I like a leaden doll, too impervious to reach any sort of ecstatic communion.

My eyes are forced closed though, so I may as well try. I'm holding a pen, because there is a pen that sits on my altar at home, reminding me that I'm asking for the grace to write, and so there's a vain hope that a thread will pass through. Magic feels easy at home – tools and time and nobody to suddenly to interrupt. The street noise of the city helps me concentrate – a constant buzzing hum. Here, it is silent, but the ripping noise of single cars is always possible, the bark of a dog and the whicker of a horse, the slam of a door down at the writers' centre. I'm only on the edge of the forest, and the magic won't come.

I cannot will it into happening, and I never seek to be alone with my thoughts. I'm waiting for ecstasy, and there is nothing. No particular sense of connection. There are midges, hanging in the air, and I can feel that I'm being bitten. 'Hello', my mouth says into the edge-wood, into the afternoon light. 'Hello.' It feels like the idiot beginning of a horror film, like something twisted and unpleasant will speak back. Or perhaps the spiders will coagulate, rise up into some wood-golem and come to join the midges in their feast.

For a while, nothing replies to my little flat 'hello's. The air settles, and the birds, indignantly interrupted, begin again. Nothing special, particularly – two blackbirds trilling territory, and wood pigeons. The ground is soft with the decaying remnants of falling trees, velveted with moss. It's damp. Unmistakeably, so am I. There is nothing less transcendent than a damp arse. It's time to go back, I think. Cup of tea, biscuit, get on with the business of writing.

And then, of course, something happens.

Two grey figures stand in the trees. They are tall. Taller than me, perhaps close to six feet. They are wearing cloaks of some kind, and from underneath the grey comes a flash of green. Their faces are half-hidden by hoods, and I cannot make out their features. Their hands are by their sides, and their feet are on the ground, exactly as you would imagine. They weren't there, but now they are. I was alone, and now I am not. They are standing behind me, deeper into the forest, and yet I can see them ahead of me. They're easy to perceive. They're easy to feel, cool and stock-still at my back. They aren't quite a man and a woman, but rather two matched and complementary forces. Sighs breathed on different winds. Their faces are impassive, and no greeting is exchanged. A meeting on neutral territory: the edge of mine, the edge of theirs. They bring no message, gift me no particular wisdom. They aren't comforting. All they are is present.

They are waiting for me to join them in the forest, to push further in until I'm walking into deep shadow. A strong pull. A strong desire to slip a hand into theirs, to roam into the grey-green dark. On that first visit, I don't. I write a little word on a bit of bark, and leave it on the ground for long enough that I can feel sure they've seen it. The word is 'perhaps'. That is all the answer I can give them. They do not nod their heads, merely acknowledge what has passed between us in a way that I can feel, like a shadow passing over a patch of sunlit grass, and disappear. They neither walk away nor fly, neither fade nor pass me. As they arrived, so they leave.

I sit, then play, in the woods for another while, gathering bark, picking up bites, accidentally upsetting spiders. My jacket sits in the moss, and I'm still sweating. I'm damp from the wet ground, and damp from the heat, and it feels as if I am in a woodland, and in a steam room. It is strange and unpleasant. I wonder, vaguely, how the tall figures came to look so comfortable in their riding habits. It is then that I realise they were almost certainly fairies. Síth, in this part of the world. It is then, in the dying light, shaken and strange, sweaty and dishevelled, that I leave the wood. It is not quite at a run. That night, they come to me in a dream, stand at my bedside, their faces shining like moonlight, their laughter deeper than Loch Ness.

The next day dawns, another hot, bright day, far more suited to August than February. The bright sky scares me, I say to a friend on the phone. She tells me it is a bridge day. That these few hot, bright days are perhaps climate change – perhaps they are just bridge days. I have no idea what these are, and so she tells me. In Scottish folklore, these are three of the days that the Prince of Summer, Angus, borrowed from August to use in February so that he could cross into the realm of winter, and rescue Bride, also known as Bridget, so that she could become the ruler of spring. These occasional, unseasonable days were his portals, the only way he could get through. This Scottish folk tale is beautiful, combines weather-lore with an understanding of the shifting seasons of the year, assigning each a figure – Bride brings the spring, Angus has the summer, and the cruel queen of winter, Beira, keeps an icy grasp on the world for as long as she can. In the retelling by Sir George Douglas, Bride is given a gift by Father Winter, who roams

Beira's lands. He hands her a bunch of snowdrops, and tells her: 'If Beira scolds you, give her these flowers . . . tell her that they came from the green rustling fir-woods. Tell her also that the cress is springing up on the banks of streams, and that the new grass has begun to shoot up in the fields.'[3]

Change has encroached on the edges of Beira's land. Even in February, I can see it. Green has crept in over the white, and the snowdrop, with its intimate patches of inner green, encapsulates the shift from snow to new life. So too does the cress, frost-sensitive as the new shoots of grass in the fields. These little green patches signal the end of Beira's reign of ice. When Bride brings Beira the message, and innocently hands her the flowers, she unknowingly signals Beira's demise. She spins into a rage, but Angus overcomes all the storms she sends, and sweeps in to rescue Bride.

One wonders if Bride actually needs rescuing. Exactly what she is – woman, witch or fairy – is not clear, but she has the power to give good harvest, and one slip of her hand into winter's icy rivers is enough to put Beira to sleep until autumn has passed. But singly or in concert, Angus and Bride herald better weather, combining their powers to shift the seasons. This story, of Angus and his bridge days, is preferable to that of the senseless heating of the planet. Thinking of everyone outside, glad in their t-shirts for some vitamin D, although it hasn't been a long winter, or a particularly hard one, is easier if it's framed by myth. Instead of the encircling arms of climate disaster, the uncharacteristic heat is caused by a prince on a rescue mission, desperate to see his beloved. The pulsing sunshine emoji on the social media accounts of all the major weather stations might feel forgivable, then.

The story is lovely, a mishmash of fairies and witches, miracles and battling seasons. It is a seasonal tale, which is to say it accounts for the reasons behind the changing world, gives the changes narrative coherence, so we can believe with faith that these things will be ok, are ordained. The central characters, Bride and Beira, spring and winter, can be considered to represent facets of a Celtic version of the tripartite goddess (Maiden–Mother–Crone) so central to many contemporary witchcraft practices. The triple or tripartite goddess appears across world mythologies – it is so pervasive as an idea that Carl Jung believed that it was part of the human collective unconscious. Triple deities can encompass any three important and inter-related ideas, for example war, work and worship.[4] But more usually, as we understand it, the triple deity describes the three archetypal phases of womanhood – youth, motherhood, and old age. Each carry strengths and weaknesses. Various alternative models have been produced, especially because a reliance on equating womanhood with reproduction doesn't hold resonance for lots of people. Hekate, the Greek goddess, is a triple goddess – she contains a variety of threes within her. She is said, for example, to have power in heaven, in earth, and in the underworld. She is also a goddess of crossroads, her three faces keeping watch where three roads meet, and of witchcraft, child-rearing and death. While the Maiden–Mother–Crone presentation of the triple deity absolutely isn't the only one, it is one which was adopted by Wiccans and became popular. The idea of the three phases of womanhood is so ingrained in much western folklore that we find the characters interacting in many myths and fairy tales. For example, Bride and Beira are both mortals and deities, both real and unreal, witches and magical beings. They represent phases of life, modes of being, ways of relating. They are archetypes, and so both flexible and rigid. They have their toes in the world and their fingers in magic, and I can feel how comforted I am by stories about them.

British folk tales – but most particularly Scottish ones – have always smudged the edges between fairies and witches. Fairies are not, in Scottish – and indeed British – folklore, the sweet, flower-inhabiting children of Victorian illustration. Rather, they are tall, serious, and extraordinarily powerful. Fairies are a strange phenomenon in the history of folk magic and myth. They kept a great hold over the imaginations of scholars until the late nineteenth century, many years after the last witch-hunts, well into the late Victorian period. A folklorist, Carole Silver, discusses the popularity of fairies and fairy-myth as being pervasive among all echelons of society, saying that 'believers were not limited to gypsies, fisherfolk, rural cottagers, country parsons . . . throughout Victoria's reign advocates of fairy exist-ence and investigators of elfin origins included numerous scientists, historians, theologians, artists, and writers'.[5] Everyone from Yeats to Sir Arthur Conan Doyle actively pursued accounts of fairy sightings, and a scholarly field of fairy research blos-somed, relating itself to archaeology and anthropology. Fairy research reached an extraordinary climax with the Cottingley fairies hoax of 1917, and then collapsed into ignominy. The hoax combined emergent photographic technology with the increasingly evolutionist and naturalist approaches to fairy research. Photographs were produced that showed fairies as 'small creatures with bobbed hair and butterfly wings', frolicking with Elsie Wright and Frances Griffiths.[6] The girls had used cardboard cut-outs of fairies, arranging them on tree-trunks to give the appearance of a fairy revel. Keen fairy researchers and spiritualists Conan Doyle and Edward Gardner supported the frisking fairy photographs as genuine. Gardner in particular treated the photographs as scientific evidence of previously undiscovered life forms, writing that fairies were 'allied to the Lepidoptera, or butterfly, genus . . . rather than to the mammalian line'.[7] The photographs were disproved, and the field of fairy research suffered its killing blow – but before then, fairies loomed large in both the cultural and scientific imagination. Familiar yet unknown, present yet invisible, fairies became representations of, among many other things, everything unseen and unaccounted for in the landscape.

The Romantic period had seen a blossoming in fairy-related interest, part of a broader folkloric revival, and the Victorians, despite their rationality, and the advances in evolutionary science and industrial proliferation, held on to these fragments of lore in the form of the 'fairy' poetry of Keats, Shelley and Coleridge, as well as serious scholarly work undertaken by figures such as Robert Southey and Sir Walter Scott.[8] As urban gardens shrank and rural populations diminished, as towns grew and man's relationship with nature became more scientific, fairies came to embody nostalgia for the natural world and became a vehicle for feelings of estrangement from nature. They were approached, however, not as sweet stories or charming oddities, but as a possibly genuine phenomenon that required rigorous investigation. Evidence of the material existence of fairyland was particularly sought after, and took the form of naturally occurring curiosities such as 'elf-shot' or 'fairy-bolts', flint shards and shaped arrows from prehistoric periods, as well as 'fairy pipes', small pipe-shards and hollow bones that the fairies used for smoking. These little objects were easily found, and easily collected, turned into sacred objects, with apophatic or malevolent powers, depending on location and folkloric significance. Elf-shot could cause 'disease or death among cattle or men', but they could also protect against lightning.[9] They were particularly terrifying when wielded by witches, who could kill men with them, as in the case of Scottish accused witch Isobel Gowdie. Their position as a fairy-crafted weapon used by witches made them part of the confusion between witch-power and fairy-power that proliferated in Britain, and they had a long history: the Anglo-Saxon healing texts referred to them as 'ylfagescot' and 'haegtessan-gescot', or 'elf-shot' and 'witch-shot'.[10] Elves are interchangeable with fairies in much British folklore, and the words are used in a variety of contexts. There is something quite wonderful about this combination of craftsmanship and use. To pick up something the fairies made and discarded, and to feel it still redolent with power, enough to be used for witches' nefarious ends. There is nothing quite like an object of power, something seemingly given up by the soil, that cannot be bought but must be looked for, and that carries in it evidence of an occult race.

I found elf-shot, when I was around eleven, on my first archaeological dig. The Young Archaeologists' Club had taken us out for the day to visit a site in the Scottish Borders, and the archaeologists graciously allowed all ten or so of us to be let loose with trowels and brushes and loud enthusiasm. There is almost nothing more genuinely geeky than extracurricular archaeology for pre-teen children. And there we were, hard-hatted and wearing our sweaters emblazoned with our logo, which was a rather inquisitive-looking worm with his own hard hat perched jauntily on his head. Sharp-eyed and desperate to find something, I remember working in a little area by myself. The sun on the soil was hot and my knees were muddy, and everything smelled of the sweet warm summer smell, when I found it. I picked it out of the soil as if it had spent thousands of years waiting for me, as if it were coming home into my hand. About the breadth of my little palm, the arrowhead was knapped flint, a weak-tea colour, its working marks clearly mappable, its arrowhead shape imperfect but distinctive. It was light, sun-warm. I wanted to keep it a secret, close it in my palm and keep it forever.

Knapped flints seem to occupy a strange place between the crafted and the uncrafted, an amalgam of shapes that look almost incidental, unless you know what you are looking for, looking at. Flint can fall away naturally from the rock, but there are ways to tell if it has been shaped by human hands. There are little secrets, characteristics that differentiate natural from shaped flint. If you find a bit of flint that might be elf-shot, hold it in good light, and see if you can see any of the various different signs of working. The first characteristic is size: if the flint is of good size, and is perhaps shaped like a raindrop or a triangle, or is about the right size to fit in a palm, then chances are you are looking at worked flint. See if you can see what is called a bulb of percussion – this is a smooth, rounded knob at one end of the flint object, where it has been struck away from a larger section. It might carry ripples, little concentric rings that mark the knapping process. Then, the ventral surface comes under consideration – this is the part of the core where flakes of flint have been removed by the flint-knapper to make the shape of the finished object. If there are faceted depressions, lozenges, a little like honeycomb, the chances are that flakes were chipped away. These are known as lithic flakes, or chip, or spall. A group of lithic flakes, the product of lithic reduction and shaping, is called debitage. Sometimes you find little piles of debitage in the ground, and can imagine a flintknapper, chipping away until a shape emerges, and sweeping away the debris.

The beauty of flintknapping language is the way it hovers between vocabularies: archaeological, geological. Thick rock words that shape like edges over the tongue. You can look also for retouching along the sides of the flint – this is where the tool has been sharpened or blunted for use, and it looks like little bites along the edge of the object, as if tiny teeth have been hard at work. Objects shaped millennia ago by human hands are intoxicating, call to us on numerous grounds – we can hold history in our hands, learn its words and work out how it was made. I am a grown-up now but have never quite managed to outgrow my enchantment with worked flint and fairy gifts.

My elf-shot didn't kill a man, didn't poison cattle, didn't corrupt witches – or at least, not by my influence. I was too honest to keep it in my pocket, and told my supervisor, who popped it into a little plastic bag, marked the coordinates, stuck it on a tray of finds. It now sits somewhere, doubtless in a box, in the still darkness of a small museum storeroom.

It was logged, and I was congratulated. I would rather have kept it.

There are questions about whether or not objects have inherent power. I think all objects sit in conversation with each other, that a witch's skill lies largely in understanding the relationships between these objects, in bringing them into new relations, in understanding how the world is not empty, not full of space, but full always of the powers and influences of things relating to one another. There is no real reason why a knapped flint in the hand should feel different from a 1970s plate, found after landfill, or a brightly patterned plastic cup, found after hundreds of years on a beach, cracked but whole. The reason flints feel different is because they are elf-shot, because they are comparatively rare, because they emerge from the earth into our sight, and because historically, it was not clear who or what had made them. Antiquity, rarity and shrouded origins make an object ripe for occult adoption. We like strange objects, things that might alarm us, unsettle us, make us wonder how the world came to be as it is.

And when we find these things, and do not know where they came from, we couple them to supernatural forces. Elf-shot for fairies. Fairies, too, claim fairy-mounds, hollow hills, fairy-rings of trees or mushrooms. Unusual geography and the traces of earlier civilisations are almost always given fairy-origin in Britain. Material evidence of fairies and their dealings with the world of men also took the form of fairy-gifts, often given to historically important houses and families. Dotted across Britain one can find metal cauldrons, borrowed from fairy-folk and never returned; more beautifully, the Luck of Edenhall, a beautiful glass vase made by the fairies, recorded at Edenhall in Cumbria and said to guarantee good fortune as long as it remained unbroken. It now sits in the V&A Museum. Perhaps the most enchanting gift is the Fairy Flag of the MacLeods, which lives in Dunvegan Castle. There are so many stories about where it comes from – it was wrapped around the shoulders of a young MacLeod chieftain as a baby, by a fairy woman who saw he was cold; it was given to a clan member by his fairy lover as a parting gift. Whatever the origin, it is understood to be a gift of great love. The fairies, moved by the innocence or brilliance of the MacLeod clan member, gave this great gift to the whole clan.

The flag itself is a sad thing, these days. The silk is so old that it is almost destroyed, brown like turned leaves. Once, it would have been butter-yellow. There are 'elf-dots' in it: little speckles of red among the yellow, like drops of blood or the dark centres of flowers. Imaging techniques have revealed that it had red crosses on it, too, although these are now faded from human sight. This crumpled, beautiful thing, too delicate to be moved, houses great powers – of course. All gifts from the fairies contain power within them. What can the flag do? The answers to this, too, are vast and varied. It is reported to have cured plagued cattle, and brought the MacLeods great success in battle. Indeed, it is supposedly capable of conjuring troops to fight for the MacLeod cause, swelling their numbers on the battlefield. It is a great gift, and one only fairies could have given. Such evidence of fairyland seems indisputable – and indeed, when a Mr Wace of the V&A Museum examined the flag and declared it to be Middle Eastern in origin, the 27th

MacLeod Chief, Sir Reginald MacLeod, gently rebutted him, saying, 'Mr Wace, you may believe that, but I know that it was given to my ancestor by the fairies.' Mr Wace was rumoured to have replied that he bowed to Sir Reginald's superior knowledge on the matter.[11]

Fairies are made of tatters and borrowings. Their gifts bestow powers in response to the prevalent anxieties of the time. Their habitat is the unexplained in the landscape, their customs reflect mysteries and fears of rural communities. Like witches, they have always been made of the things people are scared of, the things people hope for. They attract and repel – they are beautiful but untrustworthy, quick to laugh and quick to anger, and they move from tall and stately to small and sweet the further we move into the twentieth century. Fairies are a way of understanding ourselves, they are mirror-creatures, and to harness witchcraft, to understand the witch as a personal and cultural creation, it feels important to give time and consideration to how fairies are figured in popular imagination.

Fairies have always been patchworked out of amalgams of lore, created from overlapping ideas and influences. For example, the underground world of the fairies closely resembles Christian conceptions of hell as underground, and in folk tradition, the dead were often believed to have gone to the fairy-realm.[12] When folklorists and others began to approach fairies as a subject for study they tied themselves in knots discussing how fairies might relate to Christian ideas of heaven and hell. The theories were brilliant in their ingenuity. One particular theory, common in Ireland, believed that fairies were immortal, and so had no soul. Thus, when Judgement Day finally came, the fairies, being exempt from the mortal struggles between salvation and damnation, would simply cease to exist.[13]

There were concerns about this immortality, however, especially as the natural sciences and evolutionary theory became more established. Immortality suddenly seemed unlikely, the preserve of children's stories. If fairies were real but not immortal, then perhaps they had left, died out, departed for their own country. Perhaps they were extinct, and the stories told about them were ancient memories of other races of man. These theories, that fairies were a leftover memory of primitive man, touched on anxieties of race and nationhood. Fairies could be understood to be memories of an extinct aboriginal people, and there were unpleasant insinuations that they had become extinct because they were inferior to modern man. This idea, which links 'primitive' or 'uncivilised' societies with magic, and indeed classes them as so radically different as to be fairies rather than humans, also applies to witches. Tales of witchcraft and folk beliefs were preserved in rural communities in Wales, Scotland and Ireland after they had been rationalised out of existence in urban areas, particularly in England. This quickly became coupled with rural poverty and differing standards of education and 'civilisation' in these areas. These populations believed in witches and fairies, it was claimed, because they were 'simpler', less 'worldly', less scientific, and therefore, inferior.[14] These attitudes informed the implementation of brutal suppression of Celtic peoples, including the suppression of the Welsh and Gaelic languages, the Highland Clearances, and the Great Famine and other atrocities in Ireland.

Fairy-belief was ascribed to the Celtic peoples, particularly the Irish, as evidence of 'modern primitivism', but it was also celebrated among certain echelons of society, such as W. B. Yeats and his coterie, who romanticised the innocence and supernatural aspects particularly of the Irish folk tradition.[15] The Sidhe, as Irish fairies are called, came to represent both primitivism and romantic national ideals. In fact, more than that, the Sidhe embody the way nationhood and cultural value were being negotiated in Ireland during the nineteenth century. The Sidhe – and indeed folk traditions and Irish identity in general – were seen as suspect. Fairies had no part in Christian hierarchy, and represented an untamed, non-conforming quality, a loophole of belief that could not easily be stamped out, which was metonymic of Irish identity more broadly. Consequently, the Sidhe occupied a difficult position as regards Christian doctrine: perhaps jealous of mortal souls and their salvation, or perhaps ancient pagan gods who could be called on for help. Peter Alderson Smith argues that 'the Sidhe are not altogether trusted, it is not certain that they wish well to mankind. For all that, men do not exactly hate the fairies . . . they suspect that God may do so'.[16] This is the central paradox of Celtic fairies, and why they are so much like witches. Culturally, they represent a threat to order, to the primacy of certain systems, whether religious or cultural. Instead, they are illicit, strange, eerie. They cannot be fully comprehended, cannot be seen. Like witches, they become responsible for healing and harming, for what cannot be explained by any other means.

Fairies and witches overlap too in their quixotic nature, and in sudden encounters that must be carefully measured. Fairies were often credited with stealing children and replacing them with one of their own. They could travel by wind. The Gaelic word for the fairy wind is the *oiteag sluaigh*, which translates as 'the people's puff of wind', and its particular sound and pattern was referred to as 'travelling on tall grass stems' (*falbh air chuiseagan treorac*).[17] When I met my fairies in the woods, when my Sìth came to me, the wind came over the grass and the moss. It came strangely, I thought, because by rights, the trees above my head should have been shaken. But it was a low wind, a wind to shake the tall grass stems. Then they appeared, solemn and grey, bright and green, beautiful and terrible, real and unreal. No gifts for them, nothing in my pocket, and nothing to bring me back to earth if they beckoned me through their doors. The forest breathed with them, their lungs great and diffuse, pulling air from the whole forest.

Fairies are a form of animism. They are a way of speaking to the landscape. They are the human face of the landscape, a mask that it wears so we can speak to it in a shape we recognise. Spirits of a place, emanations, genii loci; these things have so many names. Fairies are one way of glimpsing something, in the landscape, that is evidence of its animation, of its aliveness. Animism has been given a bad name in anthropology, because for a long time, cultures that engaged with animism in their religious practices were seen as less advanced than those that did not. This subtly underpinned imperialist and expansionist policy: after all, primitive animists needed converting to more rational forms of thought. That these animist tendencies persisted in Celtic cultures was a source of worry. But animism, freed from repressive nineteenth-century narratives, has a huge amount to offer the witch, or anyone who wishes to reassess their relationship with the world, with everything that can be seen or felt. Previously, anthropologists believed that animism was a way of imagining life into objects that were inert. The hills were not alive with the sound of music, the furniture didn't change the energy of a room, a favourite handbag could not be lucky, a tree could not feel, the ground could not respond.

Scientific discoveries have altered how we understand perception and communication – they have altered how we understand the world around us. How things are alive, how they communicate, what they might be able to perceive. These things come to us anew, but they often reinforce previous, folk explanations for the way the world is, for the aliveness of the world. From trees that can overhear human presence to acknowledging that foraging or cutting wood can cause pain and damage, the world has long been conceived of as very alive, and every bit as sensitive as humans – these beliefs were just sidelined as no more than forms of animism, as so much irrational nonsense, alongside fairies.

Animism, then, is due for an overhaul. There is now a persuasive argument that animism is not a belief about the world – rather, it is a way of perceiving the world, a way of existing within it. It describes a heightened state of sensitivity and responsiveness in both perception and in active participation in an environment that is constantly changing, renewing, altering, moment by moment. Rather than assuming that we are the most alive, the most conscious, the most sophisticated thing in any environment we enter, this new understanding of animism asks to stop. It asks us to look around, to understand the complicated aliveness of absolutely everything. Water flowing into drains; those scrappy weeds that push up beside streetlights; the stunted little pots of herbs we keep on our windowsills. Things are not animated by our belief in them, we do not bestow the quality of 'aliveness' – rather, the world is already animate. We simply are able to perceive that animation and draw it out.

Everything is not just alive, but equal. This idea is radical, breaking down hierarchies in which humans sit at the top – it transforms our entire field of relations. We are as much animated by the grass, then, as it is by us. The trees bring us into existence in the same way we bring them. Our gaze on a meadow, picking out bees, or looking along paths in a botanic garden, a municipal park, the edge of a little pond. All things are brought into new relation, even us. We make each other real, we spin this web together, we are networking and alive in ways that are still being disclosed to us, every time we turn our attention to really perceiving what is around us and exist actively among it.[19]

It is this, perhaps, that is the beginning of believing in magic. First, it is understanding the infinite relatedness of all things. It is looking at the moorland fire, smelling the smoke, feeling the acute despair. It is also seeing the fairies. Fairies are like witches: we are visible and invisible, ordinary and magical, real and unreal. The fairies I saw in the woods didn't speak to me. They didn't need to deliver a message, to seduce me to join their dance. All they did was reveal the woods to me, just as they were. Not as I would have them exist, not as idyllic and dry and welcoming. Instead, the fairies stood in the woods, solemn and real, and made me look. Look at the spiders, the wet grass, the rotting tree trunks. The fairies came to me with human bodies, human faces. Presumably, this is because my brain is sufficiently limited that I don't imagine mycorrhizal networks as beautiful. Perhaps I don't tune into them, listen to them properly, because I can't conceive of them properly. This is my limitation, my failure of imagination. So instead, the way I see place, with my hopeless human eyes, is by conceiving of it as human-like, stern, grey, magical and unsettling. The fairies do not act as stewards, per se. Rather, they are encouraging me toward stewardship. *Come in deeper*, they seem to say, *come and get lost and understand*. If you want to do magic, you must first listen to the magic that is already being done, work out where you are needed. Witness accounts and shocking images frighten me, paralyse me, make me hide and hope for unlikely reprieve from climate change. My experience in the woods, among dripping branches and uncomfortable ground, helps me realise that my power, my alive-ness, is contingent, networked, related and inseparable from everything else. Fighting for a better climate then becomes not a distant or intellectual process – instead, it is a way of advocating for the world that is as much myself as I am, that I am as much a part of as a spider.

My solemn fairies, strange and unknowable, are figures of climate, of environment. They are reminders of network. I want to walk into the woods. Witches, if we are to do magic, must walk into the woods, into the pavement cracks, into the polluted lakes and scrubby parks and the edge-lands beside motorways. The network is under our fingers, it is inside us, we are operating inextricably within it. *Come deeper*, it says, in its voice that is not a voice. *You have already always been here.*

A Spell for Weather

What is weather but energy moving across the earth? Weather is flux, and from grey city mizzle that coats the skin to banks of rural snow, weather influences what we wear, how we live, where we go.

So let's talk to it.

This isn't a spell to summon good weather. It isn't a rain-bringing spell or a wish for a wind. These things require a lot of power, and require, too, a knack for weather-talking. They also often require a group.

You don't need anything except to go outside for this spell. You could even just open a window.

That sounds ridiculous. Barely a spell at all. You aren't casting anything, or asking for anything, it seems. You haven't made a particular ritual space, or said any special words.

Except, of course, that you have. I truly think the best way to begin a magical practice is to begin a practice of conscious attention. What you are asking for is a way into the web of the world. Not just to move through it, but to register it in multiple, careful ways. You are, in fact, asking for a lot: the reciprocal attention of the universe.

I have been singing to the wind since I was a child, and find certain songs better than others, generally Gaelic lullabies. You can find your own way to connect to the world: you could draw, you could knit, you could put two hands on the ground and just feel.

But whatever it is, you have to undertake it as a very genuine form of communication, and be very focused on whatever weather is occurring. The wind is easy to talk to, as is the rain, because you can feel them against your skin. Instead of turning away from the rain, sit with it. Notice the size of the drops, the frequency, the temperature. Are they being blown down by wind, or falling slowly? Are they sufficiently fine to hang in the air like mist, or are they great plopping splats of water? When I say talk to the weather, I think what I mean is notice it.

I once, in Croatia, at the age of thirteen, was so moved by it that I tore all my clothes off when a thunderstorm started, ran outside and danced in the rain in all my nakedness. That is not the only time this has occurred.

Perhaps you are reading this and cringing, glad that your speaking to rain will never resemble mine in its obviousness. There is sincerity in it, though: it has taught me always to notice the rain, notice its patterns and moods. The first stage of exerting one's will on the world is always to know the world. You wouldn't ask a stranger for the same sort of favour you'd ask of a friend.

If you'd like something more formal, let me give it to you:

Find a place where you will not be interrupted, and sit down. Notice the weather, and try to do this by cycling slowly through your senses. What can you see and hear? What can you touch and smell? Can you catch snow in your hand and put it against your lips to taste the cold?

Introduce yourself. You might say something informal, but if you prefer to begin with something with more shape to it, try saying, even just in your head:

Well met, rain. You were falling long before me, and will long after me, and I am glad to sit with you.

Then, see what the rain says. It might not speak back. It might ignore you altogether. You might, however, feel acknowledged, at least a little.

You don't have to stay out long: this spell works best little and often. It helps to talk to lots of weather, and find out what speaks back – the sun against your skin, the wind in your hair, the rain down your back. Get to know the world, and it will talk about itself to you.

MARCH

—◆—

Witches, Money and Protest

There are always, always money worries. I am lucky, in many ways, but I am also a freelancer, whose work is patchy and unpredictable. My partner is, too. We are precarious, and make do, but there is no settling feeling of security. In this respect, there is a sense in which we embody the current millennial workforce. I am always hustling, on something, in some direction. I always feel one bad month away from disaster, because I am.

One July, that bad month arrives, and when these things happen there is always a pattern. Fear. The hurried calculation of losses, of rent, of how far other things will stretch, of what might need to be cancelled. We do our best: commiserate over tea and then make new plans, wear brave faces. Things will be alright, but money will be tight. I hate feeling powerless. There are, of course, practical things I can do: keep an eye out for job opportunities. The situation doesn't call for anything more – it's just a hard, crap part of life. It unsettles me, though. It sits with me all day and later, when I go into the kitchen, I find myself reaching for a teacup with a wide mouth.

Once you've been practicing magic for a while, things occur instinctually. And isn't that an annoying thing to say! But they do. The shapes of spells come to you faster, and the greater your intuitive understanding of the properties of things, the more quickly and ably magic comes. And I've been dealing with money and its magical aspects for many, many years. There's a quiet confidence amid the panic: for once, I feel on solid ground.

What happens next happens almost without thinking. Opening cupboards, I empty ingredients into the cup. Firstly, a pinch of sugar to court good fortune. Then a pinch of black tea to give us the energy to carry out whatever actions are needed. Pepper, for swiftness in the charm. Oil, so that things might go smoothly. And a penny to increase fortune. It takes mere seconds. I ask the gods and goddesses of house and pocket to stir themselves, to look out for the humans who heat their home and leave them food and live with them. I mix the contents of the teacup three times, clockwise, and carry it through to the living room, where I leave it on the mantelpiece. Beside it, I then light a candle, and ask the deities who govern fortune, and harmony, to bring a little money – but only as much as is needed. Something to ease the situation. Enough to keep the wolf away. I never want to push, never want to ask for too much.

The following morning, my partner gets a copy-editing job, a day's work that brings not a fortune, but a good amount.

This charm is unusual. It differs from my normal practice, because it was cast hurriedly, in the heat of emotion, and did not involve any of the formal elements that are often the hallmark of spells – casting a circle for protection, for example, or gathering specialised ingredients. Perhaps, though, some of its power lay in its hurriedness, in working with what was immediately available, and in seeking to help not just myself. Often, magic becomes heavily formalised, and there was certainly a freedom in casting some practical magic, as it was needed, around someone I loved.

There is often a question, asked of witches and others who cast spells around money: why aren't we rich? If we're so powerful, why aren't witches living in mansions, sipping champagne while counting the money they magicked out of thin air? If a charm can contribute to gaining a small amount, why not a large amount? Why isn't magic scalable in this way? Money and witchcraft have long been contentious bedfellows. What witches do, or give, for free, or what they charge for, is difficult. Many Wiccans won't charge money for spells at all. I admire this, and don't currently charge for spells – but then nor do I frequently do them for other people. It's more common to charge for tarot readings or other services, although these still have to be carefully labelled as being for entertainment, and not to be taken seriously. Witches and their services are still often regarded with suspicion.

When the Witchcraft Act was repealed in 1951, it was replaced by the Fraudulent Mediums Act, which simultaneously implied a lack of genuine magic in the world (which was helpful to those who practised it, at least), and asserted in the same breath that gullible individuals might still be taken advantage of by those claiming to do magic. When witches are not being asked about conjuring money, they are being suspected of hoodwinking others, of parting them from their cash. We're either the devil's instruments, or mere hucksters, charlatans, con artists. And there are many con artists, of course. I'm not going to tell you that all the people who want your money won't trick you. I hold in contempt particularly those who claim to offer ease to the deeply grieving through cold-reading. Witches – true witches, who work toward the good, or at least away from harm – make neither false promises nor false communions with the dead. They offer honest attempts, and that is all.

These attempts must, as well as sincere, be proportional. In a charm-making workshop recently, an attendee made a charm for her terminally ill friend – not for healing, because the prognosis was such that this would be an insulting thing to give her friend. Rather, she asked for ease for her friend: comfort in her distress, and as little pain as possible. The will is a wonderful tool, but its exertions aren't without limit: this seemed a beautiful, tender, kind thing to ask. The same is true for money. Asking for help with subsistence is very different from asking to gain a fortune, and there are a variety of reasons for choosing the former, both magical and non-magical. Witches do not generally ask for large amounts of money when casting spells. Most witches aren't rich, and those who are almost certainly earned their money through non-occult means. In fact, witches are historically poor, societal outliers lacking in the material means to command respect and immunity to punitive action. However, Victorian magicians such as Aleister Crowley and those in various secret occult orders were often well-funded and aristocratic, and the history of magic is filled with spells and rituals that were available only to the very rich. This may be where the suspicions about moneyed witches come from. Indeed, in certain Eastern European countries such as Romania, some witches from powerful lineages are still fairly rich and well-regarded, selling expensive spells and advice.

However, in the main, spells and healing have traditionally been bartered, with witches working for subsistence. It is only rarely a profitable profession.[1] And of course, medieval and Early Modern magic, via alchemy and its professionalisation, was practised by the rich, but not as a primary profession. Magic is not a money-maker.

It is not difficult to explain why. Firstly, magical practice has long been considered suspicious by society. Being a witch has never been as easy or untroublesome as being a baker or a candlestick maker. You couldn't just open a shop: everything had to be covert. Because of this, earning money through practising magic has always been difficult. Your clients might only come and visit you in desperation, or when afraid of seeking more conventional aid. They might come to your house under shadow of night, or ask to meet you somewhere hidden. Nobody tells their neighbours they are going to visit a witch. Nobody tells their neighbours that they even know there is a witch. And witches, historically, do not tell their neighbours that they are witches, if they value their lives. Most of the pagans I know, even now, do not advertise their religious or spiritual beliefs. Most witches I know write under assumed names, or don't talk much about it. Even now, on the witchcraft courses that I run, we find that people often lie to their friends and family about the class they are attending. So it's not surprising that those seeking spells often kept it secret. Witches are rarely, then, even recommended by those they help: there are witches even today whose websites contain client testimonials, but these are almost always anonymous. For much of history, being known as a witch – or even a healer, or midwife – was potentially fatal, and so witches who practised did not usually advertise the fact. These inhibiting factors meant that witchcraft never had the opportunity to be lucrative, unlike other vocations. It has always been a shadowy place, it has always been a cash-in-hand and no-receipts way of doing business.

The second reason why witchcraft won't make you rich is, annoyingly for many people, an ethical one. When practised properly, magic should be at least an ethically neutral practice, and the accumulation of wealth is often – though of course not exclusively – predicated on the exploitation of people or resources. In order to gain great wealth, the riches must come from somewhere else. My grasp of economics might be slim, but even I am aware that money doesn't come from nowhere. So to ask for extreme wealth is to ask for harm to be done to people, by proxy. If you are getting that wealth then someone, somewhere, is being denied it. There is also the question of harmony. Under late capitalism, it can be difficult to hang on to the idea that the world might exist in any kind of harmony, but particularly harmony pertaining to resources. While the utopian ideal of each individual and community having enough resources is just that, it is nevertheless reasonable to hope for, and work towards, a fairer society. As an ethical practice, witchcraft is part of this work towards a fairer world, and so should attempt to avoid greedy or immoral spellwork. This is not to say, of course, that witches should offer free labour, or allow themselves to be exploited in turn, merely that magic is never the path to riches. We have to build a world that is rich in other things: culture, healthy green places, community. Those are the real riches. But although they are the goal, we still all need to pay rent, to buy food, to stay warm. We still need money. Of course, anyone will tell you that money won't buy happiness, but it will buy comfort, and security. And to devalue those things is to tell ourselves a lie about our needs and the needs of those around us. We all need money, and there is no shame in asking for help to get it.

Indisputably, magic is helpful when it comes to money. Magic is, as we have learned, located in, and part of, the energy exchange of all things. It is as much a part of how energy is moved around as motion, as eating, as breathing. It is the exertion of the will to change the world, and the world is made up of, and full of, energy that passes among objects. And money is caught up in energy exchange. It isn't exempt from it. We have brought money into relation with us, with everything we do. And thus, like any other aspect of energetic process, it can be focused on and called into focus. In the same way that you can conduct magic with food (from sacred offerings to spells baked into cakes), so you can make magic with money. Magic tends toward harmony, too. It likes things to be equally distributed, to move freely. As a result, money is quite good to work with, in magical terms, so long as the request is never to hold on to, or stockpile, the money. So while it might not help you win the lottery, magic is often useful for subsistence. It's also really good for helping to attract debt repayment, or outstanding invoices. As a free-lancer, this has been an excellent tip to learn.

Magic works as a flow. In fact, it is useful to remember that it is balance, rather than accretion, that is the primary concern of magic. There is money everywhere, imbalanced, and it can be slid around, a little, if we try. Perhaps not many people do it, but I like to play the game where you think about coins.

Just little coins. Pennies. And you start just casually keeping an eye out. You'll quickly notice coins on the ground if you are thinking about them. And they tend to move, for me at least, in denominations. I'll find pennies, then a few twenty pence pieces, and then a pound, or sometimes a ten pound note. And then, the game tends to reset, and slips you back to pennies for a while. Money comes and goes, even in this game. It's no solution to money woes, but it's a fun way to remind yourself of the money that sits all around us, that can appear to us in small amounts. It's also the same with anything else, from parking spaces to employment opportunities: they're more likely to appear if you have asked for them, if you have turned your mind toward them. As long as witches work toward a fair and harmonious society, it is perfectly acceptable to ask for help when it is needed. Indeed, it is our due: we are not going to suddenly become employable for our skills with the occult, so perhaps it is only fair if sometimes the universe grants us small compensations, little gifts and acknowledgements.

So we can work with money. We can work to bring it, to send it out, to help people, to change our relationships with it. But we have to remember what money is part of: a deeply difficult political system, and much of it is generated in ways that damage people and the planet. I suspect that almost all practitioners of witchcraft would object to the current devastation of the planet; to the unfair treatment of oppressed minorities; to the exploitation of humans in the name of profit.

This doesn't mean we can't do money magic: not in the least. What could be more magic than wresting money from the hands of those who have amassed it unethically? But before you reach for the tinder boxes and sharpen the guillotines, remember that witches can conduct revolutions in all sorts of clever ways. Witches are a political category: we are the bad object, the unjustly persecuted. We are present in the idea of witch-hunts in politics, we are present in the very fabric of our culture's ghost stories and fears. To be a witch is to take on an identity with political ramifications. When we walk in the world as witches, we make a statement.

Often, that statement is one that, whether we like it or not, flies in the face of much polite society. Witches often find themselves on the fringes, helping to resist society's worst tendencies. There are lots of examples of witchcraft and resistance throughout history. Witches have always protested, though not always organised into groups. But there have been a few, and among the highest-profile of these was WITCH, a series of interlinked and fairly loose resistance groups in America, formed during the 1970s. They originated in 1968 in New York, during a period in which witchcraft and the occult were having a major resurgence in popular culture. However, WITCH weren't specifically a group of occult practitioners. They weren't even a coven. Instead, they were an offshoot of radical feminist women's groups. They were formed by a break-off group of 'politicos', socialist feminists who understood the oppression of women to be a product of capitalism. They were an all-purpose liberation group in some ways, happy to join with other groups whose causes intersected with their own. WITCH allied with a diverse range of other protest groups, from the anti-war protestors to the Black liberation movement. They had a creed, a mission statement, and it emphasised women as an oppressed category, rather than a biologically defined one:

WITCH is a total concept, a new dimension of woman. It means breaking the bond of woman as a biologically and sexually defined creature. It implies the destruction of passivity, consumerism and commodity fetishism... Who is the enemy? WITCHes must name names, or rather we must name trademarks and brand names.[2]

In their manifesto they traded on the idea of accused witches giving the names of their victims to their persecutors. But instead of this act of submission to torture, WITCH made their 'naming names' into an act of speaking truth to power, of seeking to dismantle oppressive forces. These new witches, WITCH argued, would be fierce, terrifying, unafraid. WITCH was not just a feminist activist group. They also had a strong anti-capitalist stance, and their breaking of the bond of female identity was linked as much to consumption (and gendered marketing) as it was to other aspects of female experience. Although they didn't explicitly all identify as witches or all practise magic, because they fought for female rights and protested, they are often understood as a forerunner of contemporary feminist pagan groups and practices.[3]

WITCH wasn't just a name designed to strike fear: it was also an acronym, which stood for a variety of things at different times, from 'Women's International Terrorist Conspiracy from Hell' via 'Women Infuriated at Taking Care of Hoodlums' to 'Women Indentured to Traveller's Corporate Hell': and why not? There were plenty of things to be furious about, by acronym or otherwise. Even their acronyms implied that they were angry, dangerous and meant business. The group borrowed concepts and archetypes from witchcraft in their activism. They drew on ideas like the collective power of the coven, and they were among the first group of activists to employ hexes as a form of political protest. Hexes are one of the most unsettling things we have: deep curses, ways of doing evil. And they are deeply ethically questionable things to cast, especially against individuals. However, they are a highly visible and highly unsettling means of causing disruption. And WITCH didn't really hex individuals: instead, they went for big corporations or organisations. For example, when they hexed the New York Financial District in the early 1970s, Robin Morgan, a WITCH member, reported that the Dow Jones Index sharply declined the day after.[4] Their hexes, then, had been effective. They had mobilised themselves against power, using metaphysical rather than physical means. Often, women do not have violence at their disposal the way men do: that kind of magic is a proxy for it. It is safe violence, safe interference. It is action at a distance, which is one of the most potent possibilities of magic. It is using the power you have the way you have it, and WITCH did this beautifully, and paved the way for other witches to do it too. In that moment, however they self-defined, WITCH lived up to their name, in all its glory.

Although they are among the less well-known of the 1960s protest groups, is important to understand the effect that WITCH had on popular culture's association of the figure of the witch with feminist protest.[5] Existing at the edge of feminist protest culture, the members of WITCH were perceived by their peers to be wild and uncontrollable, qualities so often ascribed to witches. They were compared to revellers, bacchantes, unhinged women living outside society's strictures. According to Helen Kritzler, 'the WITCH women were wild and irreverent.'[6] This non-conforming 'wildness' was echoed in their literature, which used the language of witchcraft as a way of moving outside nice, normal, polite conversation: as a way of unsettling everyone, of demonstrating their power.

WITCH wanted people to be scared of them. They wanted people to think of them as part of a continuous trail of women throughout history. Dangerous women: renegades, protestors, practitioners of the dark arts; and so they actively aligned their cause with the plight of historically persecuted witches. You could say that perhaps they over-aligned themselves, in some ways. So keen were they to claim their witch-lineage that they repeated what is known as the 'witch-cult' hypothesis in their leaflets. The witch-cult hypothesis is a theory, now debunked, that the witches tried during the various European witch trials were the remnants of a secret pre-Christian cult. More startlingly, the witch-cult hypothesis suggests that some witches escaped persecution, and continued to practise their ancient pagan rites in deepest secret. They did this throughout history, privately, unnoticed: and they passed their practices down even to the present day. This was a very popular theory with all sorts of people, and a seductive one. After all, who doesn't want to claim ancient, sacred lineage? Who doesn't want to argue that the power they are wielding has been handed down in an unbroken line since the beginning of time? It's a great way to claim power, to claim that you are, in fact, genuinely capable of upending the order of the world.

Sadly, however, the theory isn't true. WITCH may have inherited this theory from American feminist historian Matilda Joslyn Gage, who incorrectly believed that 'hundreds' of witches were burned together at the stake in great mass burnings, 'at one time dying agonizingly by fire', and that they held in common an ancient occult religion.[7] While Gage's intention was to highlight the suffering of women and their historical oppression, she hugely exaggerated the number of women who were burned, and gave them a false history, by suggesting their part in an ancient, secret religion. This theory has been widely condemned by historians of the witch trials. Indeed, critics Jeffrey Russell and Brooks Alexander were so scathing of the assertion that they wrote:

That this 'old religion' persisted secretly, without leaving any evidence, is of course possible, just as it is possible that below the surface of the moon lie extensive deposits of Stilton cheese. Anything is possible.[8]

This is rude, of course, and dismissive. But alas, Russell and Alexander were right. The witch-cult hypothesis relied on faulty information, and manipulation of existing histories, to create a seductive narrative of secret female power. The theory relied on believing wholesale the confessions of witches on trial and forgetting that they were in fact the product of coercion and torture. Sadly, in popularising this misinformation, WITCH played a part in perpetuating glamorised accounts of early witches. The reason behind WITCH's interest in this secret cult was that it lent credibility to their enterprise, and offered an imaginative continuity between ancient female mystical power and their own direct action. This imaginative continuity allowed them to identify with imagined forebears, and assume an aura of mysterious and potent power, which empowered them to act beyond the constraints of more mainstream feminist groups. They were magic, they were chosen. They were, therefore, immune to the rules and regulations of normal life. And above all, they were absolutely not to be messed with.

WITCH didn't just want to be part of an ancient lineage of witches, they actively wanted to convert others, too. The group invited other women to self-identify as witches, create covens and engage in direct political action, writing: 'You are a woman and dare to look within yourself, you are a Witch. You make your own rules . . . You can form your own Coven of sister Witches ...'[9] WITCH's approach to the figure of the witch was, and remains, controversial – it is founded on inaccuracy and simultaneously celebrates the witch as persecuted, and as powerful. This is a common paradox in popular imaginings of the witch, and they cannot be held entirely responsible for this. WITCH were certainly complicated, but their message was radical, impactful and urgent, and while their co-opting of the idea of the witch might have had strange elements, it showed the vital importance of the witch as a political figure. It also showed the terror and power that lives inside the witch as a cultural category, even in contemporary society.

Although WITCH only existed briefly, and their political action was chaotic and not always entirely effective, they brought the figure of the witch to the forefront of the feminist protest movement. They also paved the way for subsequent manifestations of the witch figure in politics, transforming the witch from victim and resettling her to her previous status as a figure of awe and fear. Indeed, WITCH's political definition of the witch has shaped contemporary understandings of witchcraft, and planted the seeds of the current witchcraft revival. The witch as public figure, as hex-thrower, as radical sister against struggle has been cemented. Whenever we witches unite against forces that would oppress us, whenever we ask loudly for more, whenever we seek to gain knowledge or open closed doors, we should think of them.

WITCH also embedded in popular consciousness the idea of the witch as an explicitly anti-capitalist entity. Capitalism is often discussed in terms of its power to bewitch, its enchantment, its seductive magic. Marx wrote that under capitalism, the world is 'bewitched and distorted'.[10] The witch, as one who is capable of enchantment, of magic, is perhaps the only type of person who wields a similar power to capitalism, and thus is able, to some extent, to resist it. To see outside it. To look round it. Not only is the witch a reluctant operant within capitalist structures, she is also able to offer alternative bewitching. Because the witch is not entirely operant within capitalist systems, because she makes almost no money from her magic, she is able to speak back to capitalism, without requiring that those she speaks to convert to her religion. She can look at capitalism, understand that it is just another form of magic, and talk back to it, from out of the dark of the edge-places.

In their book *Capitalist Sorcery: Breaking the Spell*, critics Isabelle Stengers and Philippe Pignarre explain that the witch is able to break capitalism's 'spell', which people are under. They argue that this is because the central mystery of magic is that it cannot be entirely explained. It isn't like science, or literature, or mathematics: it lives outside the usual bounds of what is known, and it does not answer to logic. Witches know the power of speech, the power of stories. They *are* the magic: the power of the witch lies in the way they understand that the only real magic is whether or not things get done. The power lies in the implication that all forms of belief are radically strange, mysterious, and cannot be reduced. If capitalism is 'real', even though you cannot touch or see it, then why not magic? In a world of virtual currency, where money that doesn't exist can be lent, borrowed, repaid, what is to say that other forms of enchantment, of bewitchment, of collective belief in something different, could not be equally powerful?

This point can easily be demonstrated in contemporary direct action against right-wing America. Collective hexing has formed a significant means of resistance against Trump and his White House administration. It is clear that once more, a power that that comes from outside the current system can provide something valuable, and can move to effect change. In October 2018, protestors met to hex Judge Brett Kavanaugh, who was elected to the Supreme Court despite facing allegations of sexual assault. The event, held in New York City (an apparent hotbed for hexing), comprised a ritual in which the names of those to be hexed were 'thrown into vases and covered with graveyard dirt, coffin nails, broken glass, sulphur, cactus thorns, water from a thunderstorm, and urine'.[11] The ritual is described in terms of a fairly traditional hex, and certainly seems to have been cathartic for those involved. There must be a great deal of joy in the release of it, in the shouting and acting against power. Using the magic that there is, the ways that people are able to resist.

Chelsea Ritschel, a journalist who attended the hexing, explained that it was not necessarily the traditionally magical elements of the hex that she found to be the most moving. Rather, she wrote that 'while the hex to oust Judge Kavanaugh may or may not work, the real magic in the back room of the Brooklyn bookshop was the unfaltering acceptance and the belief in one another's ability to weather the storm'.[12] Again we see that the magic is inextricable from the tools used to work it: the action both affirms a belief in the magic, and is the magic itself. And by being both, this hexing lets us see how we can resist, how we can fight against the forces that seek to undo us.

This circles back, once more, to the question of belief – belief in something ineluctable, irreducible that operates its bewitching power through witches. Whether this 'something' is magic or not, whether ordinary people believe in it or not, does not matter. Witches become the individuals who can ask questions of power, who can draw on their value systems and questions as alternatives to the current forces of power. Witches, in this sense, exist partially outside, and partially in response to, political systems and contemporary cultures. This is not to say, of course, that being a witch demands radical political beliefs and a total commitment to overthrowing capitalist systems. Simply, it is important to acknowledge that the witch has an important role to play in imagining a fairer society, and in asking difficult questions of our current society. Witches can offer the world meaningful alternatives: alternative value systems, beliefs, and means of operating in the world. These are important regardless of whether or not the witch attends protests. To live in relation to a power that exists outside of our normal relations is to understand the world and its systems differently. It is important in our practice to honour the witch's unique position. As Stengers and

Pignarre assert, 'To honour the goddess is to learn . . . the "cry" of a world that demands that one learn how to join it again'.[13]

We must learn the cry of the world, and how to join it ethically, and to challenge its oppressions through our work. And we must learn, too, to ask for help when we need it.

Money is part of a corrupt system, but it is also an undeniable part of the fabric of the world, and we cannot escape from it. Instead, we can find good, small, helpful ways to ask for money, to work our magic with it, to let it redistribute itself a little. Perhaps hexing the stock exchange en masse, and regularly, is the way forward, as WITCH did. Or perhaps it is channelling our power toward keeping the wolves from the doors of those we love, and helping with charity when we can. We know that nothing we wield is powerless: we know how to look power in the eye, call to it, and have it step out of its hiding places to meet us.

A Charm for Money

It can be useful to have something in your back pocket, for when there is very little in your back pocket! This charm deals in small amounts, and seeks to maintain harmony.

You will need:

- *Green ribbon or thread*
- *Oak leaves*
- *Incense*

Oak has long been associated with increase and gain. Thread three leaves together with green thread, while at your altar, and imagine a green light running from them, and filling you up gradually. You may wish to say words such as:

Oak that grows, spreading and steady,
Grant me as much as I need and let the rest go to those who
  need it.

Keep the charm on your altar, hanging above the bed, or above where you store your handbag or wallet. When the money comes, be sure to take the leaves down, and give thanks before you return them to the ground.

APRIL

———◆———

Witches Becoming Animals

The crow is early. I see him first at the beginning of April, bobbing and weaving between cars. If he's a fledgling, then he must be among the first. He's ragged in that baby way, feathers askew from traffic. He finds his way onto one of the municipal bins, and starts to scream. We do not see his parents, although this is very normal; if he's fledged properly, they will leave him mostly to his own devices. Young crow in the big city. He's handsome, and loud, and over the next few days, he makes friends. The ladies in the flat at the end of the road speak to him. One puts down water in a cat bowl. He hops onto the post box, and warily regards them, but he drinks once they have left. Head bob, little hop, raspy noise. His scruff, his unsteady bouncing, win him admirers. I find myself leaving out bacon bits, watching him eat them from his bin-perch. He entertains like a court jester. The cool boys from the barbers take to giving him dog food. Their French bulldog is aghast at this, watches glumly from the doorstep of the shop. Eventually, the crow flies. I spend a lot of time looking out of the window at him, or going into the street to stand close by. Eventually, I begin to spot him farther away – on the side of the bridge overlooking the river, on the top of the public toilets, right down towards the riverbank itself. He cocks his head at me when he sees me, doesn't immediately take off. Does he know me now? Perhaps. I know him, he feels like a neighbour. Closer to me, in fact, than most of my real neighbours – ours is not a cosy street, and we go about our business quietly.

A little village raises that crow. We attend to him in a way we don't usually attend to anything. I spend a lot of time near him – because I can, because he intrigues me, and because I find that I like him. I feel over the weeks as if I know his life well, can empathise with his trials and tribulations, can talk to him a little, even if only through nonsense cawing sounds and slow, quiet movements. I find myself wishing we could live in a little forest, he and I, in close relation always. Even though I know that we were both born in this city, are happy clattering around behind the bins. Even though I know that all the forest is, in that thought, is a metaphor for quiet, concentrated, restful space. This is our forest – the orange shine of the pavements late at night, the way the grey twilight looks on his feathers, the way he jumps at the sound of an ambulance. He and I are already in our forest, on the edge of things and right in among them. He is a good neighbour, and when his journeys take him further from our street, I miss him.

I often want to disappear into a forest, to have time on my own, which is hardly unusual. Links are frequently made between witches and forests, between witches and any wild, lonely space with only animals for company. This preserves the safety of the community, but it also allows the practitioner to maintain their contact with whatever forces aid them. Too much comfort, too much integration into daily gossip and their power may be diminished – they might lose the skills that set them apart. This historic alienation, difference marked out through distance, still lingers in places – my godmother's experience as a doctor in rural Scotland, where she was fiercely respected but never befriended, is typical of this experience. The healer is always set apart, deferred to but not quite included. After all, to keep a knife sharp, it must be kept out of contact with blunting forces.

Witches, and often more specifically charmers, pellars, hedge-witches, healers, the shamans and spiritual leaders of diverse indigenous peoples – any category of person perceived to have links to the more-than-human world, to effect magic – these people have always lived, geographically and culturally, on the margins of civilisation. They occupy a liminal space, a setting away and apart. They are people on and of the edges of things.

The last house in the village, the strange dwelling in the woods, the cave, Baba Yaga's house raised up into the trees on its chicken-bone legs. Books could be written about edge-peoples, whose position in relation to social power, and their access to other forms of power, has made it safer, or wiser, or simply more convenient, for them to move out of the body of the community. Even in high-rises, even in rows of terraced houses, even among neatly manicured suburban lawns, we maintain ways of edging out, keeping apart from, maintaining distance with, those we think are other than us. Kicking a football into the garden of the witch-house and letting it lie; running those few steps past the place where someone we suspect is not like us lives – even holding our breath, so we aren't enchanted. The city is just another form of landscape, and it houses communities, and patches of wilderness, whether architecturally built, or psychically imagined.

This edge-dwelling displaces the individual in relation to the hierarchies of the natural world: the further they are from human networks, the closer they are to the networks of the natural world. The less in tune the witches are with their human neighbours, the more in tune they are, arguably, with their more-than-human neighbours. And this in turn puts these people into proximity with animals and plants, gives them time and space to learn about them, watch them, engage in the lived experiences of non-human life. And it is here, in this edge-place of different proximity, that animals turn into people, and people turn into animals. Or so it is said.

Witches – and indeed, all magic-effecting peoples – have a rich and global history of animal transformation. These histories differ vastly according to region and religion, and the nuances of these traditions, especially in non-Western cultures, have often not been transmitted well into Western anthropological traditions, and continue to be misrepresented. As ever, colonial bias and Western worldviews impose narratives and ignore evidence, as is their wont. Particularly in the slippery areas of magic and magical practice, it is all too easy to draw seductive parallels, or generalise in ways that are unsupportable. What is true, however, is the way in which cultures all over the world associate witches with the ability to throw off their human forms and go into animal-likeness. The ability to move from one form to another is prevalent in myths and folklore around the world, from Scottish selkies (women who were also seals), to Chinese fox spirits, Huli jing, who could transform into beautiful women.[1] The confluences between the human self and the rest of the world are of perpetual interest, and the ways in which we share the world with animals, rely on them and live alongside them, is often explored through transformation.

Dotted among these folk tales there are always stories of witches, particularly women, whose relationship to the more-than-human world was strong enough to allow them to slip right into it, to disappear out of their human forms and into those of the animals they lived alongside. Often, these are narratives of harmless domestic mischief – for example, in Irish mythology, there are versions in which witches becomes hares to steal milk from their neighbours.[2] But there are other stories, too, of women who took on the devil's work when they shed their skins.

The example that most entrances me is that of Isobel Gowdie, a cottar's wife from the Highlands, who gave the most extraordinary account of her transformative abilities. Isobel Gowdie confessed to accusations of witchcraft in Auldearn, near Nairn, in 1662. Her trial took place over three days. We know very little of her life from records, and in line with the record-keeping practices of many Scottish courts at the time, Gowdie's confessions are recorded but the verdict of her trial is not. It is widely believed that Gowdie was executed, and indeed, after such an extraordinary confession as hers, it is not difficult to understand why.

Indeed, so remarkable were Gowdie's accounts of human–animal transformation that they were circulated hundreds of years after her trial. Robert Pitcairn collected Gowdie's confessions in 1833 in a multi-volume work, called *Ancient Criminal Trials in Scotland*. Pitcairn edited a large number of court transcripts from the seventeenth century, and anthologised them for readers. He was interested in the gory details of lurid accounts, in anything that would make a trial stand out, make it worthy of publication. *Ancient Criminal Trials* reads like a series of transcripts from a bizarre reality show, with only the most eyebrow-raising trials included. Isobel Gowdie's trial, and several other witch trials, are included as curiosities – come along and read the mad woman's words, perhaps shiver a little at the possibility of witches and their wicked appetites. The context of her trial is so important – her standing in the docks, speaking to an audience of rapt listeners. As a cottar's wife in a rural village, it is unlikely she usually received such attention when she spoke, or was granted such time and length at which to speak. Even in a situation of appalling stress and with the fear of death, there was perhaps something seductive about knowing that, once in your life, you were going to be listened to. At the point of trial, the chilling truth is that the longer Isobel Gowdie spoke, the longer she might live.

And so Gowdie didn't simply recount events as they happened, or answer the spurious charges brought against her. Her confessions are all-singing, a fully embroidered tapestry of personal repentance, information about the supernatural, and perhaps most surprising of all, spells, which appear in Pitcairn's collected edition as lineated verse. They sit couched within the more prosaic aspects of the confession, alongside stories that show attention to narrative, trope and symbolism. Gowdie clearly knew how to shape a story, and these were then recorded in court. Even without lineation, the poetic sections can be easily differentiated from the rest of Gowdie's confession by their rhythm and rhyme scheme.

There has been persistent interest in Gowdie's confessions across popular culture, and it has almost exclusively focused on the theme of transformation that emerges in the poetic sections of her confession. There is one particular instance of transformation that has captured the subsequent cultural imagination as regards witches and their power to slip into animal form. Gowdie relates, quite matter-of-factly, that she could turn herself into a hare, simply by repeating four lines of poetry.

Gowdie writes that she served the devil, and gladly, because of what he could grant her in terms of power. While in the service of the devil, she often changed forms, becoming a hare, a deer, a crow. She spoke of moving out of her human form and inhabiting, with total intimacy and ease, the more-than-human environment that surrounded her. Gowdie was far from the first witch to claim magical transformations, but the uniqueness of her statement is in its detail, and in the fact that she speaks her poem-spell to the court – she reveals the devil's secrets, or invents them on the spot. Either way, the resulting charms are beautiful and unsettling:

> *I shall go into a hare,*
> *With sorrow and sych and meickle care;*
> *And I shall go in the Devil's name,*
> *Ay while I come home again.*

Then, to change back, she would say:

> *Hare, hare, God send thee care.*
> *I am in a hare's likeness now,*
> *But I shall be in a woman's likeness even now.*

These charms might read like doggerel, but they are fascinating as fragments of poetry. Their first noticeable aspect is that they are in couplets: the rhyme at the end of the line links the first two and second two lines. Rhyme and metrical forms are common in representations of spells and charms – for example in the metrical Anglo-Saxon healing charms of the *Lacnunga* and *Bald's Leechbook*. The line 'with sorrow and sych [sighing] and meickle care' reappears throughout Gowdie's spell-poems, and here it makes the transformation sound effortful, and perhaps unpleasant to undertake. This is not, Gowdie's poem tells us, a light-hearted affair, but rather a genuine satanic pact, resulting in the alteration of the whole self. The poem asks us to imagine what it might actually feel like for Gowdie's whole body to change, to shrink down, to grow fur. This idea of painful effort, of un-ordinary striving toward supernatural transformation, is reflected in the crafted poetry of the spell – the artifice of poetry is linked to the supernatural effort of transformation, both elevated from everyday experience.

Emma Wilby, in her book *The Visions of Isobel Gowdie: Magic, Witchcraft and Dark Shamanism in Seventeenth-Century Scotland*, argues that the lucidity and detail of Gowdie's confessions suggest that the accused genuinely believed her experiences were true. Self-belief in the veracity of supernatural experience is certainly possible, and may have been sincere, an expression of mental illness, or a reaction to the lengthy isolation and sleep deprivation of her imprisonment. It is simply impossible to tell from any confession extracted during the witch trials what the prosecuted person believed, or to understand it as wholly reliable. What Wilby does do, however, is ask the questions that are so important to understanding stories about witches becoming animals – what did it mean, and why are there so many accounts of human–animal transformations in many global indigenous cultures?

Gowdie's confession is remarkable among witch-trial testimonies of the seventeenth century in its length, lucidity and detail. It is made all the more extraordinary by the fact that it was, apparently, not extracted under harsher forms of torture such as the scold's bridle. Instead, Gowdie is believed to have been subjected to other, more passive, forms of torture. She was kept in solitary confinement, harshly questioned, and denied sleep. It is not known, of course, what leading questions were asked of her, or how her stories were reintepreted and told back to her. It is enough to notice the extraordinary way she speaks. So enchanting is Gowdie's confession – it holds the reader utterly in thrall – that various people have taken it as evidence of Gowdie's involvement with shamanism, or a secret witch-cult.

Gowdie's spell-poems are infamous. Her confessions have inspired folk songs such as Maddy Prior's 'The Fabled Hare' (1993), as well as James MacMillan's work for symphonic orchestra, titled 'The Confessions of Isobel Gowdie' (1990). Maddy Prior's song draws its text directly from Gowdie's confession and builds on it, linking aspects of Gowdie's animal transformation to Celtic fertility myths. MacMillan's work debuted at the 1990 Proms, and he understands it as being a 'collective act of contrition', an apology to all of those witches cruelly tried and executed during the witch-panics in Scotland. Both pieces of music are interested in alteration: the MacMillan offers eerie and unsettling fragments of horns, Gregorian chant and bagpipe drone, which catch in the ear, like the sounds of a dream, before it reaches a terrifying crescendo. Maddy Prior's song, with its exposed vocal line and chord progressions, builds to a dramatic chase, then ebbs into reflection, making the listener giddy, then gently reorienting them. The idea of Gowdie's transformation haunts Scottish culture, mutating through expressions, but seeking always to assert the strangeness, and yet familiarity, of transformations into animal form.

Gowdie offers spell-poems for almost every purpose in her confessions – for curse-work, for celebrating the devil, for destroying crops and bringing illness. Among the most unsettling is her perversion of grace, the Christian prayer of thanks before eating, which is transformed into a spell:

> *We eat this meat in the Devil's name*
> *With sorrow and sych, and meikle shame*
> *We shall destroy hows and hold*
> *Both sheip and goat in till the fald*
> *Little good shall come to the fore*
> *Of all the reste of the little store*

The grace does not thank the devil, as a traditional grace would thank God. Rather, it promises destructive acts to be undertaken in the devil's name, reversing traditional imagery of plenty, good health and good fortune. These are transformed into promises to effect destruction, and to ruin the household of the person whose house they have broken into in order to conduct their feast. Gowdie understands the power of words to upend, to reverse, to invert the natural order and offer turmoil in its wake.

The spell-poems are not, perhaps, particularly good examples of poems, or of spells. They are repetitious, and reuse both rhymes and whole lines. But one reason that popular culture associates rhyming couplets in particular with occult utterance is that rhyme is a predominant feature of verses to be memorised. Rhyming couplets feature, for example, in the King James translation of the Lord's Prayer and many other ordinary texts. Children's rhymes are often in couplets, or a similarly everyday rhyming scheme. As we can see from Gowdie's confessions, the spell-poems carry the hallmarks of perverted prayers – addressing the devil where one would expect God, for example – and their rhyme scheme also relates back to devotional utterance. Whether rehearsed or composed on the spot, they show that Gowdie understood the power of rhyme and repetition to elevate spells from everyday speech.

Spells are not just words. They are words shaped to do things, designed and spoken to have an effect on the world. The spells that Gowdie speaks in her confessions are exceptionally powerful – they are supposed to be able to rearrange the very fabric of lived experience. A woman becomes a hare. A household falls to ruin. Her spells upend the natural order of the world and upset science. Despite being slight and repetitive, Gowdie's spell-poems are a form of ritual language, similar in function to prayers. Ritual language is a designation that allows us to grasp the power that those spells would have had, even in the setting of the courtroom. Ritual language is a particular language category, in that it describes language that makes things happen, causes changes to occur in the world. Theologian Wade T. Wheelock defines ritual language as 'language that is directly used in accomplishing the ends of the ritual operation'.[3] Ritual language removes us from everyday experience, indicates that we are in a place where the words have particular meaning and resonance beyond being merely instructive or descriptive. It makes us attend to both the meaning of the words and the form in which they are spoken. By using ritual language in her confession, Gowdie signals that she possesses these stylised and particular forms of knowledge, and can understand and repurpose dominant forms of ritual language, such as Christian liturgy. Gowdie is able to capture her audience's attention, to fulfil their worst fears about how witches transform, and what they are capable of.

What is most poignant about Gowdie's confessions is that they both contain and embody ritual language. As Gowdie confesses, her words form the basis of her judgment. As she speaks in the context of the courtroom, Gowdie condemns herself. She says that she 'repents', but nevertheless recounts in vivid and unembarrassed detail all manner of extraordinary crimes, lewd acts and events that give her power as she tells them. The shocking acts reveal her to be, in the eyes of the court, not simply a cottar's wife, but a woman capable of killing men, spoiling crops, stealing possessions and transgressing the normative boundaries of reputable womanhood and female behaviours. Gowdie undergoes another magical transformation – from an ordinary woman to a powerful scion of the devil, substantiating and reinforcing the state's attitudes toward heresy and female occult activity of the time. This is why the spell-poems in Gowdie's confession are so important and extraordinary. They stand apart from this broader ritual perform-ance as small, perfected moments of power. These spell-poems are controlled by Gowdie, and represent her personal secret knowledge, her status as separate from all others in the court-room. For this alone, they are shocking and revelatory.

Gowdie uses words to change into a hare, but she herself does not change, only her body. The language used in the spell is very particular and makes it clear that Gowdie undergoes transformations of shape, of bodily vessel, rather than of inherent self. Gowdie does not become a hare, but 'goes into' one – the form is later referred to as a 'likeness' – a simulacrum, rather than the thing itself. Throughout, the witch retains her selfhood, and merely takes on a hare's likeness, assumes its shape and thus can access its qualities of speed and size. After all, she must be able to conduct the devil's business on his behalf while in the shape of a hare, and must be able to speak the second charm and return to her human form. This kind of almost-changing, where a 'likeness' is put on rather like a costume, is a feature of human–animal transformations in a number of indigenous cultures.

Gowdie is unlikely to have actually turned into a hare, of course. This would disrupt everything we understand about the limitations of the human form. What is important, however, is that she chose to relate those spell-poems to a court, to talk about transformation, to discuss intimacy with the world in those resonant terms. It doesn't matter, in some ways, whether or not she believed that the transformation occurred, or whether she was speaking metaphorically, or simply telling stories to a courtroom. How could we ever tell? She is so long gone from us. But her confessions form part of a lineage, a

global network of diverse voices, all discussing human relationships to the more-than-human world in terms of transformation
and intimacy. So perhaps the magic that Gowdie is describing,
the spell-poems she is reciting, are an attempt to capture forms
of empathetic identification, intimate knowledge and transformative watching. These experiences are difficult to describe,
and perhaps magic is the truest means of talking about them.
Then, of course, the experiences were transformed again, into
a spectacular story to please a courtroom hungry for perversion
and scandal.

It is important, I think, to explore Gowdie's spell-poems as
means of communicating with, and having meaningful relationships with, the more-than-human world. It's even more
important to understand them as part of a network of attempts
to understand and describe human means of being with the
world. These various attempts are all perhaps a form of magic
– a form of knowledge that changes the way we pass through
and experience our environment. Whatever the intention
behind Gowdie's recitation of spell-poems in her confessions,
their effect has been significant. Gowdie's confessions are
extraordinary, and allow us to relate her experiences of the
natural world out toward others whose use of language and
imagery offers similar forms of extraordinary and intimate
connection.

Witches like Gowdie were believed to have the power to transform themselves into creatures, to do the devil's bidding,
to work mischief, to gain freedom from the constraints of

human bodily life. But their power was not limited to self-transformation. Witches throughout history have also been credited with the ability to transform others. This is, perhaps, the more frightening of the two options. Certainly, it is terrifying in the *Odyssey*, when the first witch in Greek literature, 'fair-tressed Circe, a dread goddess of human speech' turns Odysseus's men into pigs.[4] Circe uses drugs, and her magic wand, to effect this transformation – a potion to create the pigs, and a salve to eventually turn them back. Her intention was cannibal: why not eat these travelling men, who had washed ashore on her land? Only an evil woman, of course, would try to eat men, would turn them into pigs. Circe's is an act of bad magic designed to sate her appetite unnaturally. In other source material, Circe is less hungry, but no less wicked – in Ovid's *Metamorphosis* she transforms men into monsters and woodpeckers when they will not love her. She is cruel, quixotic and powerful, and is among the most influential Western witch characters, in terms of cultural constructions of what a witch does and how a witch acts.

Circe's pigs demonstrate the length of this tradition of witch-transformations. The seventh-century tale finds echoes in accounts given at the witch trials of medieval Europe, where witches less often ate their victims, but put them to other uses. In medieval Europe this power to transform others was also believed to be maleficum, or bad magic. Folklorist Éva Pócs, in her book *Between the Living and the Dead: A Perspective on Witches and Seers in the Early Modern Age,* discusses these transformations. She writes that especially in Eastern Europe, victims were often reported to have been turned into horses. These horses (among other farmyard animals) were then ridden, used as transportation to get to witches' Sabbats. The idea of witches 'riding or galloping on the alter ego of a transformed human' played a significant part in European witch-beliefs.[5] Freedom to ride out at night, away from domestic commitments, and attend satanic rituals full of sex and dancing – who wouldn't want a convenient human steed? Animal transformation fitted in perfectly to religious and civil unease with female freedoms, and so it was easily incorporated into larger narratives of condemnation during the witch trials. The transformed victims were part of a larger story told about witches – that they flew through the sky to their Sabbats, using all manner of transformed household items. Brooms, sieves that could be sailed in, and pets: in the hands of a witch, even the most quotidian items transformed into occult objects of power.

Primarily it was those in positions of power – ministers, judges and those questioning the witches – who asked leading questions and circulated these tales of flying witches, able to undertake demonic activities and ride indentured humans. Often, minor disputes or unexplained acts were not only investigated but elevated into accusations of particular acts of witchcraft. It was 'suggested' to the accused witches that they must have accepted magical help from the devil, and then ridden high in the pitch-black sky to meet him. These stories have fascinating origins: they trickle through society from the top down. This is because any intellectual worth his salt in sixteenth-century Europe was well-read when it came to witches, and he drew all his information from demonologies.

Demonologies were a particular literary genre that flourished between the fifteenth and seventeenth centuries. They resembled medical or scientific textbooks, in that they were 'written by learned physicians, jurists and theologians'.[6] Their purpose was to examine 'all aspects of the interactions alleged to take place between Satan and his demons', with a focus on interactions between Satan and 'women accused of being witches'.[7]

Demonologies were primarily theological and scientific texts, interested in rationalising the supernatural phenomenon of witchcraft, and were used as practical guides to help people identify and prosecute witches. Before he translated the Bible into English, and in the relatively early days of his precarious rule, King James wrote arguably the most influential demonology, his *Daemonologie*. James was obsessed with witches, and his *Daemonologie* was doubtless influenced by those that came before it. Latin treaties on witchcraft were being produced in Latin and European languages as early as the 1430s.

There are many common sentiments shared by diverse demonology texts, which are often derivative and draw on stock images, tropes and explanations for witchcraft, cementing these in popular imagination. One oft-repeated belief was that witches 'renounced, consciously and voluntarily, the Christian faith' and entered into a pact with the devil, often in a ceremony that made a mockery of the sacrament of baptism.[8] Satanic baptism was both criminal and heretical, as it not only placed the individual into eternal damnation, but also damaged the well-being and safety of the broader community, and thus the fabric of the godly state. It is no surprise that particularly in newly Protestant Scotland, and in a newly united kingdom, King James saw any threat to the Christian community as directly undermining the stability of his rule, and indeed his very personhood.

King James' *Daemonologie* is an extraordinary document: vivid, visceral and combining the scientific and the supernatural in a maelstrom of information. It contains lengthy descriptions of witches engaging in supernatural acts, from flying to transforming victims into animals, and it would have been taken up by ministers, judges and other well-read society members, eventually trickling down to, and influencing, the way witches were forced to confess, and what they were persuaded to say. James had a fondness for vivid detail – in the *Daemonologie,* two main forms of transport are agreed upon for witches:

one way is natural, which is natural riding, going or sayling, at what houre their Master comes and aduertises them. And this way may be easelie beleued: an other way is some-what more strange: and yet it is possible to be true: which is by being carryed by the force of the Spirite which is their conducter, either aboue the earth or aboue the Sea swiftlie, to the place where they are to meet.[9]

Daemonologie is a treatise fascinated by natural science, by what it is practically, rationally possible for bodies to do. But it is fascinated by what demons can do, too. It takes the devil as a natural fact of life, as concerning as the air, or fire, or taxes. And so what is natural, and what is possible, remain in enigmatic relationship with one another – everything, more or less, remains possible. What *Daemonologie* is not concerned with, however, is the inner lives or desires of the women and men it believes to be witches. There is no sense that magical transformations might be a way to talk about how the world is experienced. Instead, the only possible explanation for anything out of the ordinary is satanic intervention, and the only manifestation of magic is evil and outward-facing. Certainly witches, rather than being complex people with interiority, are servants of the devil and act only under his will, and must be both discovered and ruthlessly eliminated.

This understanding of witches profoundly limits how testimonies of occult experience were understood. Éva Pócs believes that these stories of riding horses, flying, or squeezing through tiny holes to attend Sabbats were in fact metaphorical ways of discussing the 'transfer between levels of existence', the nuances of which were lost when witchcraft became a crime.[10] Rather than really travelling through doorframes and keyholes, Pócs argues that these are ways of speaking that try to describe profound mental experiences, perhaps dreams, visions, trances or other phenomena. In line with books on witchcraft and demonology, however, the court understood them as literal events. For example, a court asked a Hungarian witch, Ilona Vörös, 'where and through what kind of holes could you pass?'[11] By flattening metaphorical speech, or refusing to entertain the idea that these might be personal psychic experiences rather than literal events, the courts can reinscribe the ideas contained within demonologies, rather than exploring what might be 'true'.

The courts strongly influenced witches' confessions and narratives, and forced them to confess to satanic pacts, transforming humans into animals, and all manner of other extraordinary acts. As Pócs argues, there was in fact a 'a varied and multi-layered relationship between experience and narration' that characterised witch confessions.[12] This layering between experience and narrative, the gap that this creates, means that actual understandings of magic, folklore and practices of psychic experience are often lost. Of course, this is supposition on Pócs' part, and we can never know for certain the actual lived experience behind the claims of turning into animals. But what is certain is that forms of witchcraft persecution have ensured that these experiences cannot now be explored directly. Instead, they have to be examined at a slant, by interpreting court documents and other little scraps of writing, or finding fetish-objects or small material traces of folk belief. Certainly, to cultivate these psychic experiences, an intense and studied relationship with the broad world seems to have been required.

This interest in changing, in shifting from one form to another, didn't disappear along with witch trials. It changed and altered with the times, but there is still as much interest in it as ever. Contemporary Western witchcraft is still extremely invested in altering appearances, both in terms of human–animal transformations but also in terms of altering our own human appearances. One common and fairly benign form of early introduction to witchcraft is the idea of the glamour. Anyone who saw the witch films of the 1990s will remember the scene in the 1996 American supernatural horror *The Craft*. In this film, the teenage coven experiments with glamours: spells to alter their appearances. At first, they are innocent changes – hair colour, eye colour. Later, as the film takes its darker turn, glamours are used to assume the identities of others, to trick people, to stage deaths and to falsify horrendous events. At one point, one of the characters tricks another into believing her fingers have turned to snakes. The animal world is used in *The Craft* mostly as a threatening motif, an image of suppressed inner wildness. The witches want to harness all the energy of nature, and then turn it to their own ends. Power-hungry, they have gone too far, embraced the darkness – the very distillation of cultural beliefs about witches, informed by the witch trials.

When I watched it, it was terrifying. Vivid and relevant, full of all the hallmarks of powerless early teenage years, boiling with an atmosphere that felt familiar. It felt as if it had been written for me, and it radically changed the way I understood the world, and specifically, the way I understood my place in the world as a young teenage girl. Fascinated by glamours, I longed to 'go into' another form – not a hare, nor a horse, but into a beautiful, enchanting woman. Or at least, that was the beginning, as I sat in front of the mirror, candles lit, repeating the chant and hoping that, at the very least, my eyes would shift from blue to green. The world would know me as powerful, I thought. That thinking shifted fairly suddenly. From glamorous witch to the desire to hide away. What I wanted was a glamour that would make me invisible. What I wanted was to fade from view, to keep myself safe.

A sense of it can still be conjured, the day I changed my mind about what sort of alteration my appearance needed. The day I thought about things differently, came into my body as an objectionable presence, as a trick, as something to attract negative attention. I was just a teenager when I learned how to hide, and it still feels like it. The memory rises easy, vivid.

There's a tightness across my chest, and I can smell smoke: I am thirteen years old, it is a sunny afternoon, and a group of men try to set fire to me on the top deck of a bus.

The bus takes me home. Every day, after school, I take two buses across the city. The first weaves its way through Morningside, with its big houses, high windows and driveways wide enough for Land Rovers. The second bus takes me back to Leith, where I live. The two sides of the city have different codes. On the first bus, the ostentatious maroon blazers and sounded consonants are ignored, or smiled at by elderly ladies remembering their schooldays. On the second bus, you stay quiet. Eyes down. Try not to look at anyone. Try, above all things, not to attract attention.

Attention comes, of course. Name-calling, spit, and a slap once, as I sat in the seat right behind the driver. School stuff, really, from other kids who quite rightly resent everything my nice private school uniform stands for. The ache in my throat and the feeling of panic always ebbs by the time I reach our front door, tucked safe up the little dirt track. Those things I can cope with, mostly.

But the afternoon of the fire is hot and bright. The bus smells like warm dust, the red leather seats are sticky to the touch. The men at the back aren't paying attention. They are older, perhaps closer to twenty, playing tinny rap songs on their phones. Too old to be interested, and I'm comforted by that for a while. We probably look invisible to them, my friend and I. But they get bored eventually. They notice us, the blazers like beacons. They notice us, and they don't like us at all and they wait until the last stop on the main road empties the top deck of anyone else before standing up, like so many lazy tigers, and stalking up the central aisle to stand in front of our seats.

Then, in the muggy afternoon quiet, it starts. They turn to us, *wee fucking wankers, who the fuck do we think we are*, and we look at our laps, hands folded like nuns, while the men crowd the bus seat. They can't get a rise with name-calling, so they pick up dirty copies of the *Metro* from where they've been dropped under the seat. They pat pockets, get out lighters. There's no hurry, we're a captive audience. They hold the papers up, close to us, and start to set them on fire.

They don't burn convincingly. Instead they evanesce into smoke, the edges curling in. It would be difficult to actually set fire to someone using a copy of the *Metro*, but they stand around us and try. In retrospect, the scene is almost funny: a group of men lobbing smoldering newspaper at us, two teenage sacrifices, in a parodic ritual. But it isn't quite funny, even now. And it wasn't then. The smoke was acrid, and horrible, and I don't remember how we left – we probably just stood up and rang the bell. What I remember most was patting down my hair and blazer afterwards, convinced that there was an ember on me somewhere, that I was about to catch fire. Most of all, I remember walking up the road to my parents' house, dawdling until my breath was slow, and my expression carefully blank. My parents, who had sent me to my school at enormous cost. Who were working so hard. I absolutely couldn't tell them.

Since there was nobody to tell, and since I was going to have to get on that bus twice a day, five days a week, for six years, I did the only thing that I could think of. I worked out how to cast a glamour. Or rather, I copied the one from *The Craft*, embellishing where I could. I was going to hide in plain sight. I was going to sit on the bus, every single day, and work out how to disappear.

It was the first spell I ever wrote. I didn't know anything about magic, and that much was evident – it followed no rules, invoked no deities, gave reference to no great networked consciousness. But it did ask for what it needed clearly, and it was born from a place of waking nightmares, of desperate helplessness.

It is not an unknown technique. Ornithologists talk about a similar process of blending in to their surroundings while birdwatching. Making the body still, holding cramped positions, refusing to scratch noses or stretch legs, like life models draped over trees, on marshy riverbanks, behind sand dunes. The poses are not supposed to be watched, however: they are supposed to deter watching. Patience and quiet waiting let humans disappear from birds' eyes, despite their alertness. Birds are primed to spot predators, and we are predators. To let the more-than-human world reveal itself to us, we must disguise ourselves in it, remove our need to dominate land by moving through it. This stillness is also a means of letting the brain become diffuse. Birds cannot hear thoughts, of course. But perhaps our facial muscles or eyes move when we are thinking – perhaps we sigh or let out a breath. Just like when I wanted to feed the little scruffy crow, I had to hold myself in a certain relation to him. The same was true on the bus. I was holding myself apart, making myself disappear into my surroundings.

So much is luck, so much is timing, so much is statistical likelihood: once you have been threatened with burning newspapers how likely is it to happen again? There were still days when other teenagers yelled things, when my heart felt like it would burst out of my chest with terror. There were still panic attacks and running home and moving to sit downstairs on the bus. But the spell gave me a layer of protection, gave me agency in the situation, a sense of power and control. I didn't transform into a hare, of course. My eyes remained blue, and my glamour never made me glamorous. But it is amazing how we are able to hide when we need to, how we can move out of sight with the right motivation. While hiding is rarely recommended, sometimes concealment feels necessary. And having a spell I could use let me get to and from school feeling safer, feeling like I might survive.

Disappearing is important. Whether it is into a hare, or into a forest, or into the diffuse spaces of the world where eyes don't catch. Disappearing is a means of going out of the world, into oneself. Withdrawal from what is outside, to allow time for what is inside. To be able to disappear is in itself a form of magic. It is a valuable thing, to disappear, not into nowhere, but into the rich and networked world, the rich and knowable more-than-human places, where we can talk to crows, and run like hares, and know the world, and, in that knowing, care for it.

A Spell for Eating Bitterness

This is a strange spell. It is a spell to purge yourself of bitterness, and emotions that relate to it. So much destruction comes from forms of bitterness we all experience: jealousy, regret, ill-wishes, anger that sours over time. Bitterness is corrosive, and this is a spell to move through it. To experience it – and give it a place in your life, as all emotions have – but then to move it on, out of yourself and away. It can take me a long time to forgive things – the bullies from my childhood among them. This spell helps.

It isn't, as many others are, drawn from established magical traditions. It comes from my interest in bitterness. Traditional medicines often use bitter foods to heal because it is believed that they stimulate the liver to produce bile. In Ayurvedic tradition, bitters are known to reduce sweet cravings and regulate blood sugar, and in Chinese medicine, bitters are cooling and remove inflammation or 'heat' from the body.[13] There are a vast number of bitter herbs, leaves and fruits available to us. Chicory, for example, is very bitter, and can be bought easily in supermarkets. Among the bitter herbs are: dandelion, burdock, gentian, artichoke, chamomile, milk thistle, motherwort, goldenseal and angelica. Eating them on their own might be somewhat unpleasant, but taken with other foods they can be delicious. Eating something bitter is a central point of this spell, and works on the principle that if you take something deliberately into your body, it will help with the corresponding feeling that you are having. Sympathetic magic for the emotions.

You will need:

- *Chicory or dandelion leaves, washed and ready to eat*
- *A glass of drinking water*
- *Your altar*
- *Pen and paper*

Prepare your altar, cast a circle, and invoke whatever deity in your pantheon deals with negative emotions. If you do not have specific deities, then I can suggest asking those spirits from the Middle Realm of the life-tree, which govern worldly goings-on, for help. Alternatively, you can simply ask for help, from the good energies of the world. Light incense, preferably something sweet-smelling, to act as a counterbalance to your mood. Sit and write everything you are bitter about, in as much detail as you can. Then, once it has been written, fold the paper and slip it underneath the leaves in their plate or bowl. Let it sit there for a minute, while you look at the leaves. If you cry, don't worry. It's probably helpful. Let yourself sit in the hopeless unfairness.

And then, roll up your sleeves and eat. Open up the paper, but don't read it again. Instead, slowly and deliberately, eat every leaf. As you do, imagine the bitterness spreading a great bright green light through your body, starting at your mouth. It is pushing out every ounce of awful, emotional bitterness, out through your fingers and toes, where it can dissipate in the circle you have cast, and leave harmlessly. Refrain from drinking water for as long as you can, even though you will want to. You are looking to contain as much as you can of the bitter taste in your mouth for as long as you can. Between leaves, say aloud what you are doing. You could say something like:

I am eating what is bright and bitter, to purge myself of what is bad and bitter. Deliberate and slow, I regain control, and I ask the spirits to move me forward.

Once you have eaten everything in the bowl, drink the water and let it wash the bitter taste away. End the spell gently: ask the deities for help with this bitterness, and ask them to help you be in control of your own fate. Thank them, and close with a declarative. I like *So it is done*, but *So mote it be* is also common. Tear the paper into little bits. Tidy up the altar and release the circle. You can burn the scraps of paper, or recycle them. The spell is done.

MAY

——————

Magic in the Land

I n a glen that held our tents like petals in a cupped palm, two stags began fighting. Far away at first, a bashing rumble that pealed off the sides of the hills in repeats. It was dusk, and we didn't look out from the tents. We knew they were stags, but the noise was so loud, so unpleasant, that we didn't want to investigate just in case they weren't, in case they were something worse. In the long twilight, anything could have been stirring. Six girls, no more than sixteen years old, small as pebbles in the broad wilds. We'd never been so far away from other humans, and none of us had ever heard stags do this before.

They made a low growling bark, and then came the sound of antlers, like billiard balls knocking together, hard. They came closer, the noise roaring in our ears like water. They came so close that one put a hoof on another girl's tent. She saw it, plunging against the canvas as if it might come through, like a diabolical summons, like an invitation to a wild dance. It didn't, of course. Our tents were old boy-scout tents, bright orange and perpetually damp-smelling, and doubtless hardy enough to withstand the apocalypse.

The stags were locked together for a long time. They fought over our campfire, knocking over everything we'd left outside. The sound made it feel as if the hills were an arena, the stags' fight a gladiatorial match. The throwing echo made it impossible to tell where it was coming from, made it impossible to understand distance, volume, threat. Stags are more aggressive in rut, so perhaps it's for the best we didn't put our heads out until the sound drew back, until they ran off, satisfied by whatever the outcome was. We watched them go, in opposite directions, like boys embarrassed to have been caught scrapping in the street.

I'm glad we didn't go out: we were a full day's walk away from any help, across the broad bottom of the glen and over the ridge. But I'm also sad we didn't properly witness their battle. There is another reality, another version of this story, where six rather meek Edinburgh girls throw off their clothes and dance naked alongside the warring stags, gloriously sky-clad, cheering on their virility and shows of dominance. It's a terrible story, of course, at once folk horror and soft pornography, trapped somewhere between the mystic and the titillating. The reality was all mud and thistles. But as they departed, swallowed again by the dusk and the heather, there was a sense that we had somehow, narrowly, missed some sort of epiphany. We had averted our eyes during the Eucharist. We had left the theatre just before the deus ex machina, and now there'd never be a chance to get that magic back.

The stag is a magical creature, the MVP of pagan bestiaries. He is the living embodiment of the Horned God, who is one half of the two main gods, or forces, in Wiccan religion and various branches of Neopaganism. The Horned God himself, though, is older than both these practices, his name given to depictions of horned deities that date as far back as the Neolithic. He is, in contemporary practice anyway, a wilderness god, god of forests and fucking, god of hunting, of living and dying, of the parts of us that are most animal. He is impulse, both good and bad. He is internally dualistic – summer and winter, light and dark. He is both nuanced and, often, presented as very masculine. This is an issue if, like me, you find the male–female binary among the least interesting or relevant binaries. For a queer person, the Horned God can feel alienating, his power both compelling and repelling. He doesn't feel like my opposite, and I do not feel drawn to his energies in quite the right way. I am attracted to them, and covetous of them. I see them in people of all genders, and I see them in myself. He is, of course, just an archetype. His body just describes a force, a collection of attributes that need not be specifically male, but the gendered presentation and its polarity with 'female' energies is difficult.

He is loud, and dangerous. He is horns locking and stags bellowing in an empty glen while frightened girls watch. But he is also the velvet over the antlers, the deep green spaces of woodland, the great cry of the first breath, the quiet sigh of the last. He is no more male than the night or the fire or death itself, which is to say, both entirely and not at all. He is what is constructed when certain threads of reality are drawn out from others, highlighted, and put together as an archetype that we can talk to. Almost all gods are. They are the faces we give to forces we cannot control. They are the embodiments of fertility, harvest, good fortune – and bad. They are a way of making patterns in a world that often opens its jaws and shows us chaos, a world that roars at us as we sit in our tents, wondering what is outside.

The patterns on the earth are beautiful, and plentiful. Fibonacci sequences, the incidental arrangement of twigs or leaves that our brains love to give meaning. We are pattern-spotting creatures, because knowledge of patterns – of weather, behaviour, animals, time – helps to keep us safe. There is, perhaps, a particular appeal in certain patterns, however – those we enjoy because they are beautiful, and because we are not quite sure if they are useful. Often these are man-made – the Cerne Abbas Giant, the beautiful chalk horse in Uffington, the Nazca Lines of Peru. Ancient designs of largely unknown purpose. Who doesn't love the disjunct between the way a hedge maze feels – claustrophobic, incomprehensible, sinister – and its beautiful, clean, geometric overview? That shifting perspective, that visual trick that feels analogous to hindsight, or the difference between tasting wine and being drunk – seems to offer us a pattern for our lives, too. Don't worry, mazes say, in their infinite complexity and infinite simplicity – you might be lost now, but you'll work it out later.

New patterns are enthralling. And when we find them – or think we've found them – we tell them to one another as stories. One of the greatest stories ever told about landscape patterns was the story of ley lines. Ley lines have, at various times, enchanted naturalists, scientists, archaeologists, and later witches, geomancers, and all related practitioners of the occult. They have been considered real and fake, factual and wishful, archaeological and mystical, sites of enormous power and proof of the existence of a lost Atlantean civilisation. And even now, more than a hundred years after their 'discovery', they have not gone away.

The year is 1921, and successful travelling salesman and

photographer Alfred Watkins is standing on a high ridge above Herefordshire, the county where he grew up. He is also holding a map, and comparing the landscape to its representation. Suddenly, something in his vision shifts, and the various ancient man-made objects in the landscape miraculously show themselves to be aligned. He apprehends, or so he believes, that the ancient landmarks are all, in fact, connected. For him, this is no chance reading of the map, cannot simply be explained as a trick of perspective, looking down from a high point. Instead, the landscape becomes mystical in nature, releases a 'flood of ancestral memory', as he calls it, revealing the network of paths that had been hidden beneath the roads and fields of modern Britain. Further to this, he believed that many later structures were also built along ley lines – from Roman roads to defensive keeps, from churches to market squares. He wrote that 'all forms of sighting points became objects of interest, superstition, and genuine veneration', but did not at any point suggest this veneration was any more than a response to their persistence through time.[1]

Watkins never stated that the lines had mystical powers, simply that Neolithic man must have walked in straight lines between significant points, and that these tracks had persisted throughout history, and had only recently been lost. He encouraged keen amateurs to seek them out for themselves – to discover all of the lost lines of Britain. And they did, en masse. The 'Old Straight Trackers' – named after Watkins' book – were keen amateurs, and hunting ley lines was a lovely day out, particularly for motorists. Gradually, though, ley lines garnered sufficient academic interest to be widely decried as false, in particular by O. G. S. Crawford, whose view was that Watkins's work was pseudo-archaeological, and who refused to advertise his book in his literary and artistic magazine *Antiquity*.[2]

While Watkins's theory of ley lines is minimally evidenced archaeologically, it is not in itself particularly outrageous. It did catch the public interest, though: the idea of mysterious lines stitched across the landscape, of rediscovering ancient pathways, did stimulate a huge amount of interest from countercultural and fringe groups.[3] Interest in ley lines waned in the 1940s, and by 1948 the Old Straight Track club had closed due to lack of interest.

When ley lines became cool again, it was in the 1960s, as part of the explosion of small press magazines that explored consciousness-expanding hallucinogenic drug use and unidentified flying objects, and saw an explosion in occult theories, experiments and practice. The French writer and broadcaster Aimé Michel wrote a book in 1958 that proposed a relationship between ley lines and UFO sightings.[4] Michel believed that UFO sightings across France on any given day could be plotted on straight lines, and this was eagerly picked up on by scholars of such mysteries. Similarly, Buck Nelson, an American farmer who claimed he had been visited by UFOs, believed he'd seen the spacecraft picking up magnetic energy from the Earth. In England, at around the same time, a woman called Mary Long was working. Long made claims that she was in touch with UFOs, who visited her in her sleep around once a week. She passed these messages to a man called Tony Webb, who had an interest in discovering the occult truth behind the earth's patterns. She would communicate the messages these so-called Space People gave her, and Tony would use them to help map the sacred landscape. The Space People 'gave her information on scientific matters' – which she claimed were mostly related to the location of energy fields on the Earth. They worked, Long reported, from their ship, which didn't usually sit over England – and if it did it remained very high up: it was, instead, 'usually over the Pacific'.[5] These energy fields seemed to correlate in part with ley lines. In light of this interest in the relationship between extraterrestrial life and leys, the Ley Hunters Club was founded in 1962.

The fashion for contact with extraterrestrial beings occurred simultaneously with a broadening occult interest in ancient patterns and holy sites in landscape more generally. Following this trend, the Institute of Geomantic Research was founded by Nigel Pennick in Cambridgeshire in 1975 to investigate 'landscape geometry; ley lines . . . feng-shui and allied sciences; sacred geometry; cosmological town-planning; earth energies and dowsing; astro-archaeology; ancient stones and the modelling of the landscape'.[6] The cover of the leaflet showed two figures, made of space and stars, dancing. The entire organisation covered diverse subjects, including a guide to 'seismia', a means of 'charging the body with Earth waves', written by Frederick Adams, who founded a faerie religion in the 1960s, after an ecstatic vision.[7] This involves lying down on ley lines, touching your toes to the heels of someone else, who remains standing, so that you are forming an 'L' shape on the earth. The best person to do the lying-down is apparently a woman, because female bodies, Adams contends, have been shaped by 'childlike evolution . . . ever closer to the profile of the double sine curve'.[8] Adams suggests here that the relationship between land and body is pre-cultural, primal, evolutionary and biologically inflected, and this is somewhat worrying.[9] If women are better at conducting earth energy, then how quickly does this understanding of the ways in which bodies interact with landscape split bodies into 'bad' and 'good' bodies, and dictate which bodies should have access to landscape? Perhaps unsurprisingly, 'seismia' quickly devolves into fairly basic sex magic. In order to 'charge' and bless an area, Adams advises that 'after approaching one another while increasing the polar exchange through the dialectic of Land, [the practitioners] raise the current into the resounding throb of Love's Great Rite'.[10]

Unsurprisingly, the logical next step after magnifying the energies of the land through the body is sex on a ley line. The jokes write themselves. Sex magic is an important part of magical practice, just as sex is an important part of life – but here, Adams is borrowing ideas from High Magical ritual and transposing them in a pseudo-scientific setting, jumbled up amongst neologism and to no clear purpose. Sex outside is great, but I'm not sure how convincing sex on a ley line might be, while considering the 'naïve evolution' of one's body. However Adams, although he doesn't give credit to his sources, is clearly borrowing Wiccan and Neopagan tropes of male and female polarities combining to give power. The Horned God is hovering, here, antlers out.

Adams is interested in how being in patterns in landscape might change us – what we might feel when we stand on leys, specifically, but this can easily be expanded out. How do we feel when we go to ancient monuments generally? When we stand in churches, or at Glastonbury Tor, or inside Maeshowe? Does knowledge that these places are ancient or holy inflect how we feel, or does the land itself inform how holy or otherwise these places are? *The Journal* was preoccupied with these important questions, and in trying to develop responses to the landscape that honoured its perceived spirituality.

Among the most interesting of attempts to recapture the perceived spirituality of a site is the story of Wandlebury Hill Fort. People have lived at Wandlebury for over two thousand years. It was an Iron Age hill fort, and then a Roman encampment. In 1685, an estate was established there for the breeding of Arabian racehorses. The stable blocks, which date from 1729, still exist. It is a strange place, absolutely brimming with earthworks, and everything is of such a different age that it is difficult to get a clear understanding of what should go where. The same is also true of its myths and legends – Wandlebury has everything one could wish for. There's an undefeatable knight whom one can challenge with a battle cry, who rises up out of the mists. In the 1900s, children were told it was the burial place of Gog and Magog, the gods who give the hills their name.[11] Others said that Gogmagog was a giant, and that he had been thrown into the sea by a Roman.[12] There was supposed to be a golden chariot buried beneath Wandlebury, and it belonged, of course, to Helen of Troy – or King Arthur, nobody was exactly certain. Regardless of their veracity, the myths did reinforce certain beliefs about the Iron Age fort and its subsequent settlement: that it had been a site of military power, and of pagan worship, and that, perhaps, it held the remains of past civilisations.

Truth and legend and all the in-between states overlap at a site like Wandlebury, like a kind of mythical palimpsest. Walking around it alone on a muddy spring afternoon, I want everything to be true, absolutely everything. And I desire a matching experience. Even dense holly, fences, steps and signs can't quell the feeling that this place is old and wild. The way patches of crocus and lesser celandine push up through the damp woodland, softening the curve down into the Iron Age ditches, makes me think of velvet curtains over windows. I want to peel everything back and see the bones of the fort beneath the turf, even though the fort is *made* of earth, is constituted by the flowers and the soil. When I walk around the rings of the fort, the soil is full of scraps of stone, white against the dark earth. I want them to be bone. Of course I do. Wandlebury makes you hungry to shove both hands in the soil and wrench the past out, hold it, put it in your pocket and take it home. Everyone feels that Wandlebury belongs a little to them, I think. It exercises a strange reach.

As I explore, I draw from my pockets sea-glass from North Berwick, to gift to whatever energy dwells there, to buy my way in, however ineptly, to go back into its past. The air feels busy, a brush of bodies in the light spring afternoon, the tread of feet that aren't mine, the noise from the road dulled and the green smells heightened. In a place so vastly fertile to the imagination, nothing else seems possible except this – sinking into its layered history like a stone through mud. It feels easy to do magic here. I gather slips of yew, and blackthorn twigs, and chestnut casings, so old and weathered that they look like minute leather coracles. Lean against trees, put my nose into the soil, poke my shoes delicately into the ground ivy, crane my ears for birds. Everything is charged. Here, I can work magic, speak into the land and listen to it. My whole body is filled with it. A very real feeling, more physical than spiritual, one that crawls from hair to feet. The feeling is similar to standing against a bass speaker in a club, perhaps, or those experiments you do as children where you hold hands to conduct a current between two wires. There is a sense that you are in sync with something. bigger than you, that a tune is running through you, and that you could open your mouth and sing it.

Alongside the chariots and the knights there is another story of Wandlebury – that of the Gogmagog giant, existing not just in imagination, but as a hillside carving. He was said to have sat on the hill and watched over the fort, rather like the other early figures carved into chalky hillsides across England. There were rumours of his existence from local farmers and elderly residents in the 1950s, and in 1955 T. C. Lethbridge, an archaeologist at the University of Cambridge, set out to find him.

The giant was an intriguing mystery. A pattern in the landscape, lost, but now to be revealed – a sacred guardian, watching over the hill fort, gone but not forgotten – what could be more romantic? The difficulty lay in discovering him. There was grass over the whole of the hillside, and it was difficult to work out where, underneath, there might be patches of human disturbance. Lethbridge sought to find the now grassed-over pattern using metal probes. He dug these into the hillside to find soft areas of chalk among the hard, presuming the softness to be evidence of human activity. What he revealed was extraordinary: not a single, primitive line-figure. Oh no. Lethbridge found a whole pantheon of Celtic gods hiding under the grass. There was a sun-god. Then he found a triple-breasted female figure on horseback, and the horses pulled a chariot. There was even a sword-bearing warrior. The whole tableau was vast, complex and indisputably in the Celtic style. He celebrated it as a lost link, a new foundation for the understanding of Celtic art and worship. He suggested that the 'female figure Magog, at the centre of the pantheon, was the moon goddess and her horse, the surrounding figures being later additions, as the predominant religion shifted from matriarchal to patriarchal'.[13]

Lethbridge really believed that he had found a world-changing artefact, and published papers on it. Other people derided the discovery as nonsense. He had fabricated it, they said, mistakenly believed soft patches of chalk caused by water erosion and other natural forces were man-made. He had invented the pantheon for glory. He was too interested in the occult, and had let go of his rigorous training. Amid the outcry, Lethbridge was let go from Cambridge University. His discovery is now widely regarded to have been if not a hoax, then very poorly evidenced. But rather like ley lines, the idea of lost figures in the landscape clung on in popular consciousness. It was seductive, and corroborated the idea that Wandlebury was a deeply sacred place, with a host of guardian figures watching over it. The Institute for Geomantic Research, alongside others, called Lethbridge's dismissal a conspiracy, and worked to preserve the unearthed figures. However, without local support, the grass gradually covered them again, and now they can no longer be seen. The pattern has been lost to time.

It matters, of course, whether the hill fort figures were real or not. Or rather, whether they were ancient, or whether Lethbridge had simply invented them. You can imagine him up on the hill, dip-testing chalk for softness, so excited, so feverishly hopeful that he was revealing the protective gods of the hill fort. That he was unveiling a new pattern in the land-scape, one that might give information on the stars during Neolithic times, or something equally enchanting. The truth of the hill fort figures matters, because archaeology matters, because the truth of patterns matters. But there is also an extent to which the whole incident encapsulates beautifully the way we look for hidden things in landscape. The way we seek pictures and paths to tell us where we are, to show us what is special. We would like to look at the old gods, even if we aren't sure what we'd do with them. Lethbridge was drawn to Wandlebury, as so many others have been, and he found some-thing special there, which intoxicated him. What this feeling was is, of course, notoriously difficult to define.

As one letter in the *Journal of Geomantic Research* noted, 'One cannot statistically analyse the special "vibrations" one feels on entering certain places, or the sense of peace one finds in walking along some telluric pattern that only you, at a specific time and place, can feel.'[14] This subjectivity of response to landscape is one of the key reasons people wished to believe in ley lines. If they are real, and can be explained using a mixture of spiritual analysis and scientific research, then the subjective feelings that we get can be analysed, explained, shared. Like so many explorations into the unseen or unknown forces of landscape, the question that underpins ley lines really is one of power and magic. What is magic? Is it a subjective feeling? Is it a scientific fact? Why does landscape make us feel things? The desire for a definable truth is overwhelming.

Another reason that people were so keen to find explan-ations for the power of ley lines, for their force, was for the future of the planet. If leys were a source of clean, endlessly renewable power, then they might be able to replace coal or nuclear power. One theory in the 1960s was that lost Atlantean civilisations had used standing stones as giant acupuncture needles to release the earth's power, and if this could only be recovered as a technique, modern man could do the same. Adherents believed that 'in the old days of Atlantis, one could have power without ecological disaster, and these wonders were provided freely by a learned elite'.[15] There was a sense among the burgeoning hippy movement that if this lost knowledge could only be recaptured, then the planet's woes could be undone, and a utopian, clean-energy civilisation could take root once more.

For as long as people have dwelt in landscape, there have been theories as to why different places make us feel different things. There are probably as many theories as there are sacred sites, or ancient ruins, and so many of them are based around the idea that people being in a place for a long time, and affecting the landscape – shaping it, giving it meaning through continued habitual use – changes the feeling of that place. This is often the case in old houses, and is also widely discussed when we think about archaeological sites that show continuous habitation or worship in places that are now uninhabited or disused. Most of these theories are interested, at their most basic, in how time works, in whether or not places can remember the things and people connected with them.

People flock in their hundreds to see the café in Edinburgh where J. K. Rowling is said to have written much of the Harry Potter series. The claim is, as far as I am aware, unsubstantiated, but it doesn't stop people buying coffees, sitting in the knackered armchairs and – what? That is the question. What actually happens when you're in the place? The room where it happened? From J. K. Rowling's café to Pendle, the site of the infamous Pendle witch trials, people want to be in the place where an event happened, to feel the atmosphere, to perhaps access some of the residual magic of the place. One thinks of the Blue Plaques scheme by English Heritage, which marks the residences, birth-places and sites of interest of notable figures in history. What is gained, really, from knowing that someone lived at a particular address? They are no longer looking out of the window, waiting to wave to us, tossing wisdom down into the streets below.

Where we are is very important. And there are countless theories to explain why. One of the most engaging was put forward by Mircea Eliade, a Romanian historian of religion. I find it incredibly useful, because it explains not only how our minds might understand sacred places, but also how magic and persistent beliefs about place and power might best be under-stood, and, by extension, worked with. Eliade put forward a theory of 'reactualisation' of sacred space and time. He argued that sacred spaces are different from other spaces because they have a different function, and are out of the everyday flow of things. Churches, for example, tend to be preserved longer than their surrounding secular buildings. They are not subject to the same intensive use, and have a different 'feeling' – their function is not related to survival, unlike homes, hospitals, shops, or other mundane structures. Eliade believed that the same was true of sacred time. Sacred time existed outside the usual linear narrative of time and wasn't subject to the same rules of memory and distance. He argued that while you couldn't access time that has passed – you can't step in the same river twice – it remained possible to access ritual time. One of the most common touchstones here might be the Eucharist. Every time the Eucharist is taken it both commemorates the Last Supper and actually allows participants in the sacred act to re-enter the sacred time of the Eucharist. They are not just relating symbolically to the Last Supper – rather they are encountering the same space and time as Christ himself occupied. Eliade writes that the faithful participant 'must feel himself contemporary with these trans-historical events for, in repeating it, the theophanic time becomes present to him'.[16]

The sacred past opens up like a doorway, and lets us walk through. Our physical surroundings might not change, but through some ritual of access, our temporal surroundings might. The Eucharist is a neat example, because the ritual is still conducted. When we stand among standing stones, we do not know the rituals, the words or dances, the libations or sacrifices, that once opened up a holy space there. We can attempt to re-enact, or bring our own rituals to historic places, places where we feel special, but we can never exactly recreate anything. Therefore we are a little stuck – halfway between now and then, between the sacred and the ordinary. There is nothing quite as strange, to the practitioner, as being halfway into a ritual and suddenly realising what you are doing. Eliade's reactualisation theory explains why we are drawn to sites, but also why this can be a problem for magic – it is difficult to pass into sacred time without the right tools, and these tools are not easily given.

Getting stuck halfway is a strange feeling. It makes everything feel real and unreal, renders a landscape momentarily uncanny.

MAY

One midsummer, in Wigtown, in the Scottish Borders, I had coaxed a dear friend into a high field with me, overlooking the shore. It was a pleasant evening, and we had wine and bread, and had walked through pretty scenery. She didn't practice magic, so the ritual wasn't anything elaborate, but I wanted to give thanks to the ground, and I wanted to ask for good fortune for the coming year. It wouldn't do, really, I thought, to ignore midsummer altogether, but I was a bit self-conscious. I had selected the field because it was high up, with a good view, and because the hedgerows were full of hawthorn and rowan. It felt old, and green, and good. We shooed the cows away from the fence, and I made a makeshift altar, and dug a little hole in the ground for libations. Halfway through pouring the wine into the dip in the wet earth of the green field, in fairly solemn thanksgiving, the cows came back. Gently inquisitive, they wanted part of our picnic, to see what two strange grubby humans might be doing in their field at dusk. It was hilarious, and a little frightening, the way they closed round, a little curious circle. My friend noticed it first, and pointed it out, in hushed tones. There is nothing sillier than realising you're pouring perfectly decent wine into a hole, surrounded by indifferent cattle. The magic doesn't feel magic anymore. And that's fine – but that is the jarring feeling that comes, I think, with trying to move into past places without fully knowing the way.

Eliade's reactualised time certainly goes a long way to explaining how it is we come to feel connected to ancient places, holy rites or sacred historic moments. But it is a theory that, like so many theories of place magic and place-understanding, focuses on the beautiful places: the ancient ones, the holy ones, those revered throughout time and somehow maintained. For every beautiful stone circle, however, there will be a huge number of historic locations in landscapes that are simply forgotten, lying beneath development, or so far under fields that they don't show up in aerial surveys.

There is a danger to fetishising ancient landscape sites, particularly ones that are very beautiful, or very popular, or filled with the sort of layers of myth that accrete around Wandlebury. To be clear, I do not mean those sites sacred to, for example, indigenous peoples of other cultures, for whom the land is a vital sacred being. In spaces that have been colonised, and access to sacred land vastly restricted, and lands desecrated by industry, access and preservation must be fought for. Contemporary examples of this, such as the ongoing attempts to place an oil pipe across hallowed burial ground in the Standing Rock Indian Reservation, Dakota, demonstrate that sacred relationships with the land are all too often under threat. So when I think about fetishising ancient landscape sites, it is within a British framework, and references most particularly those places built by groups for purposes we cannot know, and which do not directly relate to current religious or magical practices.

For one thing, there is a false equation between something being ancient and it having particular potency. Very quickly, arguments about who relates to ancient sites and in what way become a tangle of nationalist sentiment. And additionally, the more popular these sites become, the more heavily protected they have to be. There are often fences, viewing paths that move around stones, all manner of barriers and protective layers that stand between the viewer and the monument. For good reason, of course, but there is often a feeling among those who live locally that they should be allowed access, that these barriers are for tourists who don't know how to treat the site. This is difficult – all damage is cumulative, and it doesn't matter if those wandering feet belong to tourists or locals, those seeking to worship or just to sightsee – erosion doesn't differentiate. Even annual, limited access to important sites – such as the modern Glastonbury Stone Circle during the solstice – happens for religious reasons, and so privileges one type of visitor above others. These locations are so complicated, from their owner-ship to their preservation. They are vitally important places in landscape, held in tension, in pattern, in contention. Sometimes, they can seem overwhelming.

I am not suggesting a turning-away from these sites. Nor would I say that fences or numbers or erosion could diminish whatever heavy layers of accreted history and feeling gather there. But for every Stonehenge there are hundreds of other sites that lie undiscovered, under car parks or deep under the soil. Our sense of them is different, because we don't know that they are there. Lots of people sense things at Stonehenge – far fewer detect ley lines running under supermarket car parks, or see flashes of the ancient past while standing on the tarmac at airports. There are modern sites where special things occur, and continue to occur, of course. Sacralising in real time. There are obvious examples: new church buildings, new burial plots, the places where tragedies or miracles have occurred. Anywhere people lay flowers, pay attention. There are patterns in cities, too: paths that connect hospitals to crematoria, walks through urban parks, the strange electric hum of main shopping streets. There are sacred paths in urban spaces, and sacred spaces. But they look different. They're very rarely fenced off.

They seldom appeal to many people, or to more than one group of people. But they're there.

You can almost certainly find them. Your places might be different from anyone else's, but they will become more sacred with every visit that you make. And they don't have to be man-made structures, although they can be. Ironically, in cities we are drawn to the 'natural' – or at least the green – spaces: parks, rivers, edge-lands. In rural environments, we are often drawn to historic man-made structures, both standing and ruined. We like, perhaps, that which is potent because it is comparatively rare, or rare by contrast. In my city, where history is elaborately piled on top of itself, there are so many magical places. Trying to turn away from those that are most obvious, I am a pilgrim to the less pretty ones. There is a disused lane near my parents' house, which garden gates back onto on one side. On the other side, the crematorium and graveyard, its neat rows of grey stone. The lane is full of dog shit. It is overgrown, plants greedy to cover the track, but it's brimming with nothing beautiful, choked with great purple bushes of Californian lilac, a hardy shrub beloved of municipal flowerbeds. It overspills with nettles. Every year the lane loses more stones from its pebbled surface, slides closer back to mud. It always smells of something bad. There are often broken bottles, sometimes condoms, needles, the works. I have woken up men asleep down that lane before, or interrupted them pissing. And yet, I am firm in my conviction that it is a holy place. That things move there. That the crematorium spills out into the lane, and that the air between the quick and the dead is ever so slightly thin. The back gardens are lush, full of roses and tended beds. Their gates represent the end of civilisation. On the other side, the crematorium wall, high stone, represents the edge of death. The lane threads between the two, and all of wild living is in it, contained, dredged around the edges of bushes, shoved in between nettles, thriving on dogs and neglect. When I need to talk into the air, I go there, to say spells or ask questions. I leave things there as offerings, and take nettles for spells from there. Sometimes, I hold my breath at one end, and try to make it down without breathing out, like swimming a length in a pool underwater. I've managed it in three breaths, never fewer, not even walking my fastest. What a charm for protection that is: I've been doing it since I was fifteen, and it feels so good, to pit my breath against the length of those walls. It is a charm that says: I give this place my effort, and in return I'd like it to listen to me. The lane remains quiet, but the feeling it gives me is the same feeling as at Wandlebury – that I could open my mouth and sing it out through my throat.

Ultimately, the power of sacred sites is reciprocal. The place has power, but equally, so does our attention towards it. They are linked, and form their own pattern. Our patterns are the places we go, criss-crossing around our city, our country, the world. Sometimes I imagine mine, the paths most and least worn, the paths traversed in buses, in taxis, in other people's cars. On trains.

When I leave Wandlebury, it begins to rain. The bus back to Cambridge leaves from the other side of the motorway, which must be crossed on foot in a mad dash. The bus pulls up by the lay-by, churning up loose mud that I have to run through to flag it down. I arrive back filthy, buzzing, glad to be once more among the legible order of shops and buildings and people. Getting off the bus, I think of the words of Sabrina Scott, who writes so compellingly about magic. She insists that 'magic can happen in a forest with cedar and pinecones and candles, or it can happen in a shoebox apartment downtown with some toilet paper and floss'.[17] This does not always feel true. So often, we are told that to make magic we must access power and that this power lives in sacred sites, ancient places, where holy mysteries were performed. This is not true – or it is not only true. And indeed, in this period of changing climate and increasing ecological fragility, as Scott says, it is more important than ever not simply to 'seek solace and beauty everywhere but where we live . . . forget the beauty of being rooted as it is in the flux of process, of transformation, of noticing'.[18] Rather than feeling compelled to visit ancient places, it is an excellent habit to simply find places near you that you are drawn toward. The practice of magic is not the same as the practice of place-worship, although the two are connected. Magic can happen in prison cells, it can take place in portaloos, it doesn't require ancient stones or extraordinary labyrinths to walk around. A witch's practice is related to knowledge of self, and of surroundings, of objects. And these can happen anywhere.

The gods and goddesses of Wicca and Neopagan religions are placed in woodlands, on mountains and in rivers. We see them as part of the landscape – the best parts, the most beautiful ones. Of course we do. Just as the Horned God is both masculinity and can also be understood alternatively as a cipher for particular kinds of forces, so rivers and mountains and woods are symbols for growth, for life, for fecund plenty. But gods and goddesses didn't simply move out when cities were built, because the same forces still operate in cities, still need faces to speak for them, symbols for us to interpret them. The sluggish city rivers; the particular high-rise office block that the sun glances off at 4 p.m. every day in winter; the lane choked with nettles. The gods live there, too, if they live anywhere. Scott is right – if we remove our need for grandeur, we can find patterns in the places we live and experience that are just as magical, that can help us feel rooted, give us a sense of place. It is wonderful to experience stags rutting at dusk in a glen: it is also an experience given to comparatively few. The Horned God is also present in the screech of foxes, the raucous antics of seagulls, the seething of football crowds on a full train. We work with what is near us, with what we have. We gather up what is good and work with it. Witches make magic wherever they are.

Ecological Spells

We are, as I said to a friend recently, creatures of territory. Not in the sense of conquering and owning land, but in the sense of having a stretch of the world that feels familiar, that we feel at home in. This might be our home, the streets around us, our whole city. It may even be regions of the world that we've lived in a long time. There may be several places that are our territory, spread out across the world. But each territory will be defined, have limits.

In the wake of our ongoing environmental crises, there's been a great deal of talk of sending healing magic across the world. I believe that such enormous exertion of energy is possible, but extremely difficult, even in large groups.

Once per lunar cycle, I think, is a good frequency for ecological magic. I've found my ecological magic is strongest when it becomes coupled with a definite activity: whether it's litter picking or neatening my scrap of shared garden. Our intentions become stronger the more vividly and actively they are embodied. Action and magic, paired together, make for a strong direction of energy. Ecological magic need not take place outside, and if it does it need not be somewhere conventionally beautiful or remote. The edge of a car park at dusk, when you can see the sun setting, is just as magical as the top of a mountain, in terms of effective witchcraft. Magic does not require a special setting, but will thrive wherever it is done with intention.

This is an equipment-light spell, designed to be taken around with you and used wherever you can. Try practising it in the same place, at different times of day, or on the same time at different points in the lunar cycle.

You will need:

- *A length of rope or ribbon into which you can tie nine knots*
- *Nine things you have found in the place you are in, or the local area. They don't have to be plants – scraps of paper bags, stones, moss, gaudy bits of rubbish. If they are plants, you do not have to know what they are, but it is helpful if you can identify the plants you take them from and forage responsibly.*
- *A little vial or bottle of water that you can carry in your pocket, ideally from a stream or body of water in your area. If not, then tap water, left in a bowl overnight under moonlight.*

Stand in the place you have chosen. You want to subtly call a circle of protection around yourself, and let yourself be still within it. Quietly attend to everything you can see: birds, traffic, the sun. Ask yourself how many things you can see, perhaps list them, and let yourself feel open to them. I sometimes incline my head to any trees and plants, but if you're out in public, use your judgement as to what is appropriate.

Think about the place in its best state: what might be there? Would the trees be flourishing? Would the birds be flocking here? Would there be no rubbish? Try to envisage this as clearly as you can. Repeat something in your mind, or out loud if you're alone. I like something along the lines of *A flourishing place, this place, a flourishing green place.* As this is running through your head, take the rope and lay out each of the nine things you have gathered. Tie nine knots, laying the objects out beside the knots, or tying them in if you can. Name them for each knot, and add them in to a refrain, because these little scraps of place are what will help give you the power for your spell – these are the objects you've drawn into relation with you, to help you work in this space. So for example, if you had a beech leaf, you would tie it into the first knot and say, *The first knot takes the beech tree, and helps the place to flourish.* You can do this with litter, too: *The bright red of the litter helps this place to flourish.* As you do this, imagine your energy and the energy of the objects pouring into the rope. After you've tied the nine knots, touch the vial of water against each one, and feel the energy from the knots filling up the water in the bottle. Pause, and imagine the place once more transformed, and then say something to seal the spell – I use *So it is done* for this spell, but find something you feel comfortable with. Pour the charged water onto the ground, and your spell is complete. If you can then help the place practically, too, then this is advised. Repeat as often as you can, and this will serve you well.

JUNE

Midsummer and Light Magic

June appears, bright and strange, out of May's gentleness. And I am on a train, again, stitching the miles towards the south of England. To the South Downs, which roll past the window, all soft undulation and a particular deep green that signals summer's height. The train passes the Long Man of Wilmington, a huge chalk figure who stands imposing on the hillside, from where he 'flings out a perpetual challenge'.[1] I fall instantly in love with him. He is standing proud on the hillside, and he seems to hold in his hands two long poles. I'm not sure what they are, but when I ask a local witch, whose coven worships there, she laughs. They aren't poles, of course, but the sides of a doorway. He is holding open the door between the worlds, this ancient figure, and inviting us to come through. Midsummer is the time of the looking glass, of things not being quite as they appear. Commonly, we speak of Hallowe'en as a time when the veils between our world and all other worlds is thin. Midsummer, with its excess of light, might feel less eerie, but don't be fooled. The world is made strange enough at midsummer, and it is a time of mischief, even in the long grey twilight.

We arrive in Lewes for a wedding. It is in the grounds of a stately home, in its high-walled garden, and it feels like the setting for a play. Everyone at the wedding is exceptionally tall and beautiful, and they look like flowers transformed into people. It is so hot that I burn during the ceremony. My new shoes make my feet bleed so quickly that I lose them in a herbaceous border, and let the cool, deep grass look after me. In a garden full of subdued silks and tasteful cottons, I alone am wearing sequins. I feel like one of the rude mechanicals from *A Midsummer Night's Dream*, accidentally enchanted and let loose at Titania's party, wreaking havoc.[2] There are hay bales that prick deliciously through clothes when sat on, and great bowls of food. Everything is summer-hued, and tastes of growing. Even the speeches are like spells in their fulsome wishes: health, love and happiness. The wedding is hale and healthy and whole, and I want to sneak away to work different kinds of magic, want to shake off this particular type of enchantment.

Two friends and I, hesitant, unmarried ourselves, pass through the low wooden gate into the medieval churchyard appended to the great house. We read the names of the departed aloud, bring them into the champagne-scented air. It feels strange, the churchyard. A little less than restful, on this long day. There is something unmistakeably merry about it, as if we revellers have stumbled across an even older, stranger celebration. Although I had absolutely no idea at the time, we were correct. St Peter's Church in Firle is actually very ancient. There is evidence that a Druid sanctuary existed on the site before it was a Christian site of worship. Indeed, it has also been suggested that the site was a Roman temple before it was a Saxon chapel. The church itself is sweet, with its low, welcoming twelfth-century arched doorway and its cool, quiet interior, complete with the plain altar that, on the day we see it, is decorated with beautiful wildflowers. It is a holy place in the old sense, a comfortable place for God and for many gods, and well-protected, both by the high wall of the garden, and the hills of the South Downs, which gather gloriously round it, as if cradling it from the weather.

The churchyard is lovely to look at, and we spend a while admiring the yew hedge at the entrance, the sinking graves. And then we see it. Tucked at an angle to the entrance to the church itself: a wishing tree. Short and beautiful, it is alive with ribbons. There are more ribbons than there is tree, and the faint warm breeze lifts them as if in greeting. Champagne-tipsy, we are utterly dazzled. We are warm drunk witnesses, buzzing like insects. We stand near the wishing tree, then sit near it. We don't have anything to tie to it, but I manage a thread from my dress. One more wish on its laden branches, on the most magical day of the year. From over the high wall, the sounds of the wedding drift quietly. We're able to sit and talk, keeping company with the dead and the dancing wishes. We three are deeply, strangely connected: myself, my best friend, and an old friend whom I lived upstairs from in my first week of university, come suddenly back into contact. Neither of them know each other, and yet, here we are, enfolded in the warm walls of an ancient place, touched by the magic of a wishing tree.

We are three unlikely witches, in our delicate dresses and impractical shoes. It seems that nobody else has sought out the churchyard, and we are undisturbed until a drunk, apologetic barrister with a soft face summons us for supper. Until then, we are cloistered and alone. There is always a sense, at midsummer, that I will find people to do magic with. That the magic makes itself felt, through me, because it overflows the body and spills into the world. That it summons people. Having a formal midsummer witchcraft practice is wonderful, and vital for me some years. But it's a popular date for parties and weddings, and I love both. And I have found, every year, that people similarly moved will make themselves known in time to perform some magic, some intimacy, some strange bonding or weird adventure. Neither of these women are witches, formally. Neither has an individual practice. And yet, what we did as we sat by the wishing tree was magic. The confidences we told one another, the secrets and hopes and the way we held each other so gently in our attention, was magic of the highest kind. We wished so much good for each other, and it has been borne out. When we walked back through the gate for supper, we had all changed, been given glimpses of different worlds by one another. The dead, I felt, wished us well on our way. The wishing tree glinted in the slow sunset. We walked across the grass like witches do: in concert with everything.

We return to the throng, to the party, but the magic is everywhere. You will have noticed this, if you've been lucky enough to spend midsummer in any grassy place. There is a sort of inescapable light-strangeness that animates everything. At the solstice, the magic that fills up the world spills over, charms every corner. When evening falls, the dew lies heavy. In our sheltered garden, medieval walls drank heat into their worn red brick. At night, they released it slowly, fed the espaliered fruit trees with warmth all evening. Fed us. We pressed our bodies up against the walls in the growing shadows. We huddled in a corner, three women, drinking mint tea and eating celebration cake, telling stories of how we got here, and what might happen next. We were beautiful, then, clever and sad and untouchable and excited. We watched the happy couple dance, and wished them a lifetime of dancing, and knew ourselves that we would not swap, either.

The bride had asked me jokingly, when I reached her in the shaking-hands line, if I would frolic naked on the lawn, it being midsummer. I can't remember what I said, something sweet and light, I've no doubt. There are lots of questions like that, as a witch, but midsummer especially garners interest. Even people who aren't interested in magic know vaguely about midsummer. Shakespeare has helped with this, of course. From the enchantments that wreak havoc with the lives of foolish mortals in *A Midsummer Night's Dream*, until all are brought back together, unharmed, to the chaos of *Twelfth Night*, in which pompous Malvolio is brought low by cross-gartered crossed wires, and his strange behaviour is likened to 'very midsummer madness'. Midsummer has long been said to be a time when the fairies ride abroad, leaving their homes to visit with mortals. It is a night when even those not usually possessed of magic might find themselves enchanted, confused or perhaps filled with power. It is a day of excess, of celebration, of letting body and brain feel the extraordinary power of all those hours of daylight. The sun seems to stand still and there is always a threat, on the periphery of consciousness, that it might never set again.

Midsummer is an ancient pagan celebration around the world. It is a fairly easy festival to mark, because although the exact day may not be known, the lengthening evenings toward the end of June make it clear something extraordinary is happening. The longest and shortest days have been marked in Europe for as long as evidence allows us to detect. Stonehenge is a solstitial henge, which means that when it was built it would have captured the midsummer light at sunrise, as well as the sun setting on the winter solstice. The shifting of the earth's axis means that the first rays of the sun still enter the henge through the Heel Stone on midsummer, but not as entirely centred as they perhaps once would. The trilithon (the structure of two upright stones and a doorway, like a lintel) relating to the winter solstice is no longer there, but would once have held the rays of the setting sun.

The solstice celebrations have, of course, changed as culture and religion have shifted. From the fourth century, 24 June became the fixed Christian feast of St John's Eve, the night before St John's Day, which celebrates the birth of John the Baptist. John foretold of Christ's coming and was born, in the liturgical calendar, six months before Christ. So it was simple to place his birth feast on an already-celebrated day, six months before Christmas, which sits alongside (and was intended to replace) celebrations of the winter solstice. Although traces of the pagan roots of many Christian celebrations are still visible, the feast of St John, especially in Europe, is amongst the most visibly pagan. It seems that early Christians did not wish to, or were unable to, suppress the fires and joyful chaos of solstice celebrations.

This is why much of what we know about historic pagan midsummer celebrations in Britain is intermingled with these formalised Christian celebrations. Across medieval and Tudor Europe – and almost certainly much earlier – fire played an enormous role in these celebrations. Traditionally, bonfires were lit and jumped through to ward off evil for the coming year. In Spain, especially in Galicia, the celebration of San Xoán still incorporates huge bonfires. In Ireland, they celebrated midsummer up until the nineteenth century by kindling the grimly named 'bone-fires': these literally contained the old bones of livestock saved from the previous year, and our word 'bonfire' comes from them. The fires were lit by the eldest person present, and then the youngest ones would toss in bones. These bones might have been thrown as an echo of earlier animal sacrifice, or simply as a hygienic way of getting rid of waste that was slow to decay. Equally, the popping of the marrow inside them, and the sparks they would have sent up, may have been perceived as lucky.

The 'bone-fires', or *Tine Cnámh* in Irish, were part of a network of traditions across Europe that created charms or undertook ritual actions on Midsummer Day or St John's Night in order to protect against harm, specifically harm from the supernatural realm of fairy, a particular danger at this time of year. In the 1870s, writing under a pseudonym, Reverend John O'Hanlon documented the folk customs of Ireland, and wrote that 'bone-setters' or traditional healers (we might also call them hedge-witches) would gather 'herbs and plants . . . and used [them] for charms and cures' on St John's Night. This is because herbs gathered on a holy day were thought to be 'specially impregnated by some mysterious fairy influence'.[3]

The same was true of the fires themselves: they were considered strong protective magic. The embers of the fire, or sections of burnt sod, would be brought home and sewn into women's garments in order to ward against what O'Hanlon rather romantically calls 'fairy plots and abductions'.[4] There are of course theories that the fires offered cleansing, a purging of potentially illness-bearing objects, so that their protective function was intensely practical as well as magical. These folk customs were repressed by religious reformers during the 1700s, who felt that even those aspects of the traditions that allegedly related to St John were too pagan to continue. Despite their repression, however, these customs did continue all over Europe in various guises. In Denmark, the midsummer bonfires were used to ward off witches in a festival that echoed the German Walpurgisnacht.[5] Effigies of witches were burned to guard against evil for the coming year. James Frazer writes about the Germanic tradition of the midsummer wheel, where a huge cartwheel was wrapped in straw and set alight: if 'the fiery wheel was successfully conveyed to the bank of the river and extinguished in the water', then the wine harvest would be an excellent one that year.[6] This wheel is a powerful symbol of renewal, and of the turnings of the year. Like all of the ritual fires, it also served to 'stoke the sun' to keep it strong and delay the slide into winter for as long as possible. It must also have been an extraordinary sight: a great cartwheel tearing through the gathering darkness.

In Britain, fires were often visually and magically enhanced with herbs: mugwort thrown into a fire gives a purplish hue on burning, and the purple flames were jumped through. These gaudy flames contained the very essence of the summer goddess.[7] If you have ever thrown driftwood onto a beach fire (or studied chemistry at school), you'll know what this is like. When certain chemical compounds burn they produce beautiful colours, and these most certainly add a sense of ceremony and strange magic to proceedings.

Mugwort is a fascinating herb, used across many cultures. It is an excellent insect repellent, and often used in brewing and wine-making. In Eastern medicine, there is a practice known as jiŭ, or moxibustion, which consists of burning a cone of ground mugwort leaves, or moxa, near the body's meridian points. It is commonly used in contemporary medicine to turn breech babies. Mugwort is considered to be a 'hot' herb and, as such, is burned on or near the body to stimulate the circulation. Its use was discussed in medical treatises as early as 500 BC by Bian Que, a quasi-legendary Chinese physician. Mugwort was also used in smudging (cleansing) rituals by Native American people in what is now California, and as an aid to conception in seventeenth-century medicine.[8] It has a long and illustrious history as a magical, medicinal and culinary herb. But what is it, exactly?

Mugwort is, in fact, fairly common. It is part of a huge family of herbs, the genus *Artemisia*. Greek legend states that plants of the *Artemisia* genus were the first to be used as medicine. They're sacred – as their Latin name suggests – to Artemis, the ancient Greek goddess of wildness and the hunt. Plants of the *Artemisia* genus grow all over the world, in temperate areas. Tarragon (*artemisia dracunculus*) belongs to the family, and its soft, slightly bitter leaves are regularly used in cooking, most traditionally with chicken. You might also know *artemisia absinthium* by its common name: wormwood. Wormwood is the traditional active ingredient in absinthe, which was widely banned a century ago for being hallucinogenic and causing immoral behaviour. It is wreathed in Parisian romance, an agent of chaos and dissolution among artists. It is said that the poet Paul Verlaine shot his lover, Arthur Rimbaud, when he was drunk on absinthe, and that absinthe was at play the night Vincent van Gogh cut off his own ear. And Mary Shelley, sitting in a villa near Lake Geneva, is rumoured to have written *Frankenstein* after a vision created in part by opium and absinthe. Absinthe plays the role of mischievous, dark force in legends and rumours of addiction, ill-fated romance and dissolute behaviour.

Wormwood certainly can cause hallucinations, although the active compound in wormwood (thujone) is found in absinthe in such small amounts these days that were you to drink enough to activate it, you would almost certainly die of alcohol poisoning first. That does not alter its mystique however, and absinthe, with its beautiful delicate green colour, special spoons and glasses, still feels like a very particular and magical drink. It is the Fairy Queen of drinks: its power reputedly great, its nature quixotic, depending in whose hands it is in. I love absinthe. The fussiness of its preparation, and its effect on me, which is far more likely to be its high proof than anything else. Nevertheless, it produces a particularly lovely sort of drunkenness: one in which the world and everyone in it is temporarily beautiful, glamorous, positively shining with possibility.

Wormwood is not the only *Artemisia* with mind-altering properties, it is just the most famous. Mugwort itself is a mild psychotropic.[9] Alongside all of its noble, healing and helping properties, this may well be the primary reason for burning it on fires and using it in midsummer drinks. Mugwort can be dried and smoked, or made into a sweet-tasting tea and taken to evoke strange, lucid dreams, and a mild waking high, apparently similar to that of marijuana. It is unsurprising that hours of dancing, revelry and magic were encouraged by a plant that allowed the user to get a glimpse, however small, into the fairy realm, or to have prophetic dreams.

Alongside mugwort, midsummer was traditionally a time to gather many other herbs and medicinal plants. This is for the practical reason that many herbs are at their best around midsummer, before they have bolted or become bitter through flowering. The herbs gathered are as numerous and diverse as the bonfire celebrations, but they commonly included St John's Wort, a pretty yellow-flowering plant with green leaves that look 'perforated' under the light, due to small dark spots on them. This plant is still taken as a herbal supplement believed to help manage mild depression, and is also believed to help with the treatment of alcoholism. It is named St John's Wort because of the tradition of gathering it at the feast of St John, and hanging it over windows, door lintels and crosses, to drive off unwanted and malign influences. The genus name of the plant, *hypericum,* is believed to derive from the Greek 'hyper' (above) and 'eikon' (picture), from the habit of hanging the herb above altars or holy pictures during midsummer. Indeed, it is so powerful that it was used in oil form to treat wounds during the crusades, and one medieval name for it was Fugia Daemonium or 'ghost herb' because of its supposed ability to keep the user from harm.[10]

There are many beliefs about how herbs and sacred plants effect their magic, and many of them do not involve ingesting the plant at all. One Swiss charm to guard against lightning, fire and storms (all of which were believed to be caused by supernatural influence) was a cross made of goat's beard and masterwort, blessed by a priest on St John's Day.[11] In Wales, St John's Eve was considered one of the three major *y tair ysbrydnos* or 'spirit nights' of the year. Among the other herbs that were gathered by Welsh healers – including fennel and rue – the most interesting was bracken. The tiny spores on the underside of the bracken, which become large enough to see with the naked eye around midsummer, were said to render the user invisible, but only if they were picked at the same second that the saint had been born.[12] There are a vast number of varieties of fern, and many contain psychoactive compounds, so perhaps these were also used in rituals and magics that altered revellers' perception of the world, and allowed them to feel the magic of midsummer more viscerally.

Culturally, then, midsummer has been a huge celebration, involving drinking and dancing, strange herbs and strong charms against evil. But it is in Sweden where midsummer, or Midsommar, has been most continually celebrated. Despite Sweden becoming a Christian country, many of its festivals have remained more pagan than elsewhere: indeed, they are among one of the few countries to have continuously maintained the Midsommar name, never calling it St John's Eve. The Swedes put up maypoles, which in Britain are erected, as the name suggests, for earlier celebrations, and sing traditional songs, including one that describes in beautiful and immaculate detail the biology of a 'Små grodorna', or small frog. There are drinking songs, and predictions about love and marriage. It is, of course, a popular time for weddings, but for unmarried women there are special rituals: on their way home, girls can find seven different species of flowers, from seven different fields, and take them home to place under their pillows. It is said that that night, their future husbands will appear to them in a dream. Love-divination games are a common part of folk celebrations generally – and particularly at midsummer.

Midsummer is a time of the unruly, of too much light, of dancing until your body drops. The world must keep its eyes open longer than is comfortable. Fairies appear from hedgerows, men are rendered invisible by their pocketfuls of bracken, witches must be burned and future husbands stride into dreams. What is missing from the revelry, it seems, is the presence of dread. Witchcraft, magic and misrule are all so often feared, or accompanied by legends of being stolen away, or the devil appearing. Midsummer is almost entirely free of those associations. Even though the fairies are said to walk abroad, their harm is of a more benign sort. The year is full of labour, and remains so, even though the vast majority of us now do not work the land in Britain. But midsummer is a day of relaxing, of seeing the world in its verdant glory, drinking and eating and dancing, for as long as the light holds.

As a teenager, I was taken to Orkney as part of a series of trips the school ran that involved orienteering, character building, and cramming teenagers into youth hostels around rural Scotland. The trip to Orkney was among the least physically demanding, and so we were a strange, ramshackle bunch, all weak ankles and complicated physical shortcomings. I wanted to go to Orkney, certainly, but I also didn't want to climb seven hills in ten days. We went at midsummer, accompanied by two men from the physics department, one of whom was a born-again Christian and faith healer. Alongside the puffins and cliff-tops, the strange kitchen at the youth hostel and the nesting skuas that the boys disturbed, the thing I best remember is the light. I had never seen light like it: it simply didn't get dark. It wasn't that it was bright light, the way it was in Iceland at the solstice. Rather, it was a lightly shadowed dusk that made way very briefly for stars, before the blues and pinks of dawn broke through again. It's the feeling that I remember more than anything else, an extraordinary energy.

I've always lived through light, northerly people often do – dreading the dark of winter and exulting in the longer, brighter hours of summer, when so much more can be done. But before I went to Orkney, I had never considered the light to be part of my magical practice. Still young, I had mostly been undertaking highly formalised spells, stolen from Willow in *Buffy* and the terrifying girls in *The Craft*, and any other little bits of information that I could glean. There was lots of velvet, and complicated invocations to goddesses whose importance I didn't understand. It wasn't particularly nature-based, as a practice, mostly because I had no examples to follow. But the light in Orkney changed that forever. It was as if my body had been filled with lightning, or the static energy you feel before a storm. I couldn't sleep, and spent the ten days in a strange daze, a potent mixture of sleep deprivation and intense socialising. I felt very alive, in a way that is hard to describe, and things kept happening.

The things that happened were all small, seem too minor now to mention in much detail. The most important was the overwhelming urge to gather things. All children pick up rocks, bits of grass, beachcombings, I think, if given the chance. But I'd stopped as a teen, because it was no longer sweet and my mum got tired of finding homes for buckets full of beach gravel. I could never identify anything, and what on earth was I going to do with all these bits of rock? When I got to Orkney, the urge came back. It was as if I thought I could gather up the light in my arms, store it in these rocks like batteries, and take them home with me. Rocks and shells and little strands of dried-out seaweed. Now, I am a much more sensible forager, and know what I want. But I do have tendencies. Keep your eye out for tansy, they're in flower. I wonder if the nettles are still soft enough at the tips for a second pick? Because I am disorganised, my pockets, and my handbag, are always filled with seedpods, with leaves and little berries and things I'm going to dry and use, until I forget them. That tendency comes partly from developing my witchcraft, from simply needing a wider range of materials, but also, a great deal of it is to do with wishing to hold on to things as they currently appear.

If witchcraft makes you more aware of the seasons, and how to live on the earth as it is, then it also makes you aware of how lovely but temporal, and fleeting, things are. And so you see the perfect light on a spray of rosehips, or the small crow feather dropped on the path, and suddenly you imagine you could preserve them, use them, incorporate them. The gathering impulse is such that it is half-based on future use, and half-based on wanting to hang on to that autumn, that summer, that day, that picnic, that half-hour in good company and warm, kind air. And it bloomed on Orkney, because I wanted to open my jaws and swallow the sun until it burst back out of my body. I wanted to eat light, to cram it into stones and skin and seawater and bring it back on the ferry. Briefly, I had a boyfriend who I'd met on the Orkney trip. When we kissed on the coach, teenaged and addled with performativity, I thought about sunlight. I thought about the way it might live inside us, and leak out of our mouths when we were making out.

I thought of sunlight at the wedding, too. The little bag I took is full of sequins: they fell off my dress like golden drops of light all through the evening. But it's full of other things too: borrowings from that high-walled garden. Leaves from an apple tree; a stalk of straw from the bales we sat on. Two poppy petals, crushed and rolled out of all recognition. Grass heads from the churchyard, dried and brittle. A little sprig of yew: I've been collecting yew from sites around Britain, and the Firle Yew sits among them. Wedding favours all, little remnants of midsummer's strange magic. I do not use them for spells, in this instance, although they have all the potency and power of any plants gathered on a sacred day. Instead they are just mementoes, little tangible reminders of power. They are the sods sewn into the hem of a dress or the nine herbs gathered to hang above lintels. It some ways, it is the ritual gathering that is important, the marking the occasion with something you can hold in your hand, something that can emit light for the rest of the year, can stoke you against the sun's retreat into winter.

It can be useful for me to line my home with ritual objects, things that, to the naked eye, have little to recommend them to notice. It's as if the house is lined with codes, little messages from days of noticing. Philosopher Thomas Berry writes that 'here, in its human mode, the universe reflects on and celebrates itself in a unique mode of conscious self-awareness.'[13] Berry suggests that the universe organises itself to look through us: that when we notice, it is the universe noticing itself, and being pleased. Although Berry is speaking from a Catholic perspective, the same sentiment is applicable to witchcraft. Magic, and the magic of our rituals, gatherings, attentions, is a means for the universe to work through us, for the great work of the world to be done through our practice. Whether you believe it is the universe, able to access itself through us, or the great deities working their will through us, or the ineffable energies manifesting in our work, our noticing has unmistakeable value. And on Midsummer Day, we are called to notice the light, in all its huge, vast gladness. We are asked to salute the sun, to let it know we are glad. We are asked to hold in our hands the things it has helped to make – including each other – and we are asked to dance.

A Spell to Store Up Light

I t can be easy to forget, in summer's height, that light will wane and winter come. All good things must come to an end, all cycles continue. We bottle up harvested fruit, we dry out fruit and veg and herbs, we make preparation for the winter months. The same should also be true of the emotions that, for many (although not all) of us, seem easier to access during summer. Sunshine is difficult to bottle and preserve in and of itself – and so are feelings. Both are fleeting, and once they are gone, it is difficult to conjure their complex presences again. But we can try. One sunny summer's afternoon, when the weather is good, sit in an outdoor space – a park is good for this. If you have barriers to accessing green spaces, then you can quite happily do this by a window, preferably an open one.

Take three or four candles – preferably pillar candles, nice fat ones. The colour doesn't much matter, and white or neutral tend to be the cheapest, but you can equally use sunshine colours for this – reds or yellows, or the bright green of summer grass, perhaps. Write out a list of things you like about yourself – good qualities, achievements, compliments you've received. Try to write ten. If you are struggling, this isn't because there aren't ten good things about you: it is difficult and exposing to do an exercise like this, especially if you are someone who struggles with low self-esteem. That is perfectly reasonable.

You can, instead, note down adjectives that describe the summer's day: is it hot? Is the breeze gentle? Is the air heavy and scented with flowers? Is the grass warm and comfortable? Try to be as specific as possible.

Once you have your words, you're going to carve them into the candles, dividing them between the three. You don't have to use any sort of blade or knife for this – wax can be lightly marked with a toothpick, and this still counts as carving. I find that the pointed end of a metal nail file or a skewer works well, but do be careful if you're dealing with sharps. As you carve each word, really pay attention to it – if they are words describing the sort of day, then imagine the full beauty and complexity of the day flooding into the words as you carve them. I find that repeating the words aloud is also helpful, focusing on each one as you carve it. If carving feels difficult, you can instead pop them into glass holders and write on those with permanent marker. Leave them in the sunshine for as long as possible – a couple of hours at least, and then your candles will be nicely charged with all of the good things of these light summer months.

After you've done this, wrap the candles in tissue or wax paper to keep them safe from bumps and scratches. Store them away until the winter months, to use when you have need of them. A simple ritual to use them is to light your altar, and then repeat the carved words back to yourself as the candle burns, and try to recall as many summery details of that day as you can. This is the closest magic gets, I think, to catching sunshine in a jar.

JULY

Fortune Telling and Divination

I am frightened all the time. I am frightened medically; frightened enough and sufficiently acutely that I have an official diagnosis. But even when my anxiety is controllable, allows me to do the usual things, like leave the house and be sociable, I still worry all the time. The part of my brain invested in keeping me alive (and my family, and my friends, and anyone even tangentially in my ken), works overtime. It is a good creature, fierce and constant, and it thinks that its vigilance can forewarn of, and thus dispel, disaster.

As a child, I used to have premonitions that bad things would happen to my family. Not if I was there, of course: only if they left home without me. My dad, who took me entirely seriously, used to consult the I Ching for me before they went out. He would be dressed for the evening-world, smart shirt and black jeans, and he'd smell of fancy aftershave. Mum would be upstairs, getting ready, and I'd tell him – it was always him I told – that I was worried. He would get the book down, then, and the box that he kept the coins in. And he would let me throw the coins across the living room carpet: three points for heads, two for tails. Yin or yang? Changing or unchanging? Broken or unbroken? I would add them up and he would draw the lines. We'd throw them six times, build the hexagram, and then I would be allowed to help him look them up in the book

I was not allowed to just play with, and then read the judgements. On the very few occasions that it was actually a negative result, he'd cancel the babysitter and stay at home. My father takes oracles seriously. Oracles, signs, sudden gut instincts. He respects them deeply, and never made me feel silly for having concerns. I try now, in my adult life, not to give every tremor credence, every flutter of fear a face, but I also try to respect them. What is happening, when I feel fear over something? And how can I help shape it in a way that does not cripple me, but helps inform the way I live my life?

Premonitions are not the same as simply worrying, but it has taken me half my life to tell the difference between premonitions and more nebulous, anxious feelings of things that could potentially go wrong. Throughout my life, certain things have helped to steady me, and one of them is fortune telling. Let me scry mirrors, read palms, turn cards, let me look at tea leaves and throw coins on the worn wool carpets of my childhood home: everything has meaning, everything is important, let us all see what comes to us when we look for signs in the great wide world.

The I Ching occupies a strange place in British superstition. It is a guide to right action that seems to be used by people who otherwise do not consult oracles, or look to know their fortunes. It has an air of respectability and longevity, perhaps deriving from its use as a guide to rulers, that sets it apart from other oracular systems. The I Ching is an ancient Chinese system of divination and world ordering, the origins of which are shrouded in myth, but which seems to have emerged during the Zhou dynasty (1046–256 BC). It has been in continuous use as an oracle and guide to rulers ever since, and has been, since the 1950s, among the most immediately recognised Chinese texts in Britain.[1] Emperor Wen wrote descriptions or 'judgements' for the hexagrams (blocks of broken and unbroken lines) that are cast by the user of the I Ching. Wen lived from 1112–1050 BC, and is known as an epic hero in China – the name 'Wen' means 'the civilising King', and among his achievements he also wrote a great portion of the I Ching. The hexagrams are most commonly cast by throwing three coins. This is a form of cleromancy, or generating random numbers to divine intent. Cleromancy is an ancient way to ascertain divine will, and is described in the Old Testament as 'casting lots'. In the Book of Jonah, for example, Jonah is found to be responsible for the terrible storm when the sailors cast lots to find out who caused it, and this is why he is thrown overboard.

The I Ching has gone through many translations and interpretations, in China and in the West, and it is also an important foundational text in Daoism. There is, of course, a degree of uprootedness, of vacuum, in using it apart from its situation within Chinese history and culture. It is a borrowed text among many borrowed texts that inform our fortunes and try to hint to us what might happen. Magical texts and tools are almost always palimpsests, their origins obscure, or not quite as ancient and holy as people would like to make out. We want to read the landscape, yes, but we also like fortunes we can hold in our hands. We like things we can throw: yarrow roots, coins, runes. These things take on different qualities of seriousness depending on the culture that we find ourselves in, and the extent to which we live in unsettled times.

As a child, I learned to write my name in runes at some sort of open day at the museum. They didn't have all the letters –

no exact transliteration. But it was the first time I'd seen my name made strange to me since before I could read, and it felt like magic. That something could both be and not be 'me' was very strange. I kept asking if that was really my name; if Vikings could speak it and know it; if it meant the same thing; what sort of person might call me by my name spelled out in runes. Just turning my name into symbols I didn't recognise made me feel that deep, strange, un-familiarising feeling that is so often the preserve of waking up in a new room and not knowing precisely where you are for a split second. The moment before apprehension, where you are a stranger to everything, including yourself.

Walking us out onto a thin ledge where we become unfamiliar to ourselves is one of magic's most cunning tricks. Witchcraft is interested in that moment where the familiar is made strange – for that is where interesting things begin to happen, preconceptions come loose, and things might change or be revealed. And it is in this space where we encounter pictures or letters that we both know and do not know – such as the hexagrams of the I Ching – that divination so often takes place. What I wanted to know, I realised even then, was how runes worked, what they sounded like, how I could manipulate them into telling me what I would really have been called, if I had been a Viking.

Runes are the constituent letters of the runic alphabet, which is the writing system developed to write down a range of Germanic languages before the adoption of the Latin alphabet to do so. But they are not only a historic set of characters forming various runic alphabets. They have, like many 'dead' alphabets, been latterly incorporated into occult practices. Partly, this is because runes were credited with degrees of magical power even during the time of their use, but as with many such alphabets, it is also for their feeling of ancientness and the air of mystery surrounding their origins and precise meaning. Always, before I knew that they were used in divination, I loved the idea of runes – they came, I had noticed, in boxes, inscribed on stones or round slices of wood, and so seemed to me like a much better version of Scrabble tiles. Magical letter tiles that, I was told, could tell your future. The word 'rune' means 'secret' or 'whisper' – the idea of runes, then, has always been associated in contemporary understanding with certain types of forbidden or uncommon knowledge. Even Odin, the Norse myths tell us, did not know the secrets of the runes. He watched from Asgard as the Norns carved runes into Yggdrasil, the life-tree, to shape fate. Odin wanted to know what the runes meant, to understand how fate operated. He had already given up one eye to gain other sacred knowledge, but he hungered for this, too. And to discover the meaning of the runes, he had to suffer. Because the rune-forms dwelt at the bottom of the life-tree, deep down in the Well of Urd, Odin had to work out how to get a closer look at them. And this he did. He hung down from the lowest branches of the tree, pierced by a spear to steady him there, and gazed down from the height into the watery depths. He told the other gods not to help him; to bring him no food nor water; to do nothing to ease his suffering. He hung between life and death, between existence and non-existence, sacrificing himself in the name of knowledge. And when his ordeal was over, he had learned not just the runes but what they meant, and how to work magic from them. It is said that subsequently, he learned how to speak healing words, and the symbols of 'might and power'.

Odin's quest for knowledge involved sacrifice. He sacrificed himself – the highest thing one can sacrifice is a god – to himself, in order to receive knowledge.

In the Poetic Edda (a collection of anonymous Old Norse poetry that details many Norse myths of the gods), the section on Odin's rune-quest ends with the lines: 'Thus Odin graved ere the world began / Then he rose from the deep, and came again.'[2] This quest for knowledge has parallels with depictions of Christ's crucifixion, descent into hell, and subsequent rising, having redeemed the world from sin. There are a number of close parallels: both are the sons of a father-god; both seek worldly knowledge; both are pierced by a spear; during the crucifixion, Jesus is denied food or drink by the guards, whereas Odin asks his fellow gods to deny him these comforts. Indeed, this quest makes Odin one of what we might call the 'dying and rising' gods. Odin's quest is not to bear the sins of the world away: it is a desire for knowledge; it is for insight into the mysteries of writing, reading and being in the world, and how these are all connected, that Odin is willing to sacrifice himself. The runes, then, have always held immense symbolic power, both as a system of writing and also as a means of interpreting the world.

The earliest runic inscriptions date from AD 150, and various runic alphabets were common at this time across what is now Europe. Mostly, they were used as any other written language is: for writing things down, from instructions to stories, and everything in between. They were not commonly used for divination: or at least, there is no evidence to support the idea that they were. There is some evidence to support the existence of specific magical runes, of the type that might be, for example, carved on a sword to aid in battle, or recited to aid healing.

There are also later examples of magical rune use, such as the fifteenth-century Icelandic stave runes, combinations of runes into occult symbols to aid in protection and the thwarting of enemies. They serve more prosaic purposes, too: stave runes can be carved or written to preserve against fox bites; there are runes to ensure your sheep are docile; to ensure sweet sleep. These talismanic symbols are rune-relations, never used directly in writing but developed alongside runic alphabets, much later than the Vikings, as an additional means of protection. They are also magical runes, but perhaps not those that people would link with Odin's quest for knowledge.

Icelandic stave runes were not used for divination either. In fact, the casting of runes as a means of fortune telling didn't arise until the twentieth century as part of the Northern European pagan revival. Guido von List, the Austrian occultist, published his runic divination system in 1908 in his book *The Secrets of the Runes*. List was interested in the study and revival of Germanic – and specifically ethnically Aryan – occult practices, and his work formed part of the cultural conditions from which Nazism took hold. The Nazi Party contained its fair share of individuals interested in the occult. Infamously, within the upper echelons of the Party, it was Heinrich Himmler who was particularly interested in runes and magic, and this is why runes appear in various Nazi insignia. They appear, of course, alongside the swastika, a symbol that takes its name from the Sanskrit 'swasti', a word meaning 'good' or 'auspicious', and which occurs frequently in the Vedas, the oldest scriptures in Hinduism. The symbol itself is commonly found in religious contexts across Eurasia and pre-dates the Nazis. The runes were not, then, the only occult symbols co-opted by the far right, but they are among the most immediately identifiable. The links between the rise of rune-divination as an occult practice and the ascendance of the Nazi Party in Austria and Germany amid a general culture of racism is, of course, no coincidence, and this makes runes a deeply complicated occult tool.

Divination runes were developed as part of a means of asserting Aryan supremacy in folklore and history. It can feel difficult to justify contemporary rune-work. However, the racist origins of rune-reading are complicated by the fact that those people who attempted to reclaim the runes as an esoteric system apart from their origins during the 1930s also came under significant fire. Indeed, speaking out against the appropriation of runes by racists landed one German occultist, Friedrich Bernhard Marby, in two concentration camps during the Second World War. Shocked by what he witnessed, he attempted to divorce runic divination from Aryan supremacy, and was punished for doing so. Since the Second World War, much has been done to attempt to rehabilitate runes for divination, to place them in a longer and more complex historical context as an evolution of earlier forms of rune magic, and to wrestle them from the hands of white supremacists. It is particularly upsetting for people who wish to practise witchcraft in Scandinavian and Germanic countries, as the German Völkisch movement of the twentieth century has laid a long shadow over the pagan religious practices of these places. There are small organisations (one rather lovely one is called 'Vikings Against Racism') that are seeking to reclaim runes from the far right, and to re-establish them as part of non-racist culture – and there have been multiple petitions and announcements to distance certain organisations from others. Paganism is nothing if not highly politically complex. And this brings up questions for us – should we cast runes? How do we acknowledge, beyond their co-option, the far older origins of runes?

My runes sit in a box. I haven't used them very often, and I feel a bit weird about them, although I am also very interested in the ways they operate as a divination system. It isn't the runes themselves, really – I am secure in knowing that they are, in themselves, a neutral system, and although symbols have power, the volume of actual writing in runic alphabets that occurred before any magical rune system would seem to override subsequent racist adoptions. But it is undeniable that they carry with them an air of . . . strangeness. And inevitably, perhaps, they are not entirely free from the circumstances of their production. I wish I could advise the best way round the issue: it certainly isn't dispensing with runes completely, because they are a widespread divination system that many people value, and good work is being done to delineate clearly unacceptable associations from their more general occult application. We can, perhaps, instead use them while doing our very best to actively resist and dismantle the forms of societal influence and power structures that allowed them to be co-opted in the first place. If you do not feel comfortable using runes, that is entirely understandable. I would advise anyone seeking to learn more about runes to investigate them thoroughly, and to educate themselves on the history and co-option of runes by various groups. Ignorance of the issues surrounding the darker political influences of magic is no defence: it is our responsibility as witches to do what we feel is right, and to understand and resist the darker, fascist aspects of the occult.

Harmful causes will always seek to co-opt magic – after all, many believe it confers power and status – and it is our job to recognise, resist and repulse these, and to do the active work of educating ourselves. Most particularly, of course, those of us lucky enough to benefit from the intersectional privileges of Western whiteness.

But we must think about runes both in terms of their problematic history and in terms of their effect as a divination tool. Friends who use them often have reported to me that the runes seem to work on them in different ways to other divination systems, like tarot or tea leaves. They are more knowing, somehow, speak more directly to the subconscious. This may be because, unlike the I Ching, they weren't designed for divination and, unlike something like tarot, they aren't particularly detailed or composite images. Thus, their breadth of interpretation might tend toward being narrower, their answers clearer. Runes are usually sold in sets of 24, and divination sets most usually use the Elder Futhark alphabet. Pleasingly, a blank rune (or 'Wyrd') is often included, just like the blank tile in Scrabble. This rune allows for some flexibility in interpretation, for a question mark to surface in the reading. Readings from runes are often interpreted as being not definite paths of action, but rather sets of variables offered. The interpretations of the runes are not, as in the I Ching, complete descriptions, but rather individual symbols. One nice example is that the eighteenth rune in the Elder Futhark, 'Lagus', can be taken to mean 'lake', or 'body of water', or 'tide', or 'current'. It is also credited with being the rune that represents occult power, lunar tides, psychic abilities and magical workings. It has, then, a grouping of symbolic meanings from which readings can be drawn, but is not ever prescriptive or straightforwardly advisory. Instead, concepts are lined up and 'read' together, weaving a narrative of possibility. Runes are doubtless powerful divination tools: they have a wealth of interpretation behind them, and their symbolic importance has accreted over time. They do not feel comfortable for me to use, particularly, although I am trying to work with them. I think sometimes that I learned them too late, and that my heart was already so given to tarot that I didn't quite know how to incorporate another system into my life. Runes are fascinating, but for me, there is nothing quite like tarot.

You must have noticed that everyone is learning tarot. There is an uptick, always, in magical practice as economies fail and worlds swing round to the right. Tarot, its origins and its contemporary reworking, is a huge topic, but it is interesting to note that it began as a trick-taking card game around the fifteenth century, based on the archetypes of Western medieval society and culture. Tarot cards represent the rise and fall of human lives, trace our existence around the wheel of fortune, Fate's capricious wheel, spun by the goddess Fortuna, who lifts us all up, and casts us all down. From the eighteenth century, tarot cards began to be used in divinatory practice. The system of tarot is straightforward. There are 78 cards, divided into the Major Arcana and the Minor Arcana. The Major Arcana comprises 22 cards without suits, which would originally have been used as trumps. These are numbered, from zero (the Fool) to 21 (the World). The remaining 56 cards comprise the Minor

Arcana, and are divided into four suits (Pentacles or Coins, Swords, Wands or Batons, and Cups). These are arranged as traditional playing cards, running from the lowest number to the court cards: in tarot, these are the King, Queen, Knight and Page. Each of the four suits have associated characteristics, and values are attached to each card. Thus, when a question is asked of the cards (questions are asked by a 'querent' in tarot), they can be shuffled, cards chosen and arranged – often in patterns or 'spreads' where each position carries meaning – and their advice can be read.

Similarly to the I Ching, the cards would be randomly generated after shuffling and each card would figure a concept or person, and idea, an object, or a course of action, which could be interpreted in a linear fashion, or in accordance with the layout of the cards. A fortune; a handsome stranger; a warning against rash action. The tarot's archetypes are complex, and subject to constant revision and reinterpretation. They combine elements of Kabbalah, numerology and other mystic systems. There are psychoanalytical theories of tarot, which suggest that the Major Arcana represents a cycle of internal development, moving through the various stages and facets of the self toward eventual enlightenment or congruity. There are various beliefs that the Minor Arcana represents the external world and its affairs: people you might meet, situations caused by work and love and life. Tarot is a complete system of reference, which can be applied to any question. In this respect, it functions in a space between the occult and the therapeutic: by asking us to consider things which we usually do not, tarot cards can act like a prompt to think or rethink our relationships and journeys in life.

The cards have been with me since my mum gave me hers, when I was about fourteen. Hers is a very traditional deck, well-thumbed and slightly bent. Superstitions around tarot cards abound, and one pervasive superstition is that you should not buy your own tarot cards – or at least your first set. It ought to be a gift. I don't actually use my mum's cards for reading, though. They stay talismanic in my childhood bedroom, guarding all of her desires for me. I'm not sure they'd tell me the whole truth, those cards: they'd be tempted to talk with my mum's voice, and I'm lucky – I can just telephone or pop round when I need her advice. One day, morbid though the thought is, I will be so grateful that she gave me another line to hear her voice through. For now, though, I read mostly with a set that I bought myself. It is called The Golden Tarot, and is every bit as opulent as that sounds. They are collage-cards, made up of thousands upon thousands of fragments of medieval and Renaissance art. They are extremely beautiful, complex images, and I find them easy to get lost in, but still close enough to the most prevalent tarot iconography (that of the Rider-Waite-Smith tarot) to learn from easily. Collecting tarot decks is tricky business: I love them, in their ingenious variation, but almost never read from any of my other decks. It takes a long time to learn a deck – not just its iconography but also its tendencies.

Talking to other readers, there are certain patterns that seem to recur. Our decks, when we know them well, do not give us answers to our own questions the same way they do when we are reading for other people. For other people, my deck is courteous, frames things with as much grace as it can, delivers bad news gently, offers hope. Often, it has a trick of answering whatever question they are really asking, rather than the one they think they are. When I ask my own deck questions, it affords me no such comfort. My deck tells me the truth, but it tells me the truth plainly, with no particular patience for niceties. Throughout my doctoral research, I used to ask it questions about happiness. It would show me almost exactly the same cards every single time. Keep going, keep doing the work, just do your bloody work, keep going, keep doing the work . . . and then come back and ask us about the rest of your life. Stop prevaricating, stop investing in happiness that is essentially a distraction. Get back to work. I love my cards for this. They are like a friend who will sit with you over a glass of wine and refuse to put up with your nonsense.

Tarot has a long and complicated history. There have been many tarot decks, all with differing Major Arcana, and many without any pictures at all on the Minor Arcana, except the court cards. You can still buy recreations of less popular historical decks, such as the Marseilles tarot. However, the images that you are probably thinking of when you imagine tarot are taken from the Rider-Waite-Smith deck. These images were originally published by Rider in 1910, and were a collaboration between an academic and occultist, A. E. Waite, and Pamela Colman Smith, the illustrator, whose surname was notably traditionally missing from the name of the deck: nowadays, the convention is to include her name. The deck took many traditional images from older, 'original' European decks, but changed some of them considerably. This included a move away from the Christian overtones of the Major Arcana – the Pope transformed into the Hierophant, moving him out of any particular religious path, and thus making the deck a little more occult and a little less Christian.

The work of Éliphas Lévi, the French occult author and magician, influenced much of the complex symbolism of this tarot deck. Lévi was interested in occult and arcane symbols, drawn from diverse ancient cultures. He was fascinated by what he called 'an occult and sacred alphabet' that could convey the true mysteries of the world.[3] Lévi was invested in the ancient-ness and traceability of magic, and considered magic to be – in opposition to witchcraft – a scholarly, learned pursuit. So he credits this ancient alphabet to lots of different ancient civili-sations, pointing to the idea that it is something held in common by diverse groups of people, and must therefore be true. He gives us the attributions of this sacred alphabet: 'The Hebrews attribute [it] to Enoch, the Egyptians to Thoth or to Hermes Trismegistus, the Greeks to Cadmus and to Palamedes'.[4] The alphabet, then, is an enmeshed and curious thing, moving as it does not only across time and space but also across languages. What, then, is this alphabet? And how might it be expressed? Lévi tells us that the alphabet is composed not of letters, but of 'absolute ideas attached to signs and numbers' and that 'by its combinations, it realizes the mathematics of thought'.[5] For Lévi, then, the alphabet does not spell words, but ideas: it is an alphabet of diverse symbols, and these symbols have power. For Lévi, this alphabet exists inside the tarot.

Lévi speaks of the symbols of the Major Arcana in tarot as they relate to their assigned number. And he believes that the tarot represents an extremely reliable means of fortune telling; 'an oracular instrument whose words are always clear and always accurate'.[6] Indeed, Lévi laughs at those who seek to discover wisdom or the future via other means, calling them old-fash-ioned: 'The table-turners, and those who make the spirits speak with alphabetical charts, are, then, a good many centuries behind the times'. Lévi writes that the tarot 'degenerated into superstition when it fell into the hands of the ignorant priests and the nomadic ancestors of the Bohemians who possessed the tarot in the Middle Ages' and that he alone had rediscovered its magical uses. This is a rather damning indictment of this period of the tarot's history, as well as an indictment of the priest-classes and the Bohemians (historically, peoples of Eastern Europe). Lévi asserts that these ignorant handlers 'did not know how to employ [tarot] properly, and used it solely for fortune-telling'. He credits the tarot with a far deeper and more potent symbolism, and more powerful function, than had previously been realised by the misguided fools who used it for mere fortune telling – for him it was a rich means of gathering symbolic knowledge.

One of the things that draws people to the tarot is the fact that it can be 'read' and understood at almost any level, from the most literal to the most sophisticated. Most of us, of course, are not as dogged in our pursuit of what Lévi calls the 'quabbalistic wisdom' of the tarot, but it is nevertheless a skill that rewards intuition and intellectual engagement equally. Or, at least, it does when my cards aren't being stubborn or dreadful.

You may well wonder how cards might be said to have a personality. How they might speak to one person differently than another. There are lots of theories of course, some occult, others practical. But think of any object that you know and love, the contact that builds up between you through constant interaction, the way your relationship necessarily changes over time. Think of your phone. Do you know where it is now? Is it in your hand or by your body? They can be intensely comforting, our phones, and feel exactly ours, so much so that we can feel irrationally anxious if we are separated from them or if someone picks them up. But other objects also accrue this build-up of something between user and object: a walking stick, touched every day and present through so many trials and tribulations. Hairbrushes. Favourite chairs. Objects that feel, somehow, intimately linked with the person who touches them most. Tarot cards are like that. They pick up energy in a similar way, absorb our effort as we shuffle and reshuffle, earnestly try to read them. We keep them near us: I keep mine under my altar, which I am at almost daily. And I keep them wrapped in a silk scarf that was a gift from my mum. They are treated very well, and so they have been good friends to me.

Amongst the most persuasive theories of how tarot might be understood is the theory of anagogic looking developed by Enrique Enriquez, an occult writer interested in spirituality and tarot. The word 'anagogical' comes from the word 'anagoge' and refers to 'the mystical interpretation of a text beyond the literal, allegorical or moral sense'.[7] This sounds complicated, but is in fact very simple, breaking down the process of looking at a tarot card into manageable steps. It's also good for learners, as it provides a steady means of layering meaning and complexity into tarot readings. However, I've been reading cards for over ten years, and am still delighted by the new things this technique reveals.

Enriquez states that tarot is a 'magical tool' in the sense that it uses symbols to stimulate the mind into a process that transforms it and shapes it in new ways. He argues that 'looking at the cards prompts in us a revelation', and that this revelation is brought on by anagogical thinking.[8] The tarot supplies random patterns of symbols, which differ every time we deal cards. The symbols can become familiar through study, but the combinations – or the circumstances of their appearance – will always be new to us. Because of this, we compose new narratives every time we read the cards, using the symbols to tell a story. Enriquez argues that when we do this, our brain is engaged in two distinct processes. The first is 'poiesis', which means 'to make': telling a story to contextualise the cards. The second is 'anamnesis', which is the process of recollection or reminiscence. He argues that 'by perceiving a message in tarot cards, we create a new meaning for the cards every time we observe them, taking 'an action that transforms and continues the world'.[9] So when we read tarot cards, we are transforming the world and ourselves, making something new every day. It is a process of magic because it is a process of knowingly changing things, of shaping and reshaping the world according to our understanding.

One of the ways I have often understood tarot cards is as a means of gently nudging us to think about things we have not regularly or usually considered. So often, our thinking runs along certain paths, and tarot cards can act as prompts to change these paths and consider other possibilities. We might be worried about a job, but rather than the tarot asking us to think about the position in terms of pay or security or career advancement, it might ask us to think about family or truthfulness or chaos – all of which might have a huge impact on whether we take that job, but which would not spring automatically to mind. They remind us of all of life's facets, including the ones we might overlook, or choose not to focus on. Regular readings with tarot cards – regular interactions with the cards more generally – can result in feeling more able to consider the aspects and elements of our psyches and situations that we most often overlook. This, really, is a non-occult explanation of the tarot, in which it serves as a sort of therapist, prompting us to broaden the ways we think of ourselves and others. This way, we are using Enriquez's anagogic looking, but we are not exploiting the sophisticated symbolism of the tarot to its full potential. Instead, we are probably behaving like Lévi's ignorant priests, not seeking enlightenment or oracle, but rather guidance and reassurance, and a means of ordering and reflecting upon the complex and conflicting thoughts we already have.

But some tarot readings are not so practical. Some do not follow this gentle, predictable set-up. There have been some readings that I have done, always for friends, which have seemed to reveal things that none of us could have asked. I keep my cards wrapped in their silk scarf, partly because it helps to keep them nice, and partly because I love the theatre of tarot. There is no harm in magic being a little glamorous, I always think. No harm at all. I like unwrapping them in front of people I'm reading for, laying the soft silk out over the carpet or table, and having them shuffle the cards in the low light. Having the querent hold the whole pack, feel the weight of whatever it is they think they are going to receive. Prophecy or advice, revelation or gentle guidance. Often – more often than you'd think – people do not want to tell you their question. They don't have to – instead, they can tell me a version of their question, or the general area that it addresses. Then I spread the cards out, all spilling across the scarlet silk – and I ask them to choose.

The readings that go differently do not always start

differently. Perhaps my mind is more alert, perhaps I have been reading something and it has caught in my head: numerology, medieval symbols, something about the Masons. Perhaps something in me responds to the sincerity of the other person, or their shyness, or some sort of deep need. Or perhaps it is magic, an energy between my body, their body and the cards, a good and lucky constellation that draws deeper answers out. Because I tell them things, then – things I do not and cannot know, guesses that are not guesses because they fall too certainly out of my mouth. And they are true, usually. Not in any gifted, blow-for-blow way, but in the way of the general unspooling of events and feelings. Your job did end; your mother did cry and rage; someone very dear to you unstuck themselves and walked away, leaving your heart sore but your head relieved; the defining aspects of your sexuality were tested. Often, they cry. I had one reading that ended in us both crying. Tarot is loving theatre, it is counselling with forms of answers, it is numerology and enlightenment, it is a pragmatic way of understanding where we are in the world and how to make sense of it.

It is this making sense that most appeals, I think. The laying out of possible paths to chart some sense through life's chaos, to suggest that there are patterns and ways of being that are helpful, that will bring particular results. Any oracular system that seeks to make out of chaos some sort of order always flares back into fashion when the times we live in become more than normally uncertain. And for me, tarot is one of a set of tools I can use to combat anxiety, to deal with the wide world and its undulating, untrackable forms. Nothing in our future is certain, except death – and sometimes, on those special evenings, the things the tarot hints at.

Fortune telling does not cure my anxiety. Medication cures my anxiety – or rather, manages it sufficiently that I can get on with my daily life happily. Therapy helps, too, and good routines. But fortune telling is also helpful. Divination, the communal practice of tarot, gingerly throwing my runes and squinting: these all help me understand the chaos of life, its unknowability, its risks and rewards, in ways that feel manageable. Have you thought about this? the tarot asks me gently. Have you considered this? What about that? Have you even thought about whether you want this thing, this thing you're working so hard for? All divination tools ask us questions, prompt us to reflect and question ourselves, prompt us to sort what is vital from what is optional, what we want from what we feel we ought to have. But more than anything, they teach us about change. They teach us that change is the only thing we have: fortune's wheel turns, the year turns, our lives walk us out along the narrow ledge where things become familiar, and yet unfamiliar. *You do not know yourself yet*, the fortune telling says, *perhaps you never will.* What can we do, we ask it? What can we do in this great, vast universe? *Keep going,* our cards, runes, I Ching tell us, *keep going, as the world turns, and be brave. All things will change. All things will come. Nothing will be as it was before. And we'll be here.*

A Spell Against Anxiousness

This spell uses lemon-balm balm, but it can be substituted for any other soothing hand cream or even, at a push, a little Vaseline mixed with a skin-safe essential oil, or a number of other gentle sensory interventions to help with anxiety. This is an unusual spell in that it is less concerned with reaching out into the world than it is with letting the world approach you, gently.

My anxiety, as it manifests, comes with the idea that everything that approaches is malicious: thoughts turn out to be traps to make me panic, and the outside world is overwhelming in its sensory assertions of traffic and colours and speed. This spell attempts to set up small spaces of safety, psychic and physical, into which you can retreat when it is necessary to do so. It is vitally important to note that if your anxiety troubles you repeatedly, you should speak to a healthcare professional.

You will need:

- Something comfortable to sit on (a cushion on the floor will do) from where you can see your altar
- Lemon-balm balm (or any other soothing balm – in a pinch, a moisturiser you like will do)

A Spell Against Anxiousness

- *A bowl of water (if it is tap water, let it stand for an hour or so, or ideally overnight, so the chlorine can evaporate)*
- *Something soothing to listen to: I favour Gregorian chant, but realise this is absolutely not for everyone. Ideally, nothing you're going to want to sing along to.*
- *Two candles for your altar*
- *Something to represent home, or a place you have been where you feel safe*
- *Pen and paper*

Firstly, cast a circle. You want to be very particular about this one, imagining it as a green or purple light that envelops you entirely, sort of like a large, soft bubble. If you very strongly feel you'd like another colour, go with it, but both purple and green are good calming and restful colours – consider the lavender plant. Make sure the circle takes in you and the altar.

Greet the altar and the deities or forces you speak to, and ask them for help with managing an anxious mind. I often go with something like:

The anxiety is very bad today, and I cannot manage it entirely alone. Would you please help me to find a small place of quietness and rest, where my mind can be a little more still?

Describe your anxiety aloud: is it heart-racing, are you ruminating on one specific thing, are you feeling nauseated, are you having trouble sleeping? Describe it in as much detail as you can, so that it is very clear exactly what you're asking for relief from. The important thing is that you speak your symptoms so they've gone from being private and internal to being external. After you feel you've spoken them out into the world, then it is time to apply the balm. I tend to apply it to the point between my eyebrows (where your pineal gland sits, which is also known as the 'third-eye' spot), on the pulse points of my wrists, and at the back of my neck, just a little on each spot. As I do this, I usually speak out loud, just a little refrain: *A balm on my body, a balm in my mind.* I also anoint something on the altar – usually a tiny spot of the balm applied to a statue I can wipe clean. Because it is flammable, don't put it on a candle, and if you aren't sure where to put it, then a small scrap of ribbon, rubbed in it, will do very well.

Sit by the altar, and let the balm work through your skin, and into your blood stream. You can position the bowl of water on your altar so that the candle flame is reflected in it, or you can sit with the bowl by you and blow on the surface of the water. As you watch the ripples or the flames dance, try to focus on letting the image of that gently moving water fill up your mind, working through your eyes and into your conscious-ness, as the balm does its magic. Try to feel the way the patterns have no particular meaning, are just going on, are just something that is happening. Feel that inside yourself: you are made of so many processes that are just going on, that are just happening. You can tune into them, and out of some of the urgency of your mind.

Try to look at the water for five to ten minutes. Once you're done, close the circle, extinguish the candles, and let the water feed your plants. Practise this as often as you need, and even-tually you'll be able to let the water take the place of busy thoughts or a pounding heart for a bit, automatically.

AUGUST

Protection and Sympathetic Magic

In August, I go to the British seaside on holiday, in the manner of a Victorian with a day off. There are six of us, plus two babies almost old enough to pull themselves to standing, and we stay in a big stone house at the end of the world. Or, rather, the end of England, the end of Britain; the Isle of Portland, a strange rocky protrusion out into the English Channel. It is a tide-island, joining it to the land the thinnest spit of exposed pebbles: Chesil Beach, where, when we arrive, the waves are higher than I am, and the sea a gaping, hungry, curling thing. On a clear day, the information leaflet brightly says, you can see all sorts of interesting things from the window of our Portland stone-fronted house.

There are no clear days. It is a stormy August, and cold. Dressed for somewhere far warmer, I am wretched: wet legs, sodden shoes, coats lent by exasperated friends. Didn't I know that England isn't always sub-tropical? To be fair, the Isle of Portland has palm trees, I say. Palm trees, and waves that are so hungry for the babies their mothers don't even venture down the steep-sided beach. The weather settles over us, heavier than we would like, and claustrophobic. There aren't sufficient indoor things to keep us occupied. We grow a little restless, a little fractious. The thoughts that have been gnawing at the inside of my head for most of the year start to growl a little more loudly, knock against my mood. My best friend and I are sharing a bedroom, a spinsterish twin at the top of the house, and she spends a good deal of the week attempting to comfort me as I cry, most memorably into a large plush swan that I buy on one of our outings.

There are healing places to take your bad brain, and then there are places where the grey sky skimming close to the wave-tops makes everything feel far, far worse. Places that make it feel that the world is one great pathetic fallacy, and you are holidaying inside the landscape of your own head. Chesil Beach is, I'm sure, a lovely place, but it is also an edge-place, a drowning place, a hungry sea where hungrier wreckers and smugglers did their trade. People have lived there since the Mesolithic, facing out across the Channel, seeing what the sea would turn up. People have lived along its steep cliff-edges and its hard, beautiful stone. The Vikings bumped against the island for raiding from about 793, murdering tax collectors and sailing blithely on. It is recorded in the *Anglo-Saxon Chronicle*: the boats landing, and the Vikings killing the reeve who attempted to tax their landing. This sort of casual but constant violence seems to define the Portland coastline.

It is an exposed place: all edges, beaches, angles from which someone might suddenly invade. And, as a result, it is a defended and defensive place, which has shored itself up against attack as best it could. The harsh line of its cliffs is pock-marked with the remnants of various wars, including the period in which Henry VIII feared violent retribution from Europe over the Reformation, and built fortifications and gun-batteries around the south of England. During the Second World War the island was heavily bombed, and was the site of various military tactical and intelligence centres, batteries and underground shelters. There are two prisons still on the Isle of Portland: a Young Offender Institution and HMP The Verne, which was built by inmates of Portland Prison between 1860 and 1872. Chesil Beach itself, steeply sided and entirely rocky, with the great, still Fleet behind – a quiet lagoon, perfect for making a getaway – was a site of intense smuggling activity. Legend has it that smugglers landing on the seventeen-mile stretch of coast had an advantage on those dark, moonless nights: by picking up a handful of shingle from the stony beach, they could accurately gauge the average size of the stones, which were graded from Portland back to the mainland. At the mainland end the stones are small as peas, but at the island end they are hefty, large as potatoes. The perfect guide to where you are, as you land your tub gently back against the shoreline after an evening of picking up pretty, stolen things from wrecked ships.

Perhaps it is unsurprising, then, that I spend a lot of time that holiday thinking about protection. We protect the babies from the sea, from the cold, from the wind. We protect each other from our worst moods by reading books and going on rain-scourged runs and popping to the little Tesco for things nobody really needs. We are ourselves protected – from the sea and the gales – by the Portland stone-fronted house, clad in bright limestone, so beautiful that it was quarried and shipped off to be used to build St Paul's Cathedral. And yet everything feels exposed. Raw. As if my skin has rubbed down too far in the salt air, and my nerves are singing in the cold. And so, of course, what I want is armour. Second skin. Something magical to envelop, some shield to hide behind. To be safe from harm, from job uncertainty, from relationship difficulties, from the myriad unpleasant thoughts that are nesting in my brain.

I wear all my luckiest jewellery. March into the Portland magic shop and buy a little burnt-driftwood wand, as if that flimsy object, more charcoal than power channel, might, having survived the sea's rough playing, help me survive also. I keep it under my pillow while I sleep, do not show it to my lovely but non-witch-inclined friends. Not usually one for buying equipment, I feel a little foolish: I could have walked on the beach until I found a good stick of driftwood, then carved it myself, had I had the energy and inclination. Instead, a woman with pink hair and a face like coral sells it to me, herself seeming more mermaid than human. Perhaps, in light of that, it is allowed, even if I am not entirely sure what I am going to use it for. I mutter protection spells under my breath, and keep my body braced for something to go wrong. It had already gone wrong, of course, inside my head and inside my life, but I still want to grab the universe as if it is a duvet and draw it up over my head. Instead, I know I have to keep showing up, keep standing in my life, wand drawn like a storybook character, facing whatever is coming head-on.

Arming ourselves against what is unknown is a form of protection. Magical protection is, of course, nothing new. For as long as any humans have wished safety, or to protect food supplies, or property, or to ward off personal injury or illness, or to repel enemy blows in battle, magical protections have been a key part of human responses to threat and danger. At the beginning

of 2019, the Ashmolean Museum in Oxford put on an exhibition of witchcraft artefacts and new artworks called *Spellbound*.
Many of these items were loaned from the Pitt Rivers Museum,
which specialises in natural history and anthropology. The
exhibits were precisely the sort of occult ephemera one might
imagine: crystal balls, mummified cats found walled into medieval houses, witch-bottles and poppets. The museum gift shop
traded, too, in what one might expect: fortune-telling fish, the
kind that curl and flex in response to body heat; magic-book
tricks for children; expensive velvet scarves and 'spell candles',
the operations of which were unclear.

The exhibition was based on, in the main, objects that
embodied these habits of magical protection. The displays were
mostly personal objects, designed to be worn or kept in the
home, and to ward off disease or keep away bad luck. Many of
the objects were of unknown use, but had been found in unusual
places and seemed to be part of various folk cultures of protective magic. The exhibition offered a rare chance to see so many
magical artefacts from Britain grouped together – and to gain
unusual access into the operations of folk magic of the past
six hundred years. The museum's commentary – and the book
that they produced – framed these objects in a strange way.
They referred to the motivations behind the making and using
of these magical protective objects as 'magical thinking'.

The common definition of magical thinking is the belief
that one's thoughts, desires and actions can affect external
events in particular ways. There may be very little evidence of
this, creating a false causality. 'Magical thinking' is used in
medical, psychological and anthropological contexts, although
its meaning does differ depending on the field. It is not a

term employed by practitioners or theorists of magic or witchcraft. Magical thinking is a fascinating term to apply to an exhibition of protective objects, not least because it is enormously disrespectful to the original wearers, makers and users of those objects. In the cultural context in which these people lived making and wearing protective objects was commonplace. It would not be appropriate to dismiss the beliefs of followers of Christianity or any other world religion as 'magical thinking' in a museum context. It creates a sense of distance, of us and them.

These 'primitive' people believed that shoes in the wall would bring them good fortune but we, with our post-Enlightenment rational beliefs, we know far better, thank you. We'd never believe something like that. Now we have science and medicine and clean drinking water and understand germs, we have no need of these silly superstitions. It is this attitude that makes so many people hesitant to state that they believe in magic, or practise witchcraft, in contemporary culture: the attitude that magic is something to be sneered at from a position of greater knowledge, rather than something to be engaged with seriously and understood. It's the attitude that makes me feel temporarily sheepish if someone who knows me in a professional context sees me stepping out of the witchcraft supplies shop in Edinburgh, and enquires politely as to what I might be doing in there. There is always a sense in these encounters that the desired response is laughter, that I reassure them by dismissing the whole idea of witchcraft, that we can laugh about it together. I don't do that. I stand and tell them, because I am a firm believer in being honest, but I can always tell by the look on their face that they wish I hadn't been.

However, if we look at the way that superstition has operated throughout the ages, we can see that there is no grand
moment of disproving that magic is 'true'. We find instead a
continuum, with crests and troughs. Magical thinking is a
common stress response: soldiers during the World Wars would
often have lucky items in their uniforms, from Bibles to coins.
Warding off death, hoping the bullets would pass them. Sports
competitors still engage in magical thinking, from pre-match
rituals to lucky numbers, pants, laces. However, the *Spellbound*
catalogue frames magical thinking in diagnostic terms, as if it
were a disorder of some sort: 'Magical thinking is retained from
childhood' and occurs 'in response to desire, fear, guilt and
anxiety and joy'.[1] This framing of magical thinking implies that
it is a handicap, something to be dispensed with, a fault lodged
in our wiring that invites the strange and more-than-human in,
and gives credence to the nonsensical.

This may very well be the case. But if we consider magic
to be an act of will that alters the material state of the world
then magical thinking is often just . . . magic. The thing about
magical thinking that trips even sceptics up is that superstition
works, and it is disingenuous to believe otherwise. There is a
great deal of evidence to point to the fact that what we believe
about something has an enormous effect on how we move
through the world: from optimism to protective wards, things
work for us if we imbue them with the power to do so. The
problem with this is where these beliefs and behaviours might
disproportionately impact our lives, and lead to harm or
distress. But, as the authors of the catalogue themselves
confess, 'if you believe in the power of an object, it may give
you the confidence to perform better', and the same is also

true of ritual.[2] Multiple studies have been done into the psychology of luck and superstition – and how these concretely link to performance. For example, it has been shown in studies of lucky charms, that people perform better on tasks when they have a lucky charm with them.[3] Lucky charms are considered a 'low-cost' belief: this is to say, carrying a lucky charm around may boost performance and is not usually detrimental or significantly impactful to the rest of your life. This is a complicated subject because it is so fraught: people who are not superstitious might rightly enquire as to why people believe these things enough for it to make a difference to their performance. Isn't it silly and childish, doesn't it destabilise having a balanced and logical worldview?

But nothing is balanced and logical, really. Late capitalism is not a meritocracy. We do not do well in life simply because we show up or try hard to be clever or well-behaved or good. Most often, people succeed because of the financial and institutional networks that sit behind them. From private education to parents who know important people in an industry, from being able to afford property, to living in affluent areas with better health outcomes. Institutional systems of oppression occlude progress at every turn, or allow people to rise unencumbered, like bubbles, to join the ranks of those at the top. This is an awful lesson. It goes against everything we are told in childhood. It casts our optimistic and compliant behaviour in a new light – what was the point in all our efforts if the promised rewards simply were not accessible, or even real? Good people do not live longer, the people we love do not avoid misfortune just because we love them, our hard work and effort are not enough to stop ice caps melting, to keep our children safe, to keep ourselves out of the path of harm.

On the high, grey cliffs of the Isle of Portland, this futility, this personal powerlessness against the great scrape of the world feels very real, and very close. I watch sea wear at rock, feel the cold buffet of wind against my legs, tearing through the pretty summer dresses I'd brought in the mistaken belief it would be that sort of holiday. There are so many things I am afraid of. There is illness in the family of the creeping, ill-defined sort; there is trouble in my heart, and the new babies feel like irrefutable proof that my life is a different shape from other people's, and perhaps it is the wrong one. Everywhere there are awful headlines, and the headlands feel more like walls, cutting us off from the rest of the world beyond. There isn't, I don't think, a way of stopping myself soaking everything up like pumice stone. There is no way, or no way that I can see, not to let forms of unhappiness leak into everything through my skin, my eyes, my foolish heart. I want to hurl myself against the wind to see if it will take my weight, even though I know it wouldn't. I want to scream and shout off the cliffs about things, to hear the frailty of my own voice against the over-whelming howl of the wind, but I don't want to upset the tourists, don't want to cause a coastguard incident, don't want my friends to worry. I want something to give me back a sense of myself, so that I can address the problems rather than living inside them, but I don't know how. The wand sits in my pocket, dark and frail and strange, and we don't speak to one another.

I let it be near me, but have no idea how I might use it, and, don't think much of it beyond its being a souvenir.

My luckiest things have always come to me when I needed them most, when I was looking for them, when I had nothing in the tank and desperately needed something to remind me I was going to be ok. The one that lives in my handbag now is an excellent example of that. I was walking home when I found her, peering out of a gutter. It was a week of finalities: last week in London; last week working in my glossy job in publishing; last week living at the other end of the country from my family; last week of the housemate who liked to eat cereal with her hands in the evenings and yell at me about the dirty kitchen floor. My lucky charm was lying there, in the leaf-choked gutter, face placid and smiling; it was as if she were waiting for me. A little Playmobil girl, cast in plastic, hair like mine and her little yellow legs sticking straight into the air. Who could have resisted her? She looked lost, upside down and grubby, but she also looked brave. She was brave, I decided, and I took her home and washed her. She has lived in my handbag ever since. She is a lump of moulded plastic, of course, I know this. But she is also an augur of adventure, a small self to set out across the world with. She is lucky because I found her when I needed luck. She is lucky because she looks like me, and I am vain enough to find a poppet of myself reassuring. She is lucky because I have designated her so, and because she simply is. I, after all, do not make the rules. Sitting in my bag, she is private, and hidden, and nobody needs to know that she is grinning through interviews for me, that she is being brave in the midst of rail chaos on long journeys to meet new people. And yet, all the time, she is boosting my performance for me, widening my odds. She is a nonsense lucky charm, and yet, she gives me an advantage.

One of the central practical motivations behind the practice of magic is the attempt to alter the world through the will in order to gain collective advantage. Any greedy personal gain is, rightly, demonised – we think of Faustus and his satanic pact, or Midas and his poisoning golden touch. Greed is rarely rewarded in magical practice for fairly clear reasons: hoarding of resources tilts the world off kilter. In my practice, I place more emphasis on having a rich relationship with what I would term the 'magical aspects' of the world, and a deep spiritual relationship: I do not only light my altar when I want something, as popular witchcraft so often encourages us to do. But the practical output of my magic, when I do undertake traditional spells, is very much concerned with the practical concerns of life. All of us need enough to live on; want our friends to heal from bad heartbreaks and big operations; need to protect ourselves against the forces that would harm. Folk practices that are often incorporated into the idea of magic – such as healing remedies, charms and magical protections – are usually all interested in achieving some version of these things. While the exhibition I visited might happily consign these objects and practices to a quasi-medical category of irrational behaviour, it remains true that for historic and contemporary people, objects of power played a huge part in how they understood and sought to control the world. Presumably, throughout history, these practices gave results that were perceived to be valuable and effective, given that people kept doing rituals and magic. There is a very long tradition of superstitious object-use, and these will have been made and remade, considered and reconsidered, found and repurposed. Even if what was and is considered magical has changed, the possession and use of magical objects has not changed so very much. From hare's feet and horseshoes to new coins and plastic dolls found in muddy gutters, the objects might alter radically, or be used for a range of different reasons, but their continued efficacy, or helpfulness – their continued magic – cannot be in dispute.

Lucky objects are as diverse as people, cultures, as the idea of luck itself. Even under the slightly narrower umbrella of what we might call 'European luck and superstition', lucky objects and objects to ward off bad luck vary very widely. One common feature of historic objects, however, is that the lucky object often resembles or embodies the type of luck the bearer is trying to attract or repel. This is known as sympathetic magic. My little doll would count as sympathetic magic: she looks like me, and so by treating her well and keeping her safe, I am hoping for the same for myself. The same, in reverse, is true of poppets, and dolls made to resemble people and then harmed. Or, rather, this is one small part of a much more complex multicultural set of practices that involve interacting with effigies of various kinds in various ways, some benign and others harmful. Much has been written on and around so-called 'voodoo dolls', which, contrary to what is commonly believed, do not play a major role in the Voodoo practices of Louisiana or Haiti, and often effigy practices such as ushabti (the provision of servants and companions in the afterlife in ancient Egyptian culture) or interactions with totems in various religions have been lumped alongside Voodoo, because of the shock-value of using effigies. All of these diverse practices hold in common, however, their understanding that figures made to look like humans, whether specific or archetypal, hold power.

Sympathetic magic works in other ways, too. When we research it, we find that it is often coupled with historical ideas about contagion and taintedness, many of which seem unpleasant or upsetting to contemporary practitioners. These ideas are often based on historic understandings of disease transmission, and subsequent attempts to ensure that illness did not enter an individual or household. Regardless of its difficult manifestations, however, sympathetic magic is extremely appealing and persistent as an idea. Early social anthropologists Edward Tylor, James Frazer and Marcel Mauss developed what they understood to be the three universal principles of sympathetic magic. Their research is flawed, and based on a variety of Western-centric suppositions about indigenous peoples of other cultures, but the principles they put forward are useful for understanding how sympathetic magic operates.[4] The first of these rules is the law of contagion, which declares 'once in contact, always in contact'. We can understand this in something like clippings of hair: even though they're separate from the head they came from, they are understood to always contain the essence of the person they were clipped from. We know this to be 'literally' true, now, in terms of the fact that our DNA is contained in our hair. Another example is things that have been created through hand contact keeping a sense of their maker: for example, butter keeping the character or essence of the person who churned it. While this idea that an object is always linked with, or always contains a trace of, what touched it might seem strange, it is an attitude still common today. Think of souvenirs – we like the tacky shot glasses our best friend brought us from Spain not because they are beautiful or useful, but because they bring back with them a little of the essence of that place that is full – in our imagination – of fun and sunshine. We like them, also, because they have been touched and selected especially for us, by someone who is special to us.

The same is true of the things we inherit; the mementoes we burn when we end relationships; the objects we cannot bear to touch because they came from people we hate or houses we always felt weren't quite right. Theories of contagion can be, of course, extremely harmful (one thinks of cultures where menstruation is perceived to be unclean, or rumours and scare-mongering about the spread of HIV during the AIDS crisis), but there is something potent about the idea of essences remaining tied to objects. When we speak about the story behind antiques, for example, we are really talking about all the hands that touched the thing we're holding; all the adventures that 1950s prom dress went on; all the lives lost at the end of a seventeenth-century firearm. We always want to stand in the very spot a famous person died in, or see the exact costume a film star wore on the set of a famous film. The same thing happens in established religions, too: what are the bones of saints, all bound up in gold reliquaries, if not an attempt for us to literally touch the sacred people of the past?

This is an interest, always, not only in the origin story of the objects, but in their emotional weight. What is really 'contagious' here, what can really be passed on – we suspect – are traces of emotion. The cultural critic Sara Ahmed writes on the 'stickiness' of emotions – how we think they cling to, and animate, people and things. She writes of how 'emotions do things, and they align individuals with communities – or bodily space with social space – through the very intensity of their attachments'.[5] Emotions bring us together and force us apart – and they do this through objects that wind us into proximity with each other, with the past, with ourselves. Ahmed discusses objects as gaining emotional value only when they are in circulation, says that they 'accumulate affective value over time'.[6] And this is true: our grandmother's pretty lace fan – passed down to us carefully from our mother, its tattered edges fraying, the design painted onto it a little cracked – has accumulated its preciousness over time, binds us in emotional proximity with our grandmother. A fan in similar repair, given to us, would not have the same emotions attached to it: we might not even like it. It is not the fan that we like, after all, or not on its own merits. We love it because of the value of emotion that has accumulated around it over time, and through story and association.

Think, perhaps, of the potently magical artefacts that we ourselves produce. I have friends who have kept the umbilical cords of their children; their first nail-clippings; little boxes of their milk-teeth; their first curls, tied with velvet ribbons and nestled into boxes. To anyone outside their immediate family, these bodily relics of babyhood seem, arguably, uncanny, unsettling, unpleasant – little leavings, things best burned or thrown away, biological waste. To the parents, however, they are precious objects, treasured reminders that the birth happened, that the baby came, that – yes – they were once this small. My mother keeps a selection of milk teeth – mine and my sister's – in a little metal box lined with royal blue silk. I used to think it was disgusting, a box of bones that had fallen out of our mouths – but now, on opening it, I feel a sense of strangeness: were we ever, really, that small? Did those teeth really sit in my head, bite down on things, fall out? I think about my sister's teeth, especially, although in the box we cannot tell them apart. I remember her asking me to wobble her wobbly teeth, to feel how loose they were – and I feel such affection for her baby self, now she is in her late twenties. If, at some point in the future, I am the inheritor of that box of teeth then I imagine, weird though I know it is, that I will keep them. They are, after all, in the profoundest way possible, mine. They are of me: I grew them, I lost them, and now I can hold them in my hands.

And there are some biological artefacts that exceed their person-specific beginnings. I visited the Surgeons' Hall Museum in Edinburgh recently, and there sat, nestled among the blood-letting instruments and the flayed, wax-injected nerve systems of eighteenth-century criminals, paper-thin and white as vellum, a caul. The caul, or cowl, is the amniotic membrane sac that encloses a foetus in the womb. Rarely, less than once in every 80,000 births, a baby is born with this membrane still covering its head and face. 'Caul' comes from Latin and means 'helmet' – the baby is born with an extra protective layer, gifted by the mother's body, still intact. This sense of the caul as a magical protective layer lives on in various colloquialisms for luck. In Italian and Russian, the phrase 'born with a shirt', a colloquialism for a caul birth, is used to refer to someone who is very lucky. Mothers were often given the caul by midwives to dry and preserve into heirlooms, and they were profitable, too, because in British folklore, they were believed to preserve against drowning. An advert from the late nineteenth century in *The Times* advertises a caul for sale: 'A Child's Caul to be disposed of, a well-known preservative against drowning, &c., price 10 guineas.'[7] The caul, being a protective membrane, was seen in terms of sympathetic magic – it was perceived as being like a coracle, a small boat made of animal skins that floated well on water. In shape and function, perhaps it would, in the moment of drowning, act to buoy up the individual, and keep them safe.

The caul I saw in Surgeons' Hall, pressed behind glass, so white and translucent, had been purchased from the mother at a handsome price – good recompense for giving up something so very lucky. Cauls are undeniably magical items: rare, purported to contain great powers, and sold at high prices for protection. They are also biological, rather than botanical or geological, and this is unusual – while accounts of medieval and Early Modern witchcraft practices are full of bones and noses and ears – especially those belonging to criminals and all sorts of exotic animals – there are actually very few accounts of biological parts being sold for magical protection. Animal parts – hare's feet, for example – are common, but there is something eerie, strange, about selling the caul of a baby. I spoke to several people who were caul-born, or had relatives who were. The girl whose mother told her that she couldn't drown, and they had to send a fishing boat to rescue her when she decided she'd go off swimming at the beach; the grandmother who wouldn't keep the caul of her child, because she understood the superstition to imply he'd be more likely to join the navy if she did; the vet who watched mother cats eat the kitten-cauls. All strange stories, carrying their own body magic with them. If you were born in a caul, then you are already a statistical oddity – what is there to say that your life won't follow more unusual and magical turns?

The emotional stickiness of these objects, the way meaning and emotions cling to them and are then circulated, is a form of binding. We are bound to the world by the objects we hold and pass on, and our lives are lived through these objects. Emotional stickiness is perhaps more appealing than contagion as a way of explaining how feelings and power attach to these objects, and it is also, I think, a better way of understanding how objects can become, or be seen as, magical.

The next idea that governs sympathetic magic is the law of similarity, which holds 'either that like causes like . . . or appearance equals reality'.[8] This we can see in poppets, as we have mentioned, or even in photographs stuck with pins – it is said that any actions done to the representation of the person or thing can then be found on the actual person or thing. They carry a curious weight: even people who do not believe in superstition, or magic, or anything else, are often loath to stick a pin in a photograph of someone they love. Why? It feels like desecration, like wishing someone harm, just as carrying a photograph with someone we love in it – or wearing a lock of their hair, or their name monogrammed on a ring – is a way of expressing our love for them and treasuring them, even though neither makes any 'provable' material difference.

There are other applications of this law, and it is often demonstrated in early medicine practices. It is seen in what is known as the 'doctrine of signatures', a disproven concept put forward by the medieval Swiss physician Paracelsus, who believed that 'nature marks each growth ... according to its curative benefit'.[9] It is a folk-medicine belief that God created plants to bear physical resemblance to the parts of the body they would cure. One famous example is the plant eyebright (euphrasia), the flowers of which can have a bright blue centre resembling an eye. It was believed that this plant would treat eye afflictions. While many plants – by chance – contain helpful compounds or are, at worst, harmless, other plants can be fatal.

The idea that 'like cures like' extends beyond plants. The healing stones at St Fillan's Mill in Killin, in the Scottish Highlands, which are still in use, are part of this ancient tradition. The St Fillan's stones are beautiful, heavy and strange. Eight stones, shaped like internal organs, which are still used in healing and can be visited at the mill. People lead healing sessions with them, or you can book to use them privately. They are thought to date back to pre-Christian folk healing practices, and healing is thought to occur when the stone shaped like the affected body part is placed on that body part. The stones themselves, then, contain the healing, and it is 'activated' when they are placed above their sympathetic organ. Rituals for looking after the stones have been continuously undertaken at St Fillan's Mill since, it is believed, the eighth century. There is an annual 'bedding ceremony', undertaken by local children, which 'involves replacing the layer of river wrack, straw and twigs on which the eight stones nestle'.[10] The old bedding is taken away and returned to the river, to bear it away.

Finally, in the theory of sympathetic magic, there is the law of opposites, which argues the reverse of the law of similarities: that something can be affected by its equal and opposite form. You can ward something off by using its opposite to scare it away. One fittingly terrifying example of this is the profusion of pierced natural objects found in houses in Early Modern Europe: an animal heart, for example, or a fruit, might be pierced through with a pin. This might be a reaction to the idea that a particular animal was bringing harm to the household, or it might be used as a substitute – bringing harm to an animal as a scapegoat, and sparing the house.[11] This is a sort of sympathetic magic sacrifice: taking one healthy lamb's heart to guard against the illness of the human hearts in the household.

But it wasn't just illness that was warded off that way. Sympathetic magic was also often used to scare off witches. Indeed, many folk practices of sympathetic magic were not considered witchcraft in the medieval and early modern periods, because they were instead designed to keep away witches. This is one of these difficulties with how we understand magic in history – the various nuanced strands of what was and was not lawful, godly or socially acceptable. Cunning-folk would offer to make counter-magic: charms and spells to scare off bad unnatural forces, while not considering what they were doing to be ungodly in the least. Magic and counter-magic were – and indeed remain – a matter of perspective.

We can see this in the St Fillan's stones. Although these are clearly the extension of a pre-Christian healing practice, they are considered to be holy because they had belonged to a saint, and therefore could not be witchcraft or magic. However, had they emerged in a different context, perhaps found buried in a kist in the garden of an accused witch's cottage, or discovered in the attic of a suspiciously newly rich man, they could easily have been considered superstitious or heretical. A similar phenomenon, kept as a charm to ward off witches, was the Bellarmine jug, which is now sometimes colloquially called a 'witch bottle'. Squat and imposing, but small enough to be buried under hearths or lintels, under floors or in walls, they sent a clear message against witches, for all they look to us like cursed, demonic objects, themselves full of evil. They are usually made of Bartmann stoneware (Bellarmine may be a reference to a sixteenth-century Catholic cardinal of the same name), which was made in Germany. The bottles are mostly brown, and have a little threatening figure on them, and occasionally other markings, such as a depiction of a spoked wheel. They have narrow necks and considerable, fat 'bellies' to hold their contents. During the late medieval and Early Modern period, these were the most popular choice for witch bottles. Witch bottles during this period all had one purpose: to entrap, harm or stave off witches, and repel them from the house. The bottles were all filled with remarkably uniform contents, given their geographic distribution.

They were usually crammed with metal – where the actual objects can be discerned, pins and nails are most common. In many, the pins were bent. Theories of why this might be suggest that 'killing' the pins allowed the release of 'ghost pins' that could go abroad and find the witch herself.[12] Substitutes for pins – such as small, sharp animal bones, twigs or thorns, and blades of grass – have also been found. The other main ingredient of the bottles was urine. This might have been for dousing, as a sort of territory-marking or to give a personal 'signature' to the bottle, a sense of individual creation or ownership. In terms of sympathetic magic, it would secure the pisser against harm, because their urine would be activating the spell, perhaps, or showing that it was they who needed protection. Similar magical objects were often used to ward off other things – dead cats, for example, were common, with 'the mummified cats acting as venerable scarecrows'.[13] Nobody, of course, believed that these cats would reanimate and kill any vermin in the house, but they were a symbolic deterrent. I have often felt similarly, when dealing with mice in flats, about the plug-ins that claim to emit a high-pitched deterring whine, painful to mouse-ears. They certainly are not as effective as grain-bait, or traps, or as stuffing wire wool into every visible crevice and double-sealing with expanding foam, but they give a certain comfort, and I can at least pretend that there is one more hurdle between me and an unpleasant infestation.

And that is what sympathetic magic so often is: another tool in the armoury, another means of attempting to ward off chaos, to prevent infestation, to lessen the chances of getting ill, or cursed, or having lightning strike your house. It is a type of hope or desire, a way of taking action against things that cannot necessarily be controlled. It is intimately related to the idea of foreknowledge, of perceiving possible disaster, and trying to shore up protections against it. And fear of a witch's evil could very well cause actual harm: it is understood that a fear of witchcraft and 'belief in . . . magic reflect[ed] the fact that any strong negative emotion provoked by another person's attitude or actions can cause, or contribute to, physical disorder'.[14] In other words, if you believe yourself to have been cursed, the physical manifestations of this belief (pain, illness, a sense of bad luck) are, in fact, the equivalent manifestations of the curse. There is no experiential difference in the pain. Just as lucky objects bring luck through our belief in them, so curses bring us harm through our understanding that they are real. Therefore, if the wardings we use against them are imbued with belief, then the system of sympathetic magic works. Sympathetic magic is, of course, complicated, culturally located, and changes due to how cultures understand occult threat and what they believe good action might be against it. Prayer, for example, or exorcism, are examples of warding off ill-luck or malign influence. Much like the witch bottles of the cunning folk, these are considered not to be magic. And yet – what is their effect, if not to set up a bulwark, a force to repel evil?

Crossing the road away from a stranger; carrying our keys in our hands; calling a friend. We take practical actions designed to keep us safe, and give them ritual weight. We double-lock doors, and burying witch bottles isn't much different – both are designed to keep us safe from harm, in one way or another, even if in reality, there are harms we cannot double-lock against. And we are the same with fortunes: weather forecasts, financial forecasts, having surveys done before we buy houses – everything is a form of shoring up against unknown future disaster. Charms for protection made by witches and charms for protection made against witches are not very different. It is useful to learn protective magic. It is helpful to employ it: it helps us to feel in control, to feel as if the will of the world might bend sometimes in our favour. The word for this sort of protective magic is 'apotropaic', which means to 'turn away' or 'ward off' in Greek. It is such a beautiful word, the way it pops on the tongue, the way it feels heavy. You've almost certainly come across its daily manifestations already: nazars – charms to ward off the evil eye – are prevalent on jewellery and decorations. They often take the face of a circular, stylised blue 'eye'. Or apotropaic speech: saying 'bless you' after sneezes. Or actions: knocking on wood, bypassing ladders, not sitting on cold stone lest you catch a chill. This is, as we can now see, sympathetic magic. So much of it passes uncommented on, or understood to be superstition. Superstition is, really, the dilution of sympathetic magic down into the world, into a form sufficiently unmagical to be exempt from censure. It is folk magic, popular magic, the magic we all do without thinking of ourselves as witches. So much of it forms the fabric of our daily interactions, the way we move through the world. To recognise this magic, understand it and utilise it is deeply powerful. It is a way of braving the world with skill, of recognising the systems in place and deciding to act outside of them. Apotropaic magic: in these strange days, what harm can it do? And, more compellingly – what harm might it stop from coming to pass?

On Chesil Beach, beside the cold, high, merciless sea, I asked for protection. I needed sympathetic magic. I needed something to guard me that obeyed those laws, that would stitch me back into a place where I felt safe. I picked up stones, then put them down. I sat myself uncomfortably on the shingle and spoke with the sea in low tones. I am convinced it wanted to take me: not out of cruelty, but the sea can be a blunt instrument, and swallow the person alongside their problems. I didn't want that, I realised, wretched though I felt. I wanted protection. A hand in mine, a wand, something to hold me more firmly into reality: something to protect me.

I walked a lot, that holiday. Feeling myself inside my body, moving it along the beach, every step a reassurance that I was real, and that whatever was going on, I was still myself within it. Apotropaic magic can be this, too: keeping yourself from harm by keeping yourself moving, washed, fed, by keeping yourself in the company of those who love you even when you wish to draw away. Protective magic is both what we make and how we act. In the end, the spells of protection I did were basic, perhaps. The sorts of magic that barely even count, in some ways, and yet are all-important in others. I have detailed them below, because I think that although they seem small, these protection-acts helped me enormously, both on the holiday and beyond it. Witches know, even when the world is hard, the value to be had in warding off evil. We know how to keep ourselves safe, and we know how to keep ourselves going. After all, what is magic if not a strategy for survival?

A Spell for Getting Rid of Something

*I*t is difficult, you know, to rid ourselves of the things we wish we could discard. There are things that charity shops don't want, that your neighbour won't take off your hands, that you cannot recycle. Bad habits; bad bosses; ex-lovers; loneliness; illness; the dark portions of our psyche, which do not let us achieve actualisation; declining bird populations. There are lots of things the world – and our personal lives – could do without, could happily discard.

There are lots of ways to do spells similar to this, and I chart others in the course of the book, but this spell I particularly enjoy because of its corporeality. There is something very definite in this spell. Many aspects of witchcraft are ephemeral, invisible, or require a degree of faith: this simply isn't one of them. The evidence of your actions isn't burned, isn't washed down the plughole, isn't shouted into the wind. It sits in your palm and goes into the ground.

For this spell, you will need an egg. If you are vegan, then this spell will require something else. What is important is the symbolism of the egg, with its shell-container and its interior, all trapped, secret richness. The egg, you see, is the vessel into which you are going to put everything you want to get rid of. It doesn't matter if you have the blackest mood, the worst envy,

the most wracking anxiety. The egg will absorb at least some
of it, and you can throw it away.

Sit the egg on your altar, and call a circle of protection.
Tell the deities or universe what you are going to do: *I will
put what needs to go into this egg, and it will leave me.* Then, speak
what is troubling you to the egg. As much detail as you can.
If you are angry, shout. If you are sad, you can cry. If you are
worried about something particular (moving house; an ex you
still think about; a habit you want to give up) then describe
the scenario in as much detail as you can. Here, you aren't
asking for something good: you are simply trying to get rid
of something bad. So you don't need to request anything, or
minimise any hurt or pain you feel. Direct all your speech at
the egg, and imagine it as dark-coloured waves (after all, noise
is sonic waves) leaving your mouth and permeating the shell
of the egg. If you wish, you can imagine the egg's beautiful
interior becoming slowly blackened, or withered, or disgusting,
as your words fill it. As you speak, the waves leaving your
voice gradually become lighter and clearer, like a tap running
clear. When you are finished, wrap the egg in a tissue so you
don't have to touch it, close the altar, and take it outside to
bury it. As you do so, recite a spell banishing the worry,
alongside the egg, into the ground to be absorbed: *What is
gone from me leave me and no more return to me – all of this struggle
leaves me, dissipates.* If you cannot take it outside and bury it,
then you have a number of options. You can put it in the bin,
being careful not to smash it, and let someone take it away
in the rubbish – this is a perfectly decent option. The other
option I'd go for is breaking it down the toilet, flushing the
contents and binning the shell. Not glamorous, particularly,

but it absolutely gets the job done. There are some variations of this spell where the egg is taken outside and thrown against a wall to smash it, but this, while far more fun, is a bit messily antisocial, and reminds me of teenagers on Hallowe'en.

SEPTEMBER, AGAIN

A year is a short amount of time, in magical terms. One spin of the wheel, one cycle of the seasons. Magical practice is like any other discipline: it builds with repetition, with the slow but steady accretion of skill, understanding, effort. That takes years. I do not mean this dishearteningly: instead I hope it fills you with joy. The snapshot of what it means to be a witch over one year is so different to the way you relate to that identity over a longer period of time. But conversely, a year is also a stretching and differentiating unit of time: some years feel long, and others flash past. As the seasons turn, all life is held, in miniature, within a year. It is vital that we live them as deeply, as responsively as we can. This book, I hope, moves through some of the ways that we can do that. It has been a pleasure to turn to six centuries' worth of occult tradition, knowledge and myth, to sift through it, to follow new paths, try new things, and deepen my knowledge of what it means to be a witch, or to be interested in being in the world in ways that are markedly magical.

What a deep joy I think, to spend one's life trying to find new threads to connect us to the world, new ways of speaking with its secret corners, new points and moments of connection. We are of the world, and it of us, and we are wholly bound to it: what a privilege to be able to develop our knowledge of it through our senses, through our attention, through our determination to bear witness to new ways of working and being. Witches have always shaped the world, whether through terror and revulsion in the eyes of the general public, the state and the crown, or through our acts of healing, our resistance to power, and our ability to shape new ways of being out of the wreckage of what we have. Witches transform, hide, leave and return. We are able to change ourselves, to adapt. The advantage of witchcraft as a practice, in opposition to a religion, is that we can jettison what no longer serves us and reshape ourselves and our practices to operate in harmony with the times we live in. Because witchcraft tradition is fragmentary, often lost, rarely clear or straightforward, we are free to draw on the past but keep a weather eye on the horizon of the future.

We are always seeking to make good our relationship to the planet, to the network of beings that lets our magic happen in the first place. As the pressures on those resources change, so our responses as to how we try to protect and work with them must change. Gone are the village-border cottages of our forebears. We are verge-witches, edgeland-witches, witches who stand at the end of supermarket car parks and greet the dawn. We work with plastic, with processed water, with air miles, with deforestation and communal bins that stink all summer with that sweet, cloying rot. Thinking magically is also, always, thinking ecologically, thinking about the great wide world that we inhabit. Everything is always sending messages: witches just listen to them, value them, realise how to respond. Magic is a practice of habit, and it is our job to form good habits: in our communities, in our environment, in our world. We do not have to be revolutionaries in the traditional sense, we do not have to – and not all of us can – protest or petition governments, occupy buildings or opt out of the capitalist and oppressive systems that we exist within. But then, nor can we support the current order, with its destruction of the more-than-human world, which is, of course, entirely our world too. And witchcraft is revolutionary in the true sense: being concerned with the wheel of the year, the cycles of life and death that are current, the half-lives of nuclear decay and microplastics, we are concerned with revolutions – with things going round.

Witches make things happen. We have the ability to step outside the systems that are designed to keep us inside, and we have the ability to talk back to power, or to bypass it, or to do what we genuinely think is best even it breaks the rules. After all, witchcraft has been illegal, outlawed or taboo for most of the West's recorded history. In our current cultural moment, we are allowed to practise witchcraft, and that is an extraordinary gift. We cannot all be 'out' about it: there are some people for whom, culturally, that would be extremely difficult. But those of us who can bring our practices from the shadows to the light, and use them more obviously in service of the community, should do so. Because we are the lucky ones – and to make our witchcraft common knowledge is not to 'demystify' anything – it is just a demonstration that what we do is valuable, is legitimate, is as much a part of the fabric of the world as anything else. It is almost impossible to demystify witchcraft. After all, there is something innately mysterious about any process that adapts, responds, and looks different for everyone.

There is an argument, perhaps, that witchcraft is not a set

of interlinked practices, but instead a way of understanding the world. A mode of thinking. A way of walking and looking and responding. That it isn't magic at all. That all we are doing is turning ourselves towards things, pulling them into focus. The shine of water on concrete. The way the pineappleweed pushes itself up by street lamps. The thrum of rain on our windows, and the way it bends and softens the car-lights, so that they leave traces of brightness down slick streets. As Sabrina Scott says, 'magic is the super-powerfulness of everything, just as it is'.[1] Magic isn't somewhere else. It isn't a series of distant rituals, ancient texts and expensive courses. Magic is turning to the world, and seeing it, and knowing we are indistinguishable from it, in all our embodied, strange, soft and edgeless forms. We are in the world and the world is in us, and that strange network – from birdsong to beer cans, from hypodermic syringes to sand around toes on the edge of the sea – is what thrums with power. Witches just know how to use that power. We know how to call objects into our attention, and work with them. We know how to speak to the moon when we see her face in pavement puddles. We know how to build masks for things we dare not name, and speak to them. We know how to hold all of the great, wide, grubby world inside us, and celebrate it.

Witchcraft is the practice of living in the world as it is, not as we would wish it to be. It is the practice of using our will to shape and change the world, to care for it. It is to understand that there are other systems, other ways of being, that offer care, and kindness, and transformation. We are all involved in one another, deeply, inextricably. We drink water that other people have drunk. We walk streets layered with other people's sensory information. We sit pressed up on trains. We lie in hospital beds filled with the memories of everyone else who has lain there. And that is just humans – the more-than-human world pulls spores into our lungs with every breath. It regulates us – in the millions of bacteria that operate inside our bodies. It will kiss us back to earth when we decay. It nourishes us, it poisons us and heals us. Witchcraft looks at this arrangement and asks how it can contribute. Witchcraft is the practice of holding the threads of the world, picking up a spindle, and starting to make our own. We are all witches, if we choose to be, in our vast and differing practices, and dedications to this world. The magic is in the wild, and it is also inside us. We are the wilds, and we are the hearth. Come along, won't you? All the world is waiting, and you are waiting too, and there is so much joy, and power, and there is so much work to be done. Let's get to work.

Acknowledgements

It is a great privilege to have individuals too numerous to thank.

This book would not exist without the incredible support and effort of everyone at Two Roads, and particularly my two editors, Kate Hewson and Kate Craigie, whose patience and kindness have been incredible. I also would thank the brilliant marketing and publicity teams, especially Emma Petfield, Charlotte Hutchinson, and my fab copy-editor, Lottie. They've made the experience of writing and publishing my debut really joyous.

A Spell in the Wild would never have come to pass if not for the generous friendship of Thalia Suzuma. It would also not exist without all the wonderful naturalists and occultists who have given their time so generously to my research.

There are people you can never stop thanking: my parents, Linda and George Tarbuck, who never had any doubt I'd write a book. My godmother, Cindy Brook, who I am lucky to count as a third parent. Eternal thanks, for everything you have done and continue to do.

I have leaned on innumerable shoulders, and some of them are here: I have drawn strength, succour and cold hard courage from the Difficult Aunts: Anna Scott, Christina McLeish, Emma Southon, Ella Risbridger, Eley Williams, Fiona Zublin, Kate Young, Isabella Streffen, Olivia Potts, Sarah Gulick, Sarah Perry, Sarah Phelps.

On page 90, I assert that adults dismissively tell the young that they didn't 'invent sex' – this is a quotation from AW Earl, who I am crediting here in lieu of a footnote, with thanks.

Thanks are also due to my beloved Christina Neuwirth, Dave Coates, and Sasha de Buyl-Pisco, and to Hannah and Ian Faddy-Widmann, The Dillons, and Various Babies: Josephine, Frank and Freja.

This book is indebted to Rafael Torrubia, in thanks. For conversations at weddings that mean everything: Eliza Apperly. For restoring me to myself: Laura 'Lel' Karlsen and Ray Plummer. For bravery, the good champagne, and the far horizon, A.W. Earl. For pure magic and deep joy, Claire Askew. For witchcraft beyond knowing, Simone Kotva. For pure love, always, Lucy Kelsall.

Further Reading

For a good, accessible work on the history of witchcraft:

Ronald Hutton, *The Witch: A History of Fear, from Ancient Times to the Present*. (Yale, Yale University Press, 2018).

For enjoyably contemporary spellwork, I recommend:

Rae Beth, *The Hedge Witchs Way: Magical Spirituality for the Lone Spellcaster*. (London: Robert Hale, 2018).

Lisa Marie Basile and Kristen J. Sollee. *Light Magic for Dark Times More Than 100 Spells, Rituals, and Practices for Coping in a Crisis*. (London, Quarto, 2018).

For more information on plants and their magical uses, I love:

Scott Cunningham, *Encyclopaedia of Magical Herbs*. (London: Llewellyn Publications., 1985). (This is easily found second hand online.)

Müller-Ebeling Claudia, et al. *Witchcraft Medicine: Healing Arts, Shamanic Practices, and Forbidden Plants*. (London, Inner Traditions, 2003).

Notes

A Note on the Spells and Other Magical Conduct

1. Gardnerian and Alexandrian traditions are types of High Magical practice, developed by Gerald Gardner (1884–1964) and Alex Sanders (1926–1988) respectively. The Wiccan revival encompassed a variety of different High Magical practices. Gerald Gardner drew on magical traditions developed and revived by occultist Aleister Crowley, as well as on his knowledge of world religions and spiritual practices, and Gardner himself claimed to have learned the practices he details from the New Forest Coven, who initiated him. Alex Sanders, who was a practitioner of Gardnerian Wicca, later refined and developed his beliefs into a different system. There are lots of diverse forms of Wicca, each with differing beliefs and ritual procedures, and these can be understood as in some ways similar to factions of a single religion, such as different factions of Christianity.

September: Foraging

1. This is a growing field of research, and one with a wide variety of studies. See for example: Rachel Bragg, Carly Wood, Jo Barton and Jules Pretty, 'Wellbeing benefits from natural environments rich in wildlife: A literature review for The Wildlife Trusts' (Newark: University of Essex, 2015).
2. Mitchell, Emma, *The Wild Remedy: How Nature Mends Us – A Diary* (London: Michael O'Mara Books Ltd., 2019), p. 9.

3. Ma. D. Velarde et al., 'Health Effects of Viewing Landscapes – Landscape Types in Environmental Psychology', *Urban Forestry & Urban Greening*, vol. 6, no. 4 (2007), pp. 199–212.

4. RavenWolf, Silver. *Hedge Witch: Spells, Crafts & Rituals for Natural Magick*. (Woodbury, MO: Llewellyn Publications, 2014).

5. https://www.sciencealert.com/flowers-may-not-have-ears-but-they-can-still-technically-hear-say-scientists

6. http://www.bbc.co.uk/earth/story/20141111-plants-have-a-hidden-internet

7. S. Simard, D. Perry, M. Jones, et al., 'Net transfer of carbon between ectomycorrhizal tree species in the field', *Nature*, 388, 579–582.

8. http://www.bbc.co.uk/earth/story/20141111-plants-have-a-hidden-internet

9. Rae Beth, *Spellcraft for Hedge Witches: A Guide to Healing Our Lives* (New York: Robert Hale, 2018), p. 17.

10. Ibid, p. 19.

October: Samhain and Talking to the Dead

1. L. K. Kyu, 'The Concept of Ancestors and Ancestor Worship in Korea', *Asian Folklore Studies*, 43(2), 199.

2. https://www.vice.com/en_uk/article/pgvkzv/we-spoke-to-a-druid-about-the-occult-history-of-apple-bobbing

3. https://www.bartleby.com/196/159.html

4. Sarah Iles Johnston, *Ancient Greek Divination* (London: Wiley-Blackwell, 2008), p 3.

5. Gerard Murphy, *Early Irish Lyrics: Eighth to Twelfth Century* (Oxford: Oxford University Press, 1956).

6. Anne Ross, *Pagan Celtic Britain: Studies in Iconography and Tradition* (Chicago: Chicago Review Press, 2005).

7. Ibid.

8. Ibid.

NOTES

November: Sex Magic

1. Michael Harrison, *The Roots of Witchcraft* (London: Tandem, 1975)
2. Ibid.
3. Heinrich Institoris et al., *Malleus Maleficarum*, (New York: Blom, 1970), p. 47.
4. Richard Payne Knight, *A Discourse on the Worship of Priapus, and Its Connection with the Mystic Theology of the Ancients* (London: Privately printed, 1865, reprinted 1894), pp. 234–6.
5. Margaret Alice Murray, *The Witch-Cult in Western Europe: A Study in Anthropology* (Oxford: Clarendon, 1921), p. 177.
6. Robert Pitcairn, *Criminal Trials* (Edinburgh: The Bannatyne Club, 1833), p. 610.
7. Hugh B. Urban, *Magia Sexualis: Sex, Magic, and Liberation in Modern Western Esotericism* (California: University of California Press, 2008).
8. Ibid.
9. U. D. Frater, *Secrets of Western Sex Magic: Magical Energy and Gnostic Trance* (Woodbury, MO: Llewellyn Publications, 2001), p. 6.
10. Jay, Johnston, 'Gender and the Occult' in Christopher Partridge (ed.), *The Occult World*, (London: Routledge, 2016), p. 684.
11. Raymond Buckland, *Buckland's Complete Book of Witchcraft* (Woodbury, MO: Llewellyn Publications, 1986), p. 9.
12. Skye Alexander, *Sex Magic for Beginners: The Easy and Fun Way to Tap into the Law of Attraction* (Woodbury, MO: Llewellyn Publications, 2012).
13. Livy, *History of Rome*, trans. Rev. Canon Roberts (New York: E. P. Dutton & Co., 1912), p. 400.
14. Scott Michaelson (ed.), *Portable Darkness: An Aleister Crowley Reader* (New York: Harmony Books, 1989), p. 143.
15. Hugh B. Urban, *Magia Sexualis* p. 11.
16. Janet and Stewart Farrar, *The Witches' Way: Principles, Rituals and Beliefs of Modern Witchcraft* (London: Phoenix Publishing, 1988), p. 157.

17. Janet and Stewart Farrar, *A Witches' Bible* (London: Robert Hale, 1984), p. 169.
18. Raymond Buckland, *Buckland's Complete Book of Witchcraft*, p. 167.
19. For example, articles such as: Tracey Duncan, 'Queer Sex Magic: How to Do LGBTQ Witchcraft in Bed', *Vice*, 19.08.2018
20. https://www.autostraddle.com/queer-sex-coven-fck-a-candle-to-find-your-perfect-partner/
21. Lee Harrington and Tai Fenix Kulystin, *Queer Magic: Power Beyond Boundaries* (Anchorage, AK: Mystic Productions, 2018).
22. A 'memory palace' is a memory technique that ties memories or information to objects set up around a house or 'palace' in your imagination, so you can recall the information by looking at the imaginary object. The invention is credited to Simonides of Ceos, a Roman poet born in 566 BC.

December: Midwinter and Magic in the Dark

1. Jon Kabat-Zinn, *Mindfulness Meditation for Everyday Life,* (London: Piatkus Books, 1994), p. 4.
2. See: van Tulleken C., Tipton M., Massey H., et al. 'Open water swimming as a treatment for major depressive disorder' *Case Reports* 2018; 2018:bcr-2018-225007. and the Outdoor Swimming Society for more information.
3. https://www.ncbi.nlm.nih.gov/pmc/articles/PMC4049052
4. https://news.nationalgeographic.com/2015/12/151221-winter-solstice-explained-pagans
5. https://blogs.bl.uk/music/2012/12/brief-history-of-the-christmas-carol.html
6. https://www.poetryfoundation.org/poems/44349/green-groweth-the-holly

NOTES

January: Smelling the Weather

1. Barnett, Cynthia, *Rain: A Natural and Cultural History* (London: Broadway Books, 2016).
2. Kenneth Grahame, *Pagan Papers* (London: Elkin Mathews and John Lane, 1893).
3. Ibid.
4. The Rigveda is one of the most important texts in Hinduism, and is one of a number of Vedas, which contain hymns in praise of various gods, ceremonial rituals, and cosmology. It is one of the most ancient extant texts in any Indo-European language and is thought to have originated in what is now Pakistan between 1500 and 1200 BCE.
5. http://dhlsna.bravesites.com/nr_appendix-4-pan-in-america
6. http://www.gutenberg.org/files/5319/5319-h/5319-h.htm
7. Gotzone Garay-Barayazarra & Rajindra K. Puri, 'Smelling the monsoon: Senses and traditional weather forecasting knowledge among the Kenyah Badeng farmers of Sarawak, Malaysia', *Indian Journal of Traditional Knowledge*, vol. 10(1), (January 2011), pp. 21–30.
8. Peter Grey, *Apocalyptic Witchcraft*, (Location: Scarlet Imprint, 2013), p. 1.
9. Geosmin is produced by *Streptomyces*, a Gram-positive type of Actinobacteria, when they die. See: https://www.jic.ac.uk/blog/meet-the-molecules-geosmin
10. Barnett, Cynthia. *Rain: a Natural and Cultural History*.
11. http://www.sacred-texts.com/pag/kjd/kjd11.htm
12. King James, *Daemonologie: In Forme of a Dialogie, Diuided into three Bookes* (Edinburgh: Robert Walde-graue, 1597). See also: King James, James Carmichael and Donald Tyson, *The Demonology of King James I*. (Woodbury, MO: Llewellyn Publications, 2011).

February: Fairies

1. http://www.brecon-radnor.co.uk/article.
2. P.D. Nunn, Kohler, A. & Kumar, R. 'Identifying and assessing evidence for recent shoreline change attributable to uncommonly rapid sea-level rise in Pohnpei, Federated States of Micronesia, Northwest Pacific Ocean'. J Coast Conserv 21, 719–730 (2017).
3. Donald A. Mackenzie, and John Duncan. *Wonder Tales from Scottish Myth & Legend.* (Glasgow, Blackie and Son, Limited: 1917), p.39, via sacred-texts.com
4. For an expansion and critique of this theory, which is accredited to the linguist and anthropologist Georges Dumézil, see: Belier, Wouter W. *Decayed Gods: Origin and Development of Georges Dumézils' "Idéologie Tripartie".* (Netherlands: Brill, 1991).
5. Silver, Carole G. 'On the Origin of Fairies: Victorians, Romantics, and Folk Belief', *Browning Institute Studies*, vol. 14, The Victorian Threshold (1986), pp. 141–156 (Cambridge: Cambridge University Press, 1986).
6. Silver, Carole G. *Strange and Secret Peoples: Fairies and Victorian Consciousness.* Oxford: Oxford University Press, 2009, p. 54.
7. Ibid, p. 153.
8. Ibid.
9. Canon J. A. Macculloch, 'Were Fairies an Earlier Race of Men?' *Folklore*, vol. 43, no. 4 (Taylor & Francis, Ltd. on behalf of Folklore Enterprises, Ltd., 31 December, 1932), pp. 362–375.
10. Alaric Hall, *The Meanings of Elf, and Elves, in Medieval England* (University of Glasgow PhD Thesis, 2005), pp. 107–13.
11. Canon J. A. Macculloch, 'Were Fairies an Earlier Race of Men?', p. 365.
12. Kathleen A. Heininge, "Untiring Joys and Sorrows": Yeats and the Sidhe', *New Hibernia Review / Iris Éireannach Nua*, vol. 8, no. 4 (University of St Thomas, Center for Irish Studies, Winter, 2004), pp. 101–116.

13. See, for example: Sumpter, Caroline, *Victorian Press and the Fairy Tale*. Palgrave Macmillan, 2014, p. 108 and Henderson, Lizanne, and Edward J. Cowan. *Scottish Fairy Belief: a History*. (Edinburgh, Tuckwell Press: 2011), p. 10 and passim.

14. Juliette Wood, 'Gipsy Witches and Celtic Magicians: Charles Godfrey Leland and Lewis Spence', *Béaloideas*, Iml. 76 (An Cumann Le Béaloideas Éireann/Folklore of Ireland Society, 2008), p. 22.

15. Kathleen A. Heininge, '"Untiring Joys and Sorrows": Yeats and the Sidhe', p. 103.

16. Daniel Giraudon, 'Supernatural Whirlwinds in the Folklore of Celtic Countries', *Béaloideas*, Iml. 75 (An Cumann Le Béaloideas Éireann/Folklore of Ireland Society, 2007), p. 16.

17. Sinéad Garrigan Mattar, 'Yeats, Fairies, and the New Animism', *New Literary History*, vol. 43, no. 1 (The Johns Hopkins University Press, Winter 2012), pp. 137–157.

March: Witches, Money and Protest

1. One example might be witchcraft in Romania, where clients often pay witches high sums. These witches are the exception, but include individuals such as Mihaela Minka: https://broadly.vice.com/en_us/article/kz37ny/what-happened-when-romanias-most-powerful-witch-moved-to-la. However, witches in Romania face government suppression.

2. Alice Echols, *Daring to be Bad: Radical Feminism in America 1967–1975* (Minneapolis: University of Minnesota Press, 1989), p. 97.

3. 'Although the witch theme was mostly symbolic, W.I.T.C.H. encouraged reviving midwifery, herbal and other healing practices almost entirely eradicated as quackery by 1960' Zora Von Burden interviews WITCH member Peggy Dobbins, in Burden, Zora Von. *Women of the Underground: Resistance: Progressive Instigators Speak for Themselves*. Manic D Press, 2018.

4. Susan Brownmiller, *In Our Time: Memoir of a Revolution* (London: Dial Books, 1999), p. 49.
5. Alice Echols, *Daring to be Bad*, p. 98.
6. Ibid.
7. Gage, Matilda Joslyn. *Woman, Church, and State* (New York, Arno Press, 1972), p. 122.
8. Jeffrey B. Russell and Brooks Alexander, *A New History of Witchcraft: Sorcerers, Heretics and Pagans* (London: Thames and Hudson, 2007), p. 42.
9. Margot Adler, *Drawing Down the Moon: Witches, Druids, Goddess-Worshippers and Other Pagans in America* (London: Penguin, 1979, revised ed. 2006), p. 165.
10. Karl Marx, *Das Kapital* vol. III (Hamburg: Otto Meisner, 1894), p. 969
11. https://www.independent.co.uk/life-style/brett-kavanaugh-hexing-witches-new-york-catland-books-brooklyn-trump-a8595016.html
12. Ibid.
13. Pignarre, Philippe, and Isabelle Stengers, *Capitalist Sorcery: Breaking the Spell* (London: Palgrave Macmillan, 2011), p. 357.

April: Witches Becoming Animals

1. More about the Huli jing can be found in: Anne Birrell, *The Classic of Mountains and Seas* (London: Penguin, 1999).
2. Sarah O'Connor, 'Hares and Hags: Becoming Animal in Éilís Ní Dhuibhne's Dún na mBan trí Thine' in Kirkpatrick, Kathryn J., and Faragó Borbála, *Animals in Irish Literature and Culture* (London: Palgrave Macmillan, 2018), p. 92.
3. Wade T. Wheelock, 'The Problem of Ritual Language: From Information to Situation', *Journal of the American Academy of Religion*, Volume L, Issue 1, March 1982, pp. 49–72.
4. Homer, *The Odyssey*, trans. A. T. Murray, Loeb Classical Library Volumes (Cambridge, MA: Harvard University Press; London: William Heinemann Ltd., 1919).

5. Éva Pócs, *Between the Living and the Dead: A Perspective on Witches and Seers in the Early Modern Age* (Budapest: Central European University Press, 2000), p. 80.
6. Gerhild Scholz Williams, 'Demonologies', in Brian P. Levack, *The Oxford Handbook of Witchcraft in Early Modern Europe and Colonial America* (Oxford: Oxford University Press, 2014), p. 69
7. Ibid., p. 70.
8. Ibid., pp 69–84.
9. King James, *Daemonologie*, p.30.
10. Éva Pócs, *Between the Living and the Dead: A Perspective on Witches and Seers in the Early Modern Age* (Budapest: Central European University Press, 2000), p.80.
11. Ibid., p. 87.
12. Ibid., p. 75.
13. Bitter foods can be harmful if you have a stomach ulcer or other condition related to over-production of acid in the stomach, so be careful.

May: Magic in the Land

1. Watkins, Alfred, *Early British Trackways: Moats, Mounds, Camps, and Sites.* Cosimo Classics, 2005., p. 11.
2. https://www.tate.org.uk/research/publications/tate-papers/06/lines-of-sight-alfred-watkins-photography-and-topography-in-early-twentieth-century-britain
3. Christopher I. Lehrich, *The Occult Mind: Magic in Theory and Practice* (Cornell: Cornell University Press, 2009), p. 20.
4. Aimé Michel, and Alexander D. Mebane, *Flying Saucers and the Straight-Line Mystery* (New York: S. G. Phillips, 1958).
5. http://www.jimgoddard.myfreeola.uk/tony
6. http://www.cantab.net/users/michael.behrend/repubs/j_geomancy/_common/pages/igr_leaflet_1_4.html
7. Frederick MacL. Adams, 'Ley Line Seismia', *Journal of Geomancy*, vol. 1, no. 3, (April 1977), pp. 59–62.

8. Ibid., p. 60.
9. Adams' views concerning the female body and the divine feminine are expanded on in his religious writings on Feraferia, the faerie religion he founded, and can be accessed via the Feraferia: http://feraferia.org
10. Frederick MacL. Adams, 'Ley Line Seismia' p. 61.
11. Cambridge Past Present and Future, 'Wandlebury Hill Fort' leaflet, https://www.cambridgeppf.org/Handlers/Download.ashx?IDMF=c99aa76d-9f81-40fb-81c8-25053a389bd9
12. For details of this myth, see Monmouth, Geoffrey Of, and Lewis Thorpe, *The History of the Kings of Britain*. (London, Penguin Classics: 2015).
13. Nigel Pennik, 'Wandlebury Mysteries', *Cambridgeshire Ancient Mysteries Group* (Occasional Paper 21,Cambridgeshire Ancient Mysteries Group Bar Hill, Cambridge, n.d. [1981])
14. Frederick Adams, Letters Page, *Journal of Geomancy*, vol. 1, no. 4, (Cambridge, July 1977), p. 78.
15. Lehrich, Christopher I. *The Occult Mind: Magic in Theory and Practice* (Cornell, Cornell University Press, 2009), p. 24.
16. Mircea Eliade, *The Sacred and the Profane: The Nature of Religion*, trans. Willard R. Trask (London: Harcourt Brace, 1987), pp. 68–70.
17. Sabrina Scott, *Witchbody* (Chicago: Perfectly Acceptable Press, 2010), n.p.
18. Ibid.

June: Midsummer and Light Magic

1. https://sussexpast.co.uk/properties-to-discover/the-long-man
2. William Shakespeare wrote his comedy *A Midsummer Night's Dream* in 1595/6 and it is set on a single night of the summer solstice, though part of the dreaminess and confusion of the play is that it also makes mention of May Day traditions and other pre-Christian festivals and celebrations. Part of the plot

centres around the relationship between Oberon and Titania, the King and Queen of fairies, and their enchantment of a group of actors, who are putting on a play to celebrate the season. One of the players, Bottom, is given the head of an ass, and is attended to by fairies. This forms part of a larger theme of loss of identity, enchantment and confusion that runs throughout the play − an exploration of 'midsummer madness'.

3. Rev. John O'Hanlon (writing as Lageniensis), *Irish Folk Lore: Traditions and Superstitions of the Country; with Humorous Tales* (London: Cameron and Ferguson, 1870), p. 49.

4. Ibid., p. 49

5. Jacob Ludwig Karl Grimm, *Teutonic Mythology* (New York: Dover Publications, 1966), p. 1,051.

6. James George Frazer, *The Golden Bough: A Study in Magic and Religion* (New York: The Macmillan Co., 1922), p. 623.

7. Claudia Müller-Ebeling et al., *Witchcraft Medicine: Healing Arts, Shamanic Practices, and Forbidden Plants* (Vermont: Inner Traditions, 2003), p. 11.

8. Gervase Markham, *The English Huswife* (Kingston and Montreal, Canada: McGill-Queen's University Press, 1986, originally published 1615), p. 40.

9. Among its other uses, mugwort is also an abortifacient, and should never be ingested by those who are pregnant or wishing to conceive.

10. Claudia Müller-Ebeling et al., *Witchcraft Medicine*, p. 56.

11. D. C. Watts, *Dictionary of Plant Lore* (New York: Elsevier: 2007), p. 340.

12. Mrs M. Grieve, *A Modern Herbal*, volume I: A–H (New York: Dover Publications, Inc. 1971, 1931), pp. 305–306.

13. Thomas Berry, *The Great Work* (New York: Bell Tower, 2000), p. 56.

July: Fortune Telling and Divination

1. https://www.nybooks.com/articles/2016/02/25/what-is-the-i-ching
2. *The Elder or Poetic Edda, commonly known as Sæmund's Edda, part I: The Mythological Poems*, edited and translated by Olive Bray (London: Printed for the Viking Club, 1908), pp. 61–111.
3. Lévi, Éliphas, and Aleister Crowley. *The Key of the Mysteries. Translated and with an Introduction and Notes, by Aleister Crowley.* (London, Rider & Co, 1959), p.xii via archive.org.
4. Enoch is an Old Testament figure and ancestor of Noah, apparently responsible for the apocryphal 'Book of Enoch'; Thoth is the Egyptian god of magic and writing; Hermes Trismegistus is related to the god Hermes and the god Thoth, and is the apparent author of a set of sacred texts that form the basis of Hermeticism; Palamedes, who fought at Troy, was also credited with inventing eleven letters of the Greek alphabet; Cadmus was the founder of Thebes. Ibid, p. xii.
5. Ibid, p.193.
6. Ibid, p. 194.
7. Enrique Enriquez, *Looking at the Marseille Tarot* (Vermont: Minds Eye Books, 2016), p. 6.
8. Ibid., p. 7.
9. Ibid., p. 9.

August: Sympathetic Magic

1. Sophie Page et al., *Spellbound: Magic, Ritual & Witchcraft* (Oxford: Ashmolean Museum, 2018), p. 11.
2. Ibid., p. 10.
3. https://www.theguardian.com/lifeandstyle/2016/jul/25/psychology-donald-trump-win-luck-superstition
4. P. Rozin and C. Nemeroff, 'Sympathetic Magical Thinking: The Contagion and Similarity "Heuristics"' in T. Gilovich, D. Griffin, and D. Kahneman (eds.), *Heuristics and Biases: The Psychology of Intuitive Judgment* (Cambridge: Cambridge

University Press, 2002), pp. 201–216, doi:10.1017/CBO9780511808098.013.

5. Sara Ahmed, 'Affective Economies' in *Social Text* 79 , vol. 22, no. 2 (Durham, NC, Duke University Press, summer 2004).

6. Ibid., p. 120.

7. Moore, A. W. (Arthur William), 1853–1909. *The Folk-lore of the Isle of Man: Being an Account of Its Myths, Legends, Superstitions, Customs, & Proverbs, Collected From Many Sources; With a General Introduction; And With Explanatory Notes to Each Chapter* (Douglas, Isle of Man: Brown, 1891), p. 157.

8. Rozin and Nemeroff, 'Sympathetic Magical Thinking,' (pp. 201–216).

9. http://broughttolife.sciencemuseum.org.uk/broughttolife/techniques/doctrine

10. https://www.thecourier.co.uk/news/local/perth-kinross/230362/ancient-custom-of-the-bedding-of-st-fillans-healing-stones-is-handed-down

11. Sophie Page et al., *Spellbound*, p. 11.

12. Brian Hoggard, *Magical House Protection: The Archaeology of Counter-Witchcraft* (Oxford: Berghahn Books Ltd., 2019). p. 96.

13. Sophie Page et al., *Spellbound*, p. 76.

14. Edward Bever, 'Witchcraft Fears and Psychosocial Factors in Disease' in *The Journal of Interdisciplinary History*, vol. 30, no. 4, (2000), pp. 573–590, www.jstor.org/stable/206724.

September, Again

1. Sabrina Scott, *Witchbody*, n.p.